Croner

PERSONNEL LAW & PRACTICE

**Compiled and updated
by the staff of
Croner's Employment Law
Department**

Croner Publications Ltd
Croner House
173 Kingston Road
New Malden
Surrey KT3 3SS
Tel: 01-942 8966

Croner's Personnel Law and Practice

First Edition
April 1987

© Copyright Croner Publications Ltd

ISBN 0 900319 46 1

Printed for the Publishers, Croner Publications Ltd,
Croner House, 173 Kingston Road, New Malden, Surrey KT3 3SS by
Adlard & Son Ltd, Dorking, Surrey

CONTENTS

	Preface	1
1	Personnel Management and the Law	3
2	Personnel Management	45
3	Personnel Procedures	72
4	Taking on Employees	99
5	Industrial Relations	120
6	Problem Areas	151
7	Particular Employments	185
8	Termination of Employment	228
	Index	258

PREFACE

On 20.4.77 the first issue of our newsletter *Employment Digest* was published. Since that time thousands of subscribers have come to rely on its coverage of case reports, legislative developments, news and, perhaps above all, its down-to-earth approach to issues of concern to all those involved in personnel administration.

To celebrate its 10th anniversary we have compiled this book from a selection of articles which it has carried over the past decade. The articles have been updated wherever necessary and the information in the book is as relevant today as it was when it was first published. In some ways it is a unique book: rather than setting out the legal requirements which must be observed by personnel departments, or providing an academic overview of the role of the personnel function, it aims to be a practical working tool. Whether you are interested in finding out how law is made, its practical impact, or what is good practice in areas where there is no law, this book will be a valuable guide.

Inevitably it does not cover all areas: the task of selecting articles to include in the book was difficult in that, to do justice to the scope of *Employment Digest*, at least three or four volumes would have been necessary. We do hope, however, that having sampled the quality of the information provided by *Employment Digest* in the following pages, you will wish to take out a subscription. If you are not already a subscriber and would like to be, please contact the publishers.

Croners Employment Law Department

1 PERSONNEL MANAGEMENT AND THE LAW

Over the last decade the law has had an increasing impact on the role of personnel practitioners and this trend is unlikely to diminish. In this chapter we set out the way in which laws are made, the impact of the Common Market on British laws, the way in which the effects of employment law are ameliorated for small businesses and the way that common law imposes liabilities on employers in respect of their duties of care for their employees.

We do not set out the legal requirements employers must follow in terms of maternity rights, guarantee pay, time off work, and so forth as these are amply covered in *Croners Reference Book for Employers* and *Croner's Employment Law*. Rather, the intention is to give an understanding of the basic legal system.

The Law Making Process

The way that Acts of Parliament and other legislation come into being — from their initial conception to their arrival on the statute book — is a process shrouded in mystery to much of the population. However, a glimpse behind the scenes goes a long way towards explaining some of the law's apparent absurdities and the reasons for judicial decisions on some apparently straightforward legal provisions. The procedure which must be followed in order to translate ideas into legislation is examined and the rules governing interpretation of statutes are explained.

Initiating the Process

Most proposals for new legislation are made by government Ministers and will often stem from proposals set out in party political manifestos published shortly before a General Election. The Cabinet decides each year which legislative measures it wishes to pursue in the following parliamentary year and these measures then form the basis of the Queen's Speech. Incidentally, the speech is of course written by the Government and is only read by the Queen at the State opening of Parliament.

There are, however, other sources of legislation. A decision of the European Court of Justice might force the Government into legislating in areas it might prefer to avoid. Typical examples are the regulations on equal pay for work of equal value and equalising the age at which men and women cease being able to claim that they have been unfairly dismissed. Similarly, pressure groups might be able to persuade the Government to legislate by the force of their arguments.

Members of Parliament sitting on the back benches may also introduce legislation in the form of Private Members' Bills, under the "10 minute rule" or as a result of drawing a high place in the ballot held at the start of each parliamentary session. Such bills have little chance of becoming law, mainly because the time allowed for debate on their provisions is so small. In practice they are likely to reach the statute book only if the Government takes them up.

Parliamentary Draftsmen

It is the age-old complaint of all lay people who have to try to interpret legislation that the wording of bills is almost incomprehensible. It is tempting to ascribe cynical motives to those responsible: perhaps they do not want people to understand the provisions and then adverse effects can be blamed on the judiciary rather than on the politicians, for instance.

In truth, however, the reason is generally much more prosaic. Government bills are drafted by lawyers attached to the Treasury who are called, officially, Parliamentary Counsel. Their role is to take proposals for legislation and to put them into legal language in the form of a bill. Because the practice of English law is generally to legislate by use of precise words — rather than general expressions of intent (as, for example, in the Data Protection Principles) — the lawyers will seek to cover every conceivable contingency.

A report issued in 1975 by the Committee on the Preparation of Legislation (Cmnd 6053) made the following recommendations, designed to make legislation more readily comprehensible:
- the system of issuing explanatory notes with new bills should be extended and statements of purpose and principle should be encouraged

- there should be more parliamentary draftsmen
- there should be more consolidation of statutory provisions to overcome the difficulties of having to wade through several Acts and associated regulations in order to establish just one point.

However, these very modest suggestions have made little headway in the 11 years since they were published.

The Procedure in Parliament

Most bills begin life in the House of Commons and the procedure which is followed is outlined below.

First Reading

This is a formal stage and includes no debate on the bill. It is read as a result of the House agreeing to a motion for leave to introduce it and is then printed and published. If the House does not agree, the bill is lost.

Second Reading

At this stage the person in charge of the bill — usually a government Minister — explains the purpose of the bill and the main policy issues involved and the House then debates these points. A vote on the bill is taken and, if the bill survives, it passes on to the next stage.

The Committee Stage

The bill then passes to one of three committees: a committee of the whole House; a Standing Committee; or a Select Committee. The purpose of this stage is to examine the bill, line by line and clause by clause. It is in committee that amendments are most likely to be proposed. These amendments are subject to a vote of committee members.

Report Stage

The committee chairman then reports the bill formally to the House, which considers amendments made in committee and accepts or rejects them. It may also make its own amendments which again will be subject to a vote unless they are accepted by the Government or other sponsor of the bill.

Third Reading

Finally, the bill — in its amended form — is reviewed but the debate centres only on the amendments and not on the principles of the bill.

The House of Lords

The bill is then sent to the House of Lords where it goes through the same process as outlined in points 1 to 5 above. If the Lords make further amendments the bill is returned to the House of Commons, for consideration of these amendments, after the third reading in the House of Lords.

The Parliament Acts of 1911 and 1949 provide that, should the House of Lords pass amendments to a bill which are not acceptable to the House of Commons, the House of Commons may present the bill for Royal Assent, without the agreement of the House of Lords, after one year.

Royal Assent and Commencement

Royal Assent to a bill which has successfully passed through the above parliamentary stages is a formality. The Royal Assent Act 1967 provides that the measure is enacted when the Royal Assent is notified to each House of Parliament by its Speaker.

Once Royal Assent is given the Act may come into force immediately, it may be brought into force on some future date or it might have to await a commencement order before taking effect. The Wages Act 1986 provides a good example: s.33 states that certain sections come into force on the day on which the Act was passed (July 25), others took effect on August 1, still others took effect two months from the date on which the Act was passed and the remaining provisions take effect "on such day as the Secretary of State may appoint by order made by statutory instrument".

It can sometimes take years for provisions to come into effect. Take, for instance, the Employment of Children Act 1973. This Act empowers the Secretary of State for Employment to make provisions governing the employment of young people below the minimum school leaving age. Despite its reaching the statute book 14 years ago, its provisions have not yet been given effect. Another case in point is s.131 of the Employment Protection (Consolidation) Act 1978 (EP(C)A). This section allows the appropriate Minister to make an order which would enable claims for breach of a contract of employment to be brought to an industrial tribunal rather than to a county court. No such order has yet been made and so tribunals have no jurisdiction over these matters.

Consolidating Legislation

All personnel practitioners who had to become familiar with the law as it affects employment should have breathed a sigh of relief when the Employment Protection (Consolidation) Act was enacted in 1978. This Act did not include any new provisions; rather, it took all of the measures providing individual rights to employees — previously contained in the Redundancy Payments Act, the Contracts of Employment Act, the Trade Union and Labour Relations Acts and the Employment Protection Act 1975 — and brought them into one statute. This meant that — for a period at least — there was one single source of law on matters such as unfair dismissal, notice rights, statements of terms and conditions of employment, etc.

Sadly, this happy state of affairs did not last. In addition to the 1978 Act, reference now has to be made to the Employment Acts 1980 and 1982, the

Transfer of Undertakings Regulations 1981, the Trade Union Act 1984 and the Wages Act 1986 to get a complete picture of employees' rights. Similarly, the law on collective rights is now contained in some six different Acts.

Consolidation means the combination of **statute** law. In some cases the law is codified, which means that case law on the particular subject is included in the new Act together with statute law.

Delegated Legislation

Not all legislation has to go through the same procedure as outlined above. It is often the case that Acts do not regulate every aspect of the subject they cover and the Acts will then confer power to make more detailed rules, orders or regulations by means of statutory instruments (SIs).

These SIs, known as delegated or secondary legislation, may also be used to fix fees or to vary financial limits, as is the case with redundancy payments, compensation for unfair dismissal, and so on. Over recent years there has been a considerable growth in the number of SIs issued, primarily because of the lack of time in Parliament to debate all necessary measures, because the legislation is very technical and detailed and so is regarded as unsuitable to be debated by the whole House or because urgent problems arise which warrant instant attention.

SIs are published by Her Majesty's Stationery Office (HMSO) and are subject to three types of control:
(a) consultation: in practice Ministers consult relevant experts within their own departments and outside and also consult various interest groups likely to be affected by the proposals
(b) control by the courts: the single biggest difference between Acts and SIs is that the courts may rule that SIs are void because they are *ultra-vires* (ie they go beyond the power conferred by the Act under which they were made) or are unreasonable. The validity of Acts cannot be challenged in this way
(c) control by Parliament: some SIs must be laid before Parliament before they take effect and Parliament may revoke or vary the provisions of delegated legislation. They are also subject to scrutiny by the Select Committee on Statutory Instruments.

Interpretation of Statutes

So, having reached the point of getting legislation on to the statute book, the next problem is that of interpreting the provisions of SIs and Acts — no easy feat in most cases!

There are two sources of rules governing interpretation of legislation, one derived from statute, the other from common law.

The Interpretation Act 1889 provides that, unless the legislation provides otherwise:
- words imparting masculine gender include females
- words in the singular include the plural and vice-versa
- the word "person" includes corporate bodies such as companies
- words referring to "writing" include references to printing, photography, etc.

Additionally, most statutes include an interpretation section towards the end which defines words used, eg s.153 of the EP(C)A defines 38 different words or expressions.

Where statutes cannot readily be defined in line with the statutory rules, there are three main common law rules which can be used by judges.

The Literal Rule
This rule provides that words used in statutes must be given their literal, grammatical meaning. Even if the use of this rule produces hardship, it is said, this has nothing to do with the judiciary. It is up to Parliament to produce new legislation to remedy the position rather than for judges to give their own meaning. It is for this reason that they should take no notice of what was said in parliamentary debates.

The Mischief Rule
This rule takes a very different line. It states that judges must look to see the type of "mischief" or defect in common or statute law which the legislators were trying to overcome, and they must then put such a construction on the words of the statute as will "suppress the mischief and advance the remedy".

The Golden Rule
This rule is the one that lay people would probably expect to be followed. It states that the wording of a statute should be interpreted in its grammatical and ordinary sense. Perhaps the best description of this rule was given by the judge who said: "It is a very useful rule in the construction of a statute to adhere to the ordinary meaning of the words used, and to the grammatical construction, unless that is at variance with the intention of the legislature to be collected from the statute itself, or leads to any manifest absurdity or repugnance, in which case the language may be varied or modified so as to avoid such inconvenience, but no further".

The European Dimension

As was stated above, decisions of the European Court of Justice can have a profound effect on the law within the United Kingdom. Similarly, the Treaty of Rome and EC Directives also exert a strong influence. Over the last 12 years the European Community has made a major impact on the employment legislation of the United Kingdom — on equal pay and sex discrimination, health and safety, and rights in mergers in particular — but much wider legislation is brewing at Strasbourg.

We now aim to explain the role and powers of the EC institutions, their relationship with the United Kingdom and to focus on current problems and future proposals emanating from Europe.

The Community Structure

The four principal institutions of the EC are as follows.

The Commission: akin to the United Kingdom civil service, the Commission consists of 14 Commissioners (two each from France, Germany, Italy and the United Kingdom and one from each of the other Member States) who are strictly independent of their countries. They are answerable to the European Parliament and their duties are:
- to initiate all Community action by preparing and presenting proposals for Community legislation
- to steer its proposals through the Council (which can only amend them by unanimous vote)
- to ensure that the European treaties and secondary legislation are properly applied and respected
- to administer and implement common rules.

The Council: known as the Council of Ministers, it consists of one member of the Government of each Member State. The Council is the final arbiter on what action the Community will take.

The European Parliament: there are 518 elected members of the Parliament, with elections taking place every five years. Parliament's role is three-fold: to provide opinions on legislative proposals; to agree the Community budget; and to exert some control over the Commissioners. This last power is limited in practice as the Parliament's only sanction is to dismiss all Commissioners, for which it needs to pass a motion of censure by a ⅔ majority, with over half of all members voting in favour.

The European Court of Justice: the European Court's role is similar to that of the House of Lords and other appeal courts: its duty is to ensure that any measures taken by the Council or the Commission are compatible with European treaties and to decide, on request, on the interpretation or validity of national Acts of Parliament which give effect to Community law.

The Law Making Process

The way in which legislation evolves at Community level is shown diagrammatically overleaf.

9

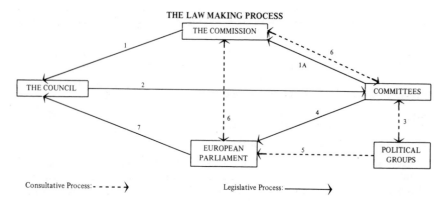

THE LAW MAKING PROCESS

Consultative Process: - - - - - →   Legislative Process: ——————→

The key to the numbers shown is:

1. The preparation of proposals for legislation is formally the prerogative of the Commission. In practice there are often discussions with the appropriate Committee of Members of the European Parliament before proposals are formulated.

1A. It is also possible for Committees themselves to make proposals to the Commission for legislation, through an "own initiative" report.

Proposals, once formulated, are then passed from the Commission to the Council.

2. On receiving the proposals the Council sends them immediately to the appropriate Parliamentary Committee for its opinion. The committee stage is very detailed, with the proposals examined line by line by MEPs.

3. At the same time, political groups (eg Christian Democrats, Socialists, Liberals and Democrats, etc) of the Parliament usually hold parallel meetings to determine the "party" line.

4. The final report of the Committee is presented to Parliament by the Committee's *rapporteur* for debate.

5. Further amendments may still be made to the proposals at this stage. The debate ends with a vote on the formal resolution and of course this is when the political groups can exert pressure, although individual MEPs are subject to Party "whips" to a much lesser extent than is the case at Westminster.

6. The Commission will normally incorporate the opinion of Parliament and the Committee into its own proposals.

7. It is these proposals that are finally passed back to the Council, which can then decide whether they should be given legal effect.

The final stage of the action can be in the form of a:
- **Decision:** this is binding in its entirety on those to whom it is addressed
- **Regulation:** binding and directly applicable to all Member States without the need for national legislation

- **Directive:** which is binding on each Member State as to the principle it incorporates, but leaves them free to decide on the form and method of giving it legal effect
- **Recommendation:** this is not binding; merely an exhortation as to the action to which Member States should aspire.

Impact on United Kingdom Legislation

To date, the European Community has had a greater impact on equal pay and sex discrimination law than on any other area of interest to personnel practitioners, although the Transfer of Undertakings Regulations 1981 have caused many headaches.

When the United Kingdom is required to introduce new legislation — either in response to a directive or to a decision of the European Court of Justice (ECJ) that existing legislation fails to comply with the country's obligations under the Treaty of Rome — it may do so by seeking the approval of both Houses of Parliament for regulations made under the European Communities Act 1972. This Act provides Parliament with only two options: it may reject the regulations wholesale or it may approve them. It cannot introduce amendments. Thus the traditional role of parliamentary committees cannot be used to ensure that the regulations will mean what they set out to mean, nor that they will achieve the objectives laid down by the EC.

This problem was highlighted recently by the equal pay regulations which set out to provide equal pay for work of equal value. The House of Lords took the view that the regulations did not satisfy the provisions of the Council Directive of 10.2.75 which, in Article 1, provides that:
"The principle of equal pay for men and women outlined in Article 119 of the Treaty . . . means, for the same work or for work to which equal value is attributed, the elimination of all discrimination on grounds of sex with regard to all aspects and conditions of remuneration".

The House of Lords, by the implied threat that it would reject the draft regulations, was able to exert pressure on the Government to modify them to a certain extent, but the House itself was unable to change them. As a result the regulations are widely regarded as incomprehensible and there is a strong belief in some quarters that the United Kingdom will again be found wanting when the European Court of Justice is asked to rule on the question of whether they meet the requirements of the Treaty of Rome.

Membership of the EC has also influenced the interpretation of legislation. For instance, in the case of *Macarthys Ltd v Smith* [1980] IRLR 209, the case was referred by the Court of Appeal to the ECJ for it to decide whether a woman could claim equal pay with her predecessor. The ECJ decided that she could, under the provisions of Article 119 of the Treaty of Rome, and so the Court of Appeal upheld Mrs Smith's claim.

Laws Derived from the EC

Other than the equal pay regulations, legislation has been necessary on sex discrimination, redundancies, mergers and health and safety.

The Council Directive of 9.2.76 aims to put into effect the principle of equal treatment for men and women as regards access to employment, including promotion; vocational training; and working conditions and social security, although the principle of equal treatment in this last area was implemented by stages. Although the Sex Discrimination Act was already on the statute book, this directive has caused problems, as is shown below.

So far as the law on redundancies is concerned, there is a Council Directive of 17.2.75 which requires employers to consult with workers' representatives in the case of collective redundancies. The objectives of this Directive were given effect by s.99 of the Employment Protection Act 1975.

The Council Directive of 14.2.77 concerning the rights of employees in the event of the transfer of the business in which they are employed, gave rise to the Transfer of Undertakings (Protection of Employment) Regulations 1981.

The Problem Areas

The difficulty of interpretation of regulations made under the European Communities Act has been mentioned above in connection with equal pay, but the problems are no less acute as regards the Transfer of Undertakings Regulations. Despite the fact that they have now been in operation for over five years, it is extremely difficult to predict the outcome of tribunal cases centring on such issues as whether a dismissal is for economic reasons, whether it is a "relevant transfer" and even whether people were in the employment of the transferor "immediately before" the transfer.

In addition to these problems, however, the United Kingdom ran into particular difficulties with the Sex Discrimination Act. The ECJ held that it failed to meet the requirements of the Treaty of Rome and the Directive in that:
- the exemptions in the Act in respect of organisations employing five people or less and private households were too broad to be permissible and
- the Act did not outlaw discriminatory provisions in collective agreements, internal rules or rules governing independent occupations and professions.

The Court in its decision stated that:
"Even if (collective agreements) are not legally binding as between the parties who sign them with regard to the employment relationship which they govern, collective agreements nevertheless have important *de facto* consequences for the employment relationships to which they refer, particularly insofar as they determine the rights of workers".

As a result, the Sex Discrimination Act 1986 has been enacted to resolve these problems.

New Proposals

There are a considerable number of proposals still in the European pipeline which, if agreed by the Council, will have a strong impact on employment policies.

The draft "Vredeling" and Fifth Directives, on the provision of information to employees and on employee participation, were summarised in ED in issues 146 and 147. Other draft directives concern the rights of part time and temporary workers and are designed to give them the same rights as permanent full time workers. There is also a draft recommendation which calls for the creation of more jobs through a reduction in working time, but without higher production costs.

To date these proposals have been resisted by the British Government. It is, however, possible that the right of individual Member States to veto proposals will eventually be withdrawn, since little progress can be made on legislative proposals when opposition from just one country can block them. Progress on all these measures could then be expected.

Employment Law and the Small Company

There are several areas of employment law where specific reference is made to small companies and, in some circumstances, separate legislative provisions apply. The problem for an employer who thinks his or her company may be covered by such provisions is knowing how a "small company" is defined, and exactly which areas of the law are affected.

Unfair Dismissal Rights

One important aspect of employment law which is affected by the size of the company is that of unfair dismissal. In the first place, the qualifying service needed to claim unfair dismissal used to be different for employees of a small company. For employees whose employment began before 1.6.85 the necessary qualifying service for unfair dismissal rights is one year. However, it is two years for employees of any company which employs 20 or fewer employees.

In order for the extra year of qualifying service to apply, at no time during the relevant two years must the number of employees have gone above 20; and, when calculating the number employed, account must be taken of any employees of an associated employer (see below). Employers who wish to rely on the two year qualifying service must, therefore, check carefully that no temporary or casual employees (taken on to cover a busy period, perhaps) took their total workforce over 20 at any time.

Of course, since the qualifying service for unfair dismissal is now two years for **all** employees whose employment began on or after 1.6.85, the small company provisions will soon lose their significance.

Reasonableness of Dismissal

The size of the company may also have a bearing on the actual fairness or otherwise of a dismissal, as assessed by an industrial tribunal. S.57(3) of the Employment Protection (Consolidation) Act 1978 as amended states that, once the employer has proved that the reason for dismissal was a fair one, the decision on whether the dismissal was fair or unfair will depend on whether in the circumstances (including the size and administrative resources of the employer's undertaking) the employer acted reasonably in treating it as a sufficient reason for dismissing the employee.

In other words, tribunals must consider all the circumstances of a case and they are particularly directed to look at the size of the business. An example of how this might work in practice is where a tribunal considering an unfair dismissal claim refers to the ACAS Code of Practice on Disciplinary Practice and Procedures in Employment. Although the code of practice has no legal status, it is admissible in evidence in tribunal proceedings and tribunals often use it as a guide to reasonableness.

The code recommends that an appeals procedure should be made available to employees who have been disciplined. However, it also acknowledges that smaller establishments may not be able to adopt all the detailed provisions. Therefore, in a very small company, a tribunal would be unlikely to hold a dismissal unfair just because the right of appeal was not granted. In a larger organisation it is possible that this factor alone could render a dismissal unfair.

What small companies cannot do, however, is try to rely on their size to justify other failings when dismissing an employee. In *Henderson v Granville Tours Ltd* [1982] IRLR 494 the EAT held that the smallness of the undertaking was not an excuse for failing to carry out a proper investigation prior to dismissing an employee.

Sex and Race Discrimination

The Equal Opportunities Commission (EOC) code of practice on sex discrimination makes special reference to small businesses. It acknowledges that small companies require much simpler procedures than larger, more complex organisations and that it may not always be reasonable for them to carry out all the code's detailed recommendations. For example, when it comes to monitoring an equal opportunities policy, the code states that in a small firm with a simple structure it may be adequate to assess the distribution and payment of employees from personal knowledge.

It should be noted that there are no small company exemptions from the provisions of either the Equal Pay Act 1970 or the Race Relations Act 1976. However, once again, in the Commission for Racial Equality (CRE) code of practice on race relations, specific reference is made to the application of the code to small companies and the fact that there may be less need for formality in assessing whether equal opportunity is being achieved in arrangements for monitoring, etc.

Maternity Rights

Employees who work for small companies still have the right to receive maternity pay and to go on maternity leave, provided they satisfy the necessary qualifying conditions. However, what may be affected, if the company they work for is small enough, is their right to return to work. In order for the different provisions to apply the total number of employees employed in the company (added to the number employed by any associated employer) must be five or less immediately before the woman's absence on maternity leave.

Where this is the case, if the employer can show that it is not reasonably practicable to allow the woman to return to her old job, or to offer her suitable alternative work, she loses her right to return to work. If suitable alternative work is available it must be offered to the woman and, if the woman takes a complaint to a tribunal over her lost rights, the onus will be on the employer to show that the company is small enough to rely on the exemption, and that it was not reasonably practicable to give her the old job back or offer her another. Other employers can also argue that it was not reasonably practicable to give a woman her old job on her return from maternity leave, but if they do so they *must* offer her suitable alternative employment — they cannot put forward the defence that there was none available.

Health and Safety

S.2(3) of the Health and Safety at Work Act 1974 states:
"Except in cases as may be prescribed, it shall be the duty of every employer to prepare and as often as may be appropriate revise a written statement of his general policy with respect to the health and safety at work of his employees and the organisation and arrangements for the time being in force for carrying out that policy, and to bring that statement and any revision of it to the notice of all his employees".

One of the prescribed exceptions referred to is that of the small company. Any employer who carries on an undertaking in which for the time being

15

fewer than five people are employed is exempted from the requirement to provide a written safety policy statement.

In *Osborne v Bill Taylor of Huyton Ltd* [1982] IRLR 17, the High Court had to consider exactly what the wording of the exemption meant. First of all it looked at the construction of the word "undertaking". The case involved a chain of betting shops and the court held that the correct question to ask was whether each shop was being carried on as a separate undertaking from the others, ie was it a single business carried on through a number of outlets or was it a case of a single company carrying on a series of businesses? The sort of factors which it suggested should be taken into account included the fact that: each shop had its own manager (indicating separate undertakings) and each shop was subject to close central control (indicating a single undertaking). What is an undertaking must be a question of fact to be decided in each case.

Secondly, the court considered what was meant by the phrase "for the time being he employs less than five employees". It held that "for the time being" should be interpreted as "at any one time". Therefore, if an employer employs fewer than five people at any one time, even if he or she employs four in the morning and four others in the afternoon and provided the two sets of employees do not overlap, the exemption will apply.

In line with its policy of lessening the administrative burdens on small businesses, the Government has floated the idea, in a White Paper, of amending the small firms provision. It suggests that the minimum number of employees required before a written health and safety policy need be prepared should be increased to 20.

Redundancy Rebate

Until July 1986, all employers who dismissed employees on grounds of redundancy, and who made them statutory redundancy payments, could claim a rebate of 35% of the payments from the Redundancy Fund. However, for most employers, payment of the rebate ceased for redundancies which took effect on or after 1.8.86. The only exceptions are those companies which employ fewer than 10 people; they are still eligible for a rebate. These changes to the system of redundancy rebate were contained in the Wages Act 1986.

Directors' Reports

The definition of "small company" for the purposes of statements which must be included in directors' reports is substantially different from that in other areas of employment law.

All companies, where the average number of people employed in each week during the financial year exceeded 250, must include the following in their directors' report for that year.

1. A statement describing the policy the company has applied that year:
   (a) for giving full and fair consideration to applications for employment made by disabled people
   (b) for continuing the employment of, and arranging training for, employees who have become disabled
   (c) for any other training, career development and promotion of disabled employees.
2. A statement describing the action that has been taken during the financial year to introduce, maintain or develop arrangements aimed at:
   (a) providing employees systematically with information on matters of concern to them as employees
   (b) consulting employees on a regular basis so that their views can be taken into account in making decisions which are likely to affect their interests
   (c) encouraging the involvement of employees in the company's performance through a share scheme or some other means
   (d) achieving employees' awareness of the financial and economic factors affecting the company's performance.

Note that the requirement is to include a *statement* as to any action taken in respect of these matters; there is no legal obligation on companies actually to *do* anything in respect of disabled employees or employee involvement if they do not do so already. Also, of course, even the requirement for a statement does not apply to companies employing 250 or less.

Associated Employers

When establishing the number of employees in a company for the purposes of some of the provisions for small employers, the employees of any associated employers must also be taken into account.

In the EP(C)A it states that "any two employers are to be treated as associated if one is a company of which the other (directly or indirectly) has control, or if both are companies of which a third person (directly or indirectly) has control". This means that, if employers are trying to establish whether they can rely on one or more of the small company exceptions described above, they may have to look beyond their own company — perhaps to others in the same group.

Another rather disconcerting point for small companies to note is that just because any associated employers are overseas it does not mean that they can be disregarded. In *Cox v ELG Metals Ltd* (1985) ICR 310, the Court of Appeal felt that — in the case of unfair dismissal rights — the underlying purpose of the provision was to protect employees, while giving genuinely small, independent companies limited protection. It held that, although employees ordinarily working outside Great Britain are excluded from the unfair dismissal provisions, there is no suggestion that they stop being employees within the meaning of the Act. It was therefore held that associated employers overseas must be taken into account when calculating the number of employees for the purpose of unfair dismissal rights.

Employment Protection Exclusions

Under the provisions of the Employment Protection (Consolidation) Act 1978 the rights of most individuals in employment are protected. Given the qualifying service necessary in certain cases, people working 16 hours or more per week (or eight hours after five years' service) have the right to claim unfair dismissal and to receive redundancy pay and maternity pay with the right to leave and return after the birth. Other provisions in the Act cover the right to receive a written statement of terms and conditions; an itemised pay statement; and the right to notice and written reasons for dismissal. Guarantee pay and medical suspension are also included, together with various time off rights. Some categories of worker, nonetheless, fall outside some or all of these provisions and here we look at some of the "excluded groups".

Non-Employees

First of all, to qualify for employment protection, the worker has to be an employee engaged under a contract of service and not a contract for services. Thus independent contractors and genuinely freelance agents are not employees for the purposes of the Act. Whether a person is an "employee" is by no means easy to determine in all cases. Recent events have highlighted the problems of categorisation with regard to temporary, casual and homeworkers. This remains an obscure area where caution should be exercised before assumptions are made about the employment status of the people concerned.

It is sometimes believed that, by virtue of being a director, a person cannot be an employee. The position as far as directors is concerned is that when they hold salaried employment in addition to a directorship, which makes them a "servant" or employee, they enjoy employment protection rights separate from the rights they enjoy as holders of the office of director. Indeed in the case of *Chapman v Beacon Auto Electrics Ltd* (unreported) the EAT's opinion was that there might well be an implied contract of service where the director received regular payment, whether it is called "director's remuneration" or "wages". On the other hand, in a company where no fees or salaries were agreed and remuneration was voted by resolution each year, and where self-employed NI contributions were paid, the Court of Appeal held that the director was not an employee (*Albert J Parsons & Sons Ltd v Parsons* [1979] IRLR 117).

True partners are not considered "employees". Where a person has entered into a partnership agreement with a firm recognising him or her as a partner and it is quite clear to the public (for example from his or her name appearing as a partner on the firm's letter-head) that the person is a partner, he or she will not be classified as an employee even if he or she is taxed and pays NI contributions as an employed person. A tribunal will look at the reality of the situation. Where it is evident that the status of an individual is that of a partner, the person will not be an employee even if payment is made by salary or commission.

Office-holders, such as JPs, are not employees; they are appointed to an office, are not paid a salary, and are not working under direction. There has been some debate as to whether club secretaries can be employees for the purposes of the 1978 Act. Much will depend upon the size and method of payment, the extent of duties and degree of control exercised.

Co-Operatives

The question has been raised also as to whether members of a workers' co-operative can be considered employees of the co-operative. In a reported case covering this situation (*Drym Fabricators Ltd v Johnson* (1981) ICR 274) the EAT held that, since this co-operative was registered as a limited company, it was capable of employing and dismissing its own workforce. In an obiter passage, however, the EAT remarked that, had the co-operative not been registered, it would still be open to a co-operative to have a "legal personality", to have different members who could receive instructions from the body as a whole and for the body itself to appoint and dismiss. Given the above statement and the fact that most co-operatives are registered in the same way as Drym Fabricators, it would seem that in the majority of cases co-operative members are also employees for the purpose of employment protection rights.

Together with non-employees there are also some groups of employees who are not protected under the terms of the Act.

Working Abroad

One large excluded group is that of people employed outside Great Britain, as detailed in s.141 of the 1978 Act. An employee who under his or her contract of employment ordinarily works outside Great Britain is *not* entitled to a series of rights including:
- an itemised pay statement
- written reasons for dismissal
- guarantee pay, medical suspension
- the right to complain of action taken against him or her in respect of trade union membership and activities
- various time off rights

- maternity pay/leave and the right to return
- rights to claim unfair dismissal
- rights on insolvency of employer (unless based inside the EC).

Needless to say, the seemingly innocuous phrase "ordinarily working outside Great Britain" is far from innocuous when it comes to interpretation. The most contentious cases arise when an employee has spent time both in Great Britain and overseas during the course of employment.

The Court of Appeal in 1977 held that the correct approach in determining whether or not an employee ordinarily works outside Great Britain under his or her contract of employment is to look at the express or implied terms of the contract — the whole period contemplated by the contract should be considered. Where a contract of employment has an implied term leaving it to the employer's discretion as to whether the work should be carried out inside or outside Great Britain, all relevant terms of the contract should be analysed to determine where the employee's base is to be. If there are no special factors leading to a contrary conclusion, it is the country where the employee's base is to be which is likely to be the place where he or she is to be treated as ordinarily working under the contract of employment. This guidance arose out of the case of *Wilson v Maynard Shipbuilding Consultants AB* [1977] IRLR 491. Mr Wilson's contract contained no express terms on where he was to work and he had spent 40 weeks in the United Kingdom and 50 weeks in Italy. Rejecting the EAT's finding that an employee could work ordinarily both inside and outside Great Britain, the Court of Appeal sought to establish where the employee was based: factors such as his headquarters; where the travels in the course of his employment began and ended; where his home was; where and in what currency he was paid; whether he was subject to NI contributions in Great Britain — all were important indications of his base. It was not sufficient merely to look at the relative length of time spent overseas and in Great Britain when deciding if an employee ordinarily worked in Great Britain.

The "base" test has since been applied by the Court of Appeal in the case of a pilot who spent most of his time on overseas flights but whose employment base had at all material times been in Great Britain (*Todd v British Midland Airways Ltd* [1978] IRLR 370), and by the EAT in *Iran National Airlines Corporation v Bond* (unreported) where the employee, a flight attendant, spent over 80% of her time on flights abroad and was managed from Iran but paid in London and had income tax and NI contributions deducted. In both cases the employees were found to be ordinarily working in Great Britain.

When employees are posted abroad from Great Britain, contractual terms must be analysed to ascertain whether or not a secondment under the terms of the contract has taken place or, alternatively, whether a variation of the contract has occurred. Where there is an implied mobility clause and transfers are normal practice, no contractual change is involved when a person is moved outside Great Britain. In that case the person remains ordinarily working inside Great Britain and is not excluded (*Waring and Gillow Ltd v Hodgson* EAT 30/84). On the other hand, where an employee is transferred to a post abroad on different contractual terms and it is not envisaged as a temporary posting, there is a fundamental change in circumstances so far reaching as to vary or rescind the original terms of the contract and exclude the employee from the provisions of the 1978 Act.

"Great Britain" for the purposes of the Act includes British territorial waters and designated areas of the Continental Shelf (other than those under Northern Ireland law), thereby including in the protected category oil rig and gas installation employees who work in those sectors.

Redundancies

When employees are outside Great Britain on the relevant date for redundancy purposes they are not entitled to redundancy payments unless under their contracts of employment they ordinarily work in Great Britain (s.141(3)).

Employees who ordinarily work outside Great Britain are not entitled to redundancy payments unless, on the relevant date, they are in Great Britain — in accordance with instructions given to them by their employers (s.141(4)). Simply being on leave in Britain when the employer has paid the fare will not be sufficient to indicate that the employee was "under instructions" to return (*Costain Engineering Ltd v Draycott* [1977] IRLR 17). In view of this disparity between the statutory rights of employees at home and those posted overseas, employers may wish to consider including in the contract a provision for overseas workers to receive payments comparable to statutory redundancy pay, should the occasion arise.

Ships, Boats and Docks

For the purpose of deciding whether a person working on board ship is excluded by virtue of the "ordinarily working outside Great Britain" provision, s.141(5) makes the position clear. Someone employed to work on board a ship registered in the United Kingdom (but excluding Northern Ireland) is regarded as ordinarily working in Great Britain, unless the employment is *wholly* outside Great Britain or the employee is not ordinarily resident in Great Britain.

Even if the employee has worked only on a British-registered ship this may not be sufficient, where the contract made with the employer is to serve on any of the ships irrespective of the port of registry (*Royle v Globtik Management Ltd* (1977) ICR 552).

Having established the preliminary point of being employed to work on ships registered in the United Kingdom, seafarers then face two further questions if, for example, they wish to bring a claim for unfair dismissal:
– were they employed wholly outside Great Britain?
– were they ordinarily resident outside Great Britain?
If the answer to *either* of these questions is yes, a tribunal will not have jurisdiction.

An employee working on a ship which is not registered in Great Britain still has to pass the test of ordinarily working inside Great Britain.

While not being excluded from statutory provisions in respect of redundancy pay, most merchant seamen are covered in practice by the National Maritime Board Agreement.

With regard to fishermen, it has for some considerable time been assumed that all share fishermen are excluded from most employment rights under the EP(C)A. A recent case reaching the Court of Appeal, however, has cast doubt upon that interpretation in a situation where a fisherman is remunerated by a share in the profits of a fleet of vessels as opposed to the profits of the vessel on which he is employed (*Goodeve v Gilsons* CA 31.1.85).

One further group of people connected with the sea and ships who are largely excluded from the EP(C)A provisions are registered dockworkers engaged wholly or mainly on dock work. They do, however, retain the right to: an itemised pay statement; time off work for trade union duties/activities and public duties; and complaints of action short of dismissal in connection with trade union membership and activities.

Illegality

When an illegal contract has been entered into, the employee will not have employment protection rights. If employment is in breach of statutory requirements — for example an alien working without the required work permit or an under-age child employed during school hours — the contract is unenforceable because it is illegal. The same applies to contracts drawn up for an unlawful purpose.

The situation may be less clear-cut when the contract is "tainted" with illegality. This most frequently occurs when a contract, legal in itself, involves a tax dodge. If it is known to both employer and employee from the start that the Inland Revenue is being defrauded, the contract will not be enforceable. In circumstances where an employee claims to be unaware of the employer's fraud, tribunals will examine carefully the likelihood of the employee being an innocent "victim" before deciding on the illegality issue.

Other Groups

National Health Service employees may claim unfair dismissal but are specifically excluded from redundancy rights under the EP(C)A as they are covered by other arrangements. However, an apprentice who is not re-engaged by the employer *when the apprenticeship expires* is not able to claim a redundancy payment, since it has been held by the Employment Appeal Tribunal that the dismissal does not amount to dismissal on grounds of redundancy within the meaning of the Act.

Finally, where a dismissal procedures agreement which provides unfair dismissal remedies, on the whole as beneficial as those provided in the Act, has been drawn up jointly by management and an independent trade union, the parties to the agreement may apply to the Secretary of State to make an order designating the agreement. The employees covered will then be excluded from the statutory unfair dismissal provisions. An example of this sort of agreement is that between the Electrical Contractors' Association and the EETPU.

Signing Away Employment Rights

Although at common law employers and employees are free to agree between them whatever conditions they wish to apply to the employment relationship, the influence of statute law serves to invalidate certain terms. For example, agreements which provide that wages will be paid without any deduction for tax and national insurance contributions run counter to the relevant Finance and Social Security Acts. Similarly, a contract term which excludes or restricts a person's liability for death or personal injury resulting from negligence is deemed ineffective by virtue of the Unfair Contract Terms Act 1977. When it comes to statutory employment protection rights granted under the Employment Protection (Consolidation) Act 1978, s.140 of the Act ensures that the position is no different in principle, apart from certain limited exceptions.

What Does S.140 Say?

S.140 states that, subject to particular exceptions:
". . . any provision in an agreement (whether a contract of employment or not) shall be void in so far as it purports:
   (a) to exclude or limit the operation of any provision of this Act or
   (b) to preclude any person from presenting a complaint to, or bringing any proceedings under, this Act before an industrial tribunal".

The effect of this is that, where an employer and an employee agree between them that certain statutory rights will not apply to an employment, this will be rendered invalid and the employee will still retain those rights in the eyes of the law. A simple example of this can be shown in relation to an employee's right to receive a certain minimum period of notice to terminate the employment. Under s.49 of the Act, an employee's right to notice from the employer is a statutory minimum of one week if the period of employment is more than one month but less than two years, and a week for each complete year of continuous service after that, up to a maximum of 12 weeks' notice for a period of employment of 12 years or more. It may be the case that a new employee is taken on by a company, and that as part of the terms and conditions of the contract there is a clause which provides for one month's notice to terminate the contract on either side.

There would be no problem with this term as far as notice from the employee to the employer is concerned, since s.49 provides that statutory minimum notice for the employee to terminate the contract is one week, once that employee has at least one month's service and this does not increase with length of service. The contract provides for more than that statutory minimum, therefore it is binding. Indeed, even in respect of notice from the employer to the employee, the contract will be binding for the first four years, as that term would either be more generous than or the equivalent of the statutory minimum. However, as soon as the employee has accrued five years' continuous service, the entitlement to statutory minimum notice (of five weeks) would automatically override the contractual provision of one month, regardless of the fact that the employee had agreed to such a term when taking up the employment.

Interpretation by Tribunals

There have been a number of significant cases which have illustrated some of the circumstances in which tribunals have seen fit to invoke s.140. It is worth noting that, even if an agreement is reached in all honesty and with good intentions, the ignorance of both parties to its unlawful effect on a statutory right will not prevent s.140 rendering it null and void. In *Joseph v Joseph* (1967) 1 Ch 78 the High Court held that the words "in so far as it purports to exclude or limit" should be taken to mean "in so far as it has the effect of excluding or limiting". It is easy to see how such an unlawful agreement might be unintentionally reached over an issue such as continuous service. The rules on calculating continuous service are very complicated and, even assuming an employer knows of their existence, many of them are open to interpretation. It would, therefore, be relatively easy unwittingly to contract an employee out of his or her statutory entitlement to previously accrued continuous service. The problem is that the validity of that agreement may not be known unless and until it is tested before an industrial tribunal.

In *Hanson v Fashion Industries (Hartlepool) Ltd* [1980] IRLR 393, the Employment Appeal Tribunal looked at the legality of a statement in the employee's contract which said that "No employment with a previous employer counts as part of your continuous service with us which accordingly began on 4.7.77". In fact, Mrs Hanson began working for the company in 1970. However, in May 1977 she took part in a strike for which she was dismissed; 4.7.77 was the date on which she was re-engaged following the strike. The need to establish her true continuous service arose because she stopped work on March 30, 1979 to have a baby and claimed maternity pay. This was refused by her employer on the grounds that she had insufficient continuous service. An industrial tribunal agreed with the employer, but the EAT overturned the decision. It held that the paragraph of Schedule 13 which preserves continuity between the periods before and after a strike protected Mrs Hanson's continuity of service. It also held that the employer's attempt to rely on the term in her contract, which discounted previous service, failed since the term was void under s.140 of the EP(C)A, her continuity being automatically preserved through Schedule 13 of that Act.

Another case which looked at the effect of an agreement on working hours on the accrual of continuous service, pointed to the possibility of a much wider application of the s.140 restriction. In *Secretary of State for Employment v (1) Deary and others (2) Cambridgeshire County Council* [1984] IRLR 180, school dinner ladies who worked under a "variable-hours" contract of employment were made redundant within two years of having their working hours reduced to less than eight per week. Prior to that they had all worked for more than five years at more than eight hours per week. The employers refused their claims for redundancy payments on the grounds that the reduction in their hours to below eight broke their continuity of employment. The EAT finally decided the case on the basis that what had to be looked at was how the contract had been performed in terms of hours over the whole period of employment. However, the industrial tribunal, as part of its decision, felt that — in any case — s.140 effectively precluded the agreement to vary the employees' hours to below eight per week as it prevented them from accruing continuous service. As the case was decided by the EAT on the basis of how to calculate continuous service, the industrial tribunal's alternative view was not considered. This leaves the matter very much open to other tribunals to interpret as they wish, and some may take the view (as did the employers in the *Deary* case) that such an application of s.140 as was put forward by that tribunal would lead to absurd results.

Another type of agreement which was made null and void by s.140 was a redundancy "bumping" agreement (*Tocher v General Motors Scotland Ltd* [1981] IRLR 55). The agreement in question provided the employers with the right to transfer otherwise redundant employees to alternative employment. When Mr Tocher's job as a lorry driver ceased, he was transferred to the job of washer operator in the assembly department, which resulted in a £6.00 per week reduction in pay and a drop in status. After two weeks in the new job the employee resigned and claimed a redundancy payment. The employers contended that they were entitled to redeploy him by virtue of their bumping arrangement, but the EAT disagreed. It held that the bumping agreement had the effect of depriving the employee of his statutory right to a trial period (where alternative employment is offered in a redundancy situation) and to a redundancy payment (when that alternative work is turned down as unsuitable or because the employee is reasonable in doing so). The agreement was, therefore, invalid.

Other cases where s.140 applied were: *Inner London Education Authority v Nash* [1979] IRLR 29 in which a staff code provided for the cutting down of statutory maternity rights; and *Council of Engineering Institutions v Maddison* [1976] IRLR 389, where an agreement not to pursue a claim in return for an ex gratia payment was rendered null and void.

Overstaying Leave Agreements

Probably the most important case on this area of law recently has been that of *Igbo v Johnson Matthey Chemicals Ltd* [1986] IRLR 215. The agreement in this case was regarding an employee's failure to return to work after a period of extended leave. Prior to going on extended leave to Nigeria, Mrs Igbo signed a document which stated ". . . you have agreed to return to work on 28.9.83. If you fail to do this your contract of employment will automatically terminate on that date". Although Mrs Igbo returned to the United Kingdom two days before she was due to return to work, on September 28 she was unwell and did not attend work, forwarding a medical certificate to cover her absence. The employers wrote to her saying that her employment was terminated in accordance with the terms of the agreement. When she tried to claim unfair dismissal, both the industrial tribunal and the EAT found that there was a consensual termination and, therefore, no dismissal. This followed a previous EAT decision, in *British Leyland (UK) Ltd v Ashraf* [1978] IRLR 330, which had been followed in a number of other cases since then and had been frequently relied on as a precedent.

However, the Court of Appeal saw things rather differently. It held that such an agreement, introduced by way of a variation to the contract of employment, did in fact serve to "exclude or limit" the operation of a provision of the EP(C)A, namely the right of the employee not to be unfairly dismissed. Although the agreement did not expressly exclude that right, it had that effect in practice, since in order for there to be a claim for unfair dismissal there must be a dismissal in law. An agreement such as that in Mrs Igbo's case results in a termination by mutual consent, which is not a dismissal in the eyes of the law and therefore deprives the employee of the right to proceed with an unfair dismissal claim. The Court of Appeal thus held that since the agreement had this effect in practice, it was null and void under s.140, and that the Ashraf case had been wrongly decided and must be overruled. The case obviously has far-reaching implications, as many employers have been relying on the Ashraf case when drawing up extended leave agreements. However, the Court did stress that it distinguished an agreement such as Mrs Igbo's from cases where the employee is genuinely willing to leave and has agreed to do so in return for a financial consideration.

Conciliated Settlements

As stated above there are some exceptions to the restrictions otherwise imposed by s.140. The two most commonly used are the provision which allows for certain terms in fixed term contracts, and the one which excludes the operation of s.140 from agreements reached through a conciliation officer. It is possible to include terms in some fixed term contracts which legitimately deprive the employee of rights to claim unfair dismissal and redundancy payments.

As far as conciliated settlements are concerned it is the duty of conciliation officers from ACAS "to endeavour to promote a settlement" of any complaint that has been presented to an industrial tribunal. Under s.140(2), any agreement to refrain from instituting or continuing any proceedings before an industrial tribunal, which has been reached through a conciliation officer, will be binding, regardless of the operation of s.140(1)(b). This does not often cause a problem, but in *Gilbert v Kembridge Fibres Ltd* [1984] IRLR 52 the question was considered of whether a settlement reached through a conciliation officer must be in writing to be enforceable. In that case, Mr Gilbert was offered a sum of money by his ex-employers to settle his claim for unfair dismissal prior to the hearing. An agreement was reached orally but was never confirmed in writing as Mr Gilbert changed his mind and refused to sign the COT3 form. The EAT held, nevertheless, that an enforceable agreement had been created (on the grounds that it is an established principle that legal agreements can be made orally and will still be binding on the parties to them), that the restrictions under s.140 could not be invoked, and that the employee was barred from proceeding further with his unfair dismissal claim.

In a more recent case, *Courage Home Trade Ltd v Keys* [1986] IRLR 427, the operation of s.140 after proceedings had started was considered. The industrial tribunal had reached a reserved decision that the applicant had been unfairly dismissed, and the question of remedy, therefore, had to be settled at another hearing. However, in the meantime, the applicant accepted a payment from the respondents which was said to be in full and final settlement of the claim before the tribunal. It came to the EAT to decide whether the applicant could return to the tribunal for still further compensation, or whether he was prevented from doing so because of the agreement reached. It was held that, since the agreement had not been reached via the offices of a conciliation officer, it could not preclude the applicant from "bringing any proceedings" (ie continuing to bring proceedings) under the Act. However, the EAT also upheld the industrial tribunal's decision to make an award of nil compensation, on the grounds that it would be"taking advantage of a section of the statute and . . . that it is not just and equitable to award any further compensation to the applicant".

Pre-Complaint Conciliation

The exemption of conciliated settlements from the restrictions of s.140 also applies to any agreement to refrain from proceedings, where a conciliation officer has acted in accordance with s.133(3) of the EP(C)A. This provides that, as long as an individual claims that action has been taken in respect of which a complaint could be presented to a tribunal, a settlement can be reached through the offices of a conciliation officer even if a complaint has not actually been presented. Once made, such an agreement has the same status under s.140 as a settlement reached after a claim has been presented. Such agreements are regularly used by employers, but can present some problems. In *Hennessy v Craigmyle & Co Ltd and ACAS* [1985] IRLR 446, the employee who signed a COT3 form prepared by ACAS sought to demonstrate before the EAT that it was void because it was made under economic duress. Although the EAT felt that economic duress was capable of rendering an employment contract voidable, they considered that "only in the most exceptional circumstances" was it likely to be claimed successfully. Since Mr Hennessy had taken legal advice, had not considered social security and would receive a substantial benefit from the settlement, it held that there had been no economic duress and that the agreement was binding.

Employers and Negligence Law

The common law duty to "take reasonable care", which is the basis of the law of negligence, has considerably increased in importance in recent times. It is no longer confined to the common law of tort but now forms the basis of many statutory duties from the Factories Act 1961 to the duties imposed under the Health and Safety at Work Act 1974 and regulations made thereunder.

What is Negligence?

In *Riddell v Reid* (1943) AC 1, Lord Potter said that "negligence is the failure to use the requisite amount of care required by the law in the case where a duty to use care exists". In *Donoghue v Stevenson* (1932) AC 562, Lord Macmillan said that:

"The law takes no cognisance of carelessness in the abstract. It concerns itself with carelessness only where there is a duty to take care and where failure in that duty has caused damage. In such circumstances carelessness assumes the legal quality of negligence. . ... The cardinal principle of liability is that the party complained of should owe the party complaining a duty to take care, and that the party complaining should be able to prove that he has suffered damage in consequence of a breach of that duty".

For the tort of negligence to be proved, therefore, there must be three elements present:
- a duty of care owed by the person who has been negligent to the person who has suffered because of that negligence
- a failure by the person under a duty to take proper care
- damage suffered by the complainant due to the other's failure to take proper care.

Duty to Take Reasonable Care

Because the duty to take reasonable care (ie not to be legally negligent) does not stem from a contract, the persons to whom a duty is owed have to be specifically defined for purposes of liability for negligence. The general test which has been accepted by the courts is one of "reasonable foreseeability": the people to whom a duty is owed are those who it is reasonably foreseeable might be damaged by the employer's failure to take care.

In *Donoghue v Stevenson* (above) the plaintiff (ie the person bringing the case) suffered from shock and gastro-enteritis when she drank some ginger beer which contained a decomposing snail. (The shock was caused when the offending snail floated to the top of her glass and she realised what she had been drinking.) Although she drank the ginger beer at a cafe, she could not pursue an action against the cafe owner because the drink had been bought for her by a friend. She therefore sued the manufacturer for his failure to take reasonable care that the opaque bottle in which the ginger beer was sold was clean and uncontaminated. The House of Lords in this case had to consider whether there was any duty owed by the manufacturer to the plaintiff (until this time the law of negligence had been confined largely to protect those whose property or other proprietary rights had been damaged). Lord Atkin, giving the leading judgment of the House, held that:

"The rule that you are to love your neighbour becomes, in law, you must not injure your neighbour. . ... Who, then, is my neighbour? The answer seems to be — persons who are so closely affected by my act that I ought reasonably to have them in contemplation as being so affected when I am directing my mind to the acts or omissions which are called into question".

Clearly, manufacturers of soft drinks must have the ultimate consumer in mind when they make and bottle these drinks for sale.

The "neighbour" principle enunciated by Lord Atkin in this case gives rise to the modern concept of the tort of negligence. By application of the "neighbour" principle the class of people to whom a duty is owed can immediately be seen to be a wide one. The extent of this class is well illustrated by *British Railways Board v Herrington* (1972) AC 877 where a six year old child who was trespassing was injured on a railway line, having got through a gap in a fence. It was held that British Rail owed a duty to take reasonable care for the child's safety.

What is the Duty?

The duty of care which is owed is primarily a duty to take reasonable care. What is reasonable or what is reasonably foreseeable for purposes of the tort of negligence is always objectively assessed: what would a normal, right-thinking person think in the circumstances? This objective test is reflected by the time-honoured example: the man on the Clapham omnibus. A striking example of the objectivity of the test occurred in *Nettleship v Weston* (1972) 2 QB 691, where the plaintiff (ie the person bringing the action), an experienced driver, agreed to give a friend's wife some driving lessons using the friend's car. They started with the plaintiff controlling the gears and the handbrake whilst the defendant operated the pedals and the steering. The defendant made a mistake and panicked as a result of which the car drove up onto the kerb and hit a lamp-post. The plaintiff was injured in the collision and sued in negligence. The plaintiff could only succeed in his claim if the defendant had failed to take reasonable care. The defence pleaded that the defendant had used all the skill and competence which could be expected of a learner driver who was out on the road for the first time. The Court of Appeal, however, re-emphasised the objectivity of the test: a driver owes a duty to drive with the skill and competence of an experienced driver regardless of the individual driver's actual knowledge, competence or experience.

Foreseeability of the Plaintiff

The duty of care owed to employees is thus high. Obviously in any undertaking it will be apparent that unless proper care is taken in operating the business, employees are liable to be injured. This high duty of care would also apply to visitors to the premises, for example, prospective employees coming for interview, sales representatives and those carrying out work on the premises. Again, the duty of a manufacturer or retailer to the ultimate consumer will be high.

At the other end of the scale the duty of care owed to trespassers will be very low indeed. As we noted above, in *British Railways Board v Herrington* it was held that there was a duty of care owed to a six-year-old child trespasser. The House of Lords, in this case, held that there was a low duty of care owed to a trespasser who has, after all, thrust the "neighbour" relationship upon the occupier. An occupier's duty in such circumstances is to take precautions in respect of any danger on the land which is actually known about; there is no obligation in such cases to make inspections to ascertain whether there is such danger.

Dangerous Things and Activities

The greater the intrinsic danger of the thing which causes harm to the plaintiff, the higher the duty of care owed by the person responsible for that thing. It is obvious that employers who have explosives on their premises will be under a high duty of care towards anyone who might be injured by those explosives. In such cases the nature of the substance or thing puts the user on notice that care will have to be taken to ensure that no one will be injured.

Breach not Causing Damage

Since the damage suffered must be due to the defendant's failure to take proper care, the defendant will not be liable if the accident would have occurred even if proper care had been taken. In such circumstances there is no "causal connection" between the defendant's breach of duty and the damage suffered by the plaintiff. In *McWilliams v Sir William Arrol & Co* (1962) 1 AER 623, the plaintiff was the widow of a steel erector (M) who had died in an accident at work. M was working in a shipyard some 70 feet above ground on a platform held up by four "needles". One of the needles was not properly fixed and when M put his weight on it it gave way, as a result of which he fell to his death. No negligence in erecting the scaffolding was alleged (indeed, it appeared that M might have been responsible for erecting the platform himself). The plaintiff alleged that the defendant employers had been negligent in not providing safety belts. These safety belts had some 15 feet of rope attached to them and, if fixed to the main structure on which the employee was working, would prevent him from falling further than the length of the rope. Up until two days before the accident, safety belts had been available at the site but for some unknown reason the safety belts had then been removed.

The evidence, however, showed that it was not the practice for steel erectors to use the safety belts and, in particular, M had never used a safety belt. Nor, during the days preceding the accident, had M enquired about or sought to obtain a safety belt from the company. The House of Lords held that in these circumstances any breach of duty by the employers in failing to provide safety belts did not contribute to M's death since he would not have worn the safety belt even if it had been provided; the employers were not, therefore, liable for M's death. (**NB** The duty on an employer to ensure that safety equipment is used is considerably greater now than when this case was decided.)

Different Types of Damage

Even where a causal connection is established between the defendant's negligence and the plaintiff's damage this is still not the end of the matter. Since the defendant's duty is to take reasonable care, the plaintiff will not be able to recover for types of damage which are too remote from the breach of duty which gave rise to the damage. In *Gorris v Scott* (1874) LR 9, for example, the plaintiff was suing for the loss of some sheep which had been washed overboard whilst being carried on the defendant's ship. The animals had not been properly penned as was then required by the Contagious Diseases (Animals) Act 1869. If they had been properly penned the sheep would not have been washed overboard. The Court of Exchequer held that the plaintiff could not succeed in his action: the purpose of the Act was to prevent animals from infecting each other whilst in transit; it was not to prevent the animals from being washed overboard. The type of damage which had occurred (ie death by drowning) was too remote, or outside the contemplation of the duty imposed.

In *In re Polemis* (1921) 3 KB 560, the Court of Appeal considered the principles governing the question of the types of damage which could be compensated for in a case of negligence. Here the charterers of a ship had employed some stevedores in Casablanca to unload the ship. One of the stevedores dropped a plank into the ship's hold. The falling plank had, in turn, caused a spark which resulted in the ship catching fire and, ultimately, being totally destroyed. The Court of Appeal held that because the plank was the direct cause of the fire and some damage, however trivial, was foreseeable, the shipowners were entitled to recover damages from the defendant's charterers.

The Privy Council Judicial Committee* in *The Wagon Mound (No. 1)* (1961) 1 AER 404 took a different approach. Here oil was negligently allowed to spill from The Wagon Mound, a ship under the defendant's control. The oil spread to a wharf some 200 yards away where another ship, the Corrinal, was being repaired. The plaintiff wharf owners asked if it was safe to continue repairing the ship with welding equipment and were assured that it was. It was accepted at the trial that it was not reasonably foreseeable that oil spread on water would catch fire. A piece of molten metal from the welding set fire to a piece of floating rag as a result of which the oil was ignited and the wharf was destroyed. The Supreme Court of New South Wales affirmed the proposition that, since some damage to the wharf could be anticipated, if only by fouling, the defendants were liable for the fire which was a direct, though

---

*The Privy Council Judicial Committee hears appeals from Commonwealth countries. In England its judgments are not binding on other courts, but are of persuasive authority. The Privy Council is composed of the same judges as the House of Lords.

unforeseeable, consequence of the spillage. The Privy Council overturned this decision holding that *In re Polemis* was no longer good law: the type of damage for which a plaintiff could recover was that damage which was reasonably foreseeable as a consequence of the negligence. In this case the evidence was that damage by fire was not reasonably foreseeable and the defendant was not, therefore, liable. This case, although only of persuasive authority in the United Kingdom, has been accepted in subsequent cases as laying down the correct test for the type of damage which is recoverable by a plaintiff in a negligence action.

The decision in *The Wagon Mound (No. 1)*, that a particular type of damage must be foreseeable, is much more in accordance with the duty in negligence which is to take reasonable care for the plaintiff's safety — if no damage of a particular type can be foreseen the defendant should have no duty to guard against it.

Extent of the Recoverable Damage

Whilst *In re Polemis* (above) is no longer good authority for the type of damage for which the defendant is liable it is, nonetheless, the leading case on the extent of recoverable damage. Provided that the type of damage is foreseeable the defendant will be liable for all the damage which is directly caused by that negligence. *Hughes v Lord Advocate* (1963) AC 837 is a good example of this distinction. In this case the defendants opened a manhole cover to carry out telephone repairs. Above the manhole workmen placed a tent and warning paraffin lamps. Two boys, aged 8 and 10, took a lamp whilst the workmen were at tea and went down the manhole. As they re-emerged the paraffin lamp was knocked over into the hole. A violent explosion caused one of the boys to fall back into the manhole where he suffered serious burns. The judges in all the courts below the House of Lords accepted that it was reasonably foreseeable that the paraffin in the lamp might spill out and ignite outside the lamp (eg if it had fallen over and the glass broken) but, equally, all the lower courts held that an explosion was not reasonably foreseeable. The House of Lords held that this was analysing the "type" of damage too closely. An explosion, it was held, was merely one way in which burning could be caused. Since damage by fire was reasonably foreseeable the defendants were liable for the boy's injuries.

Chain of Causation

Another way of considering the extent of damage which is recoverable is to look at the "chain of causation": once there is a foreseeable type of damage, the defendant is responsible for all the damage which is caused until the chain of causation is broken. In *Scott v Shepherd* (1773) 2Wm B1 892, a live squib was thrown at B by A. B, in self-defence, threw the squib away, injuring a third person. B was held not liable for the resulting injuries. They were a direct consequence of A's unlawful act which had put B in the position where, as a reflex action, he had thrown the squib away.

In *Philco Radio & Television Corporation v J Spurling Ltd* (1949) 2 AER 882, the defendants were carriers who accidentally delivered five cartons of celluloid film scrap to the plaintiff company. The celluloid was highly inflammable and explosive and the cartons were unmarked. The plaintiff's foreman, recognising the material, told the men not to smoke and went off to try and contact the defendants. Meanwhile, a typist employed by the plaintiff came along and lit a piece of the cellulose with her cigarette. The plaintiff's premises were severely damaged in the ensuing conflagration. The typist's motives in starting the fire and what she expected to happen were unclear since, by the date of the hearing, she was no longer employed by the company. The Court of Appeal, holding that the typist could not possibly have meant to do more than "make a small and innocuous bonfire of some of the material which she probably took to be ordinary packing", found that her action did not relieve the defendants from liability for their admitted negligence in delivering highly inflammable material to the wrong address without any warning. In other words, the chain of causation was not broken by the typist's "innocuous" bonfire.

Breaking the Chain

There are, however, cases where the chain of causation is broken. An action which breaks the chain of causation is called a *novus actus interveniens*. In *McKew v Holland & Hannon & Cubbitts (Scotland)* (1969) 3 AER 1621, the employee's left leg was injured as a result of the admitted negligence of the employers. Three weeks after the accident he was going down a staircase when, allegedly because of the weakness in his left leg, he decided to jump down the remainder of the stairs. His right leg was injured in the fall. The employee claimed that the employers were also responsible for the damage to his right leg on the grounds that his leap was provoked by, and was directly attributable to, the damage to his left leg for which his employers were responsible. The House of Lords held that his jump amounted to a *novus actus interveniens* and, therefore, broke the chain of causation from the earlier accident.

"Thin Skull" Cases

Finally, it should be borne in mind that in law a defendant "takes his victim as he finds him". The classic example of this was in *Smith v Leechbrain & Co* (1961) 3 AER 1159 where the plaintiff, S, was employed by the defendants as a labourer and galvaniser. Part of his job was to galvanise articles by dipping them into the molten metal in the galvanising tank. In 1950 S's lip was splashed and burned by a drop of molten metal which flew out of the tank when a large object was dipped into it. The defendants were negligent in not providing adequate protection for S against being splashed by molten metal. At the time of the accident S had an existing, pre-malignant, cancer condition which could be made malignant by a scratch or a burn. As a result of the burn on his lip the cancer became malignant and S died of cancer in 1953. The defendants were held liable for not only the burn on S's lip but also for his death from the cancer which had been induced thereby. Lord Parker CJ held: "The question is whether these employers could reasonably foresee the type of injury he suffered, namely, the burn. What, in the particular case, is the amount of damage which he suffers as a result of that burn depends upon the characteristics and constitution of the victim". A reduction in S's damages was made, however, for the possibility that S might anyway have died of cancer, at some stage, induced by some other agency.

Vicarious and Personal Liability

An employer can be made liable for the negligent and unlawful acts of an employee, even though he has given express instructions to the contrary, which have been disobeyed. This is known as the doctrine of vicarious liability, whereby one party becomes liable for the actions of another. Whilst the guilty or negligent employee does not escape liability, it will be the employer who pays the price. If the employer is party to the negligent or unlawful act, or aids and abets the activities of another, he or she assumes personal liability along with that other person. Both principles have been clearly embodied in three notable employment statutes: the Health and Safety at Work, etc Act 1974, the Sex Discrimination Act 1975 and the Race Relations Act 1976.

Health and Safety at Work

The Health and Safety at Work Act 1974, provides (s.37(1)) that "Where an offence. . . committed by a body corporate is proved to have been committed with the consent or connivance of, or to have been attributable to any neglect on the part of, any director, manager, secretary or other similar officer of the body corporate. . . he, as well as the body corporate, shall be guilty of that offence and shall be liable to be proceeded against and punished accordingly". Here we are talking in terms of personal criminal liability. The penalty in such cases may be a fine of an unlimited sum and/or imprisonment for a maximum period of two years. Any personnel managers or safety officers who neglect to take reasonable steps to ensure the health, safety and welfare at work of each employee may literally find themselves "behind bars". Whilst employers may be prepared to pay a fine, they may not recover the money from their insurers.

In one case (*Armour v Skeen* [1977] IRLR 310) Mr Armour was prosecuted for failure to devise a sound safety policy for employees in his charge, even though he had argued that he was not a director, etc within the meaning of the Act. Earlier cases had determined personal liability on the criterion of whether the employee was within the "brain area" of the company; that is to say, if he could be identified with the controlling mind and will of the Company. In *Tesco v Nattrass* (1972) AC 153, a case on the Trade Descriptions Act 1968, a Branch Manager was regarded as a subordinate and not within the"brain area" of his employers. It appears that the wording of the Health and Safety Act is rather wider than this, but each case will be determined on its merits, especially the function assigned to the individual in the company.

Discrimination: Sex and Race

S.41 of the Sex Discrimination Act 1975 states that "anything done by a person in the course of his employment shall be treated for the purposes of this Act as done by his employer as well as by him, whether or not it was done with the employer's knowledge or approval". Thus, discrimination by a supervisor may very well devolve on the personnel manager or company secretary, if it can be shown that either of the latter was responsible for ensuring compliance with the law and had taken insufficient steps not only to devise a suitable non-discriminatory employment policy but to convey the message loud and clear to those responsible for administering that policy on the shop floor. The only defence that a personnel manager (or equivalent) would have in such cases would be to "prove that he took such steps as were reasonably practicable to prevent the employee doing. . . acts of that description" in the course of his employment. Additionally, the employer would assume personal liability if he or she knowingly aids and abets a discriminatory act, or turns a blind eye to the actions of people known to be breaking the law.

These provisions contain both doctrines. The employer may be personally or vicariously liable, whilst employees will similarly assume personal liability for their actions. The defence that all reasonably practicable steps were taken does give the employer a greater chance of success than at common law, because, as we shall see, an express prohibition does not necessarily absolve the employer from liability.

In the case of *Read v Tiverton and Bull* [1977] IRLR 202, Mrs Read claimed that she had been discriminated against on grounds of sex in failing to be appointed to the post of Chief Land Charges Clerk. She sued Mr Bull, Solicitor to the Council, and described him as her employer. In a preliminary hearing the question was whether Mr Bull could be sued as well as the Council. He conceded that he had played a prominent part in the decision not to promote Mrs Read but claimed he was acting on behalf of the Council. It was held that he could be sued personally and the tribunal said it was implicit from s.41, especially from the words "as well as by him", that Parliament recognised that an agent should personally be responsible. The tribunal added that s.42 also gave support to that interpretation. Although the decision was on a preliminary point, namely whether Mr Bull could be joined as a respondent, the case should be regarded as a clear statement of the law. It should also be noted that the tribunal also referred to almost identical provisions (ss.32–33) in the Race Relations Act, 1976; the same interpretation would be applied to that Act.

Outside the Scope of Employment?

If an employee's negligent or illegal acts occur "outside the scope of employment" it can generally be assumed that the employer is not liable for the damages which result. The legal test is not so much whether an employee was acting in defiance of an express instruction to the contrary, but whether or not, in doing so, he or she was"engaged in his (or her) employment" at the time. This general principle was first propounded in 1862 (*Limpus v London General Omnibus Company* (1862) I H & C 526). Drivers of omnibuses were each issued with a card saying that they "must not on any account race with or obstruct another omnibus". Nevertheless, a driver did so obstruct another omnibus, thereby causing injury. The employer was held vicariously liable on the basis that the employee's act was done for the employer's services. It was not done in the furtherance of his own interests.

There have been a number of cases on this point, all of which turn on whether the act was within the sphere of employment. Thus, a heavy goods vehicle driver would be acting "outside the scope of his (or her) employment" if he or she gave an unauthorised lift to a hitchhiker and injury ensued (*Conway v George Wimpey* (1951) 1 AER 363).

Express Prohibition

In a recent case (*Rose v Plenty and Co-op Retail Services Ltd* [1976] IRLR 60), Mr Plenty, a milkman, had been expressly prohibited from (a) giving lifts on his float and (b) obtaining help in his work. Nonetheless, he invited a young boy to assist him and, while making deliveries, the boy was injured as a result of Plenty's negligent driving. The High Court awarded damages against the employee, but not his employer, as it was held that Plenty had been acting "outside the scope of his employment". The Court of Appeal, by a majority decision, reversed the earlier decision holding that, even though Plenty had acted in a prohibited manner, he had done so in the course of his employment and in his employer's interests.

This is all a matter of policy; the doctrine is a reflection of the fact that the employer is in a better financial position to pay damages and will have an insurance policy to meet contingent civil liabilities.

Employers' Liability (Compulsory Insurance) Act 1969

In the latter context, an employer should not need reminding that, since 22.10.69, it has been a criminal offence not to insure against "liability for bodily injury or disease sustained by. . . employees, and arising out of and in the course of their employment . . .". In addition, the Certificate of Insurance must be duly framed and exhibited for the information of employees. There is a neat irony in this context. S.5 of the above Act provides that:

"an employer who on any day is not insured. . . shall be guilty of an offence and shall be liable on summary conviction to a fine not exceeding two hundred pounds; and where an offence . . . committed by a corporation has been committed with the consent or connivance of, or facilitated by any neglect on the part of, any director, manager, secretary or other officer of the corporation, he as well as the corporation shall be deemed to be guilty of that offence and shall be liable to be proceeded against and punished accordingly".

Conclusion

Whilst an employer may have observed the letter of the law in, for instance, producing and distributing a statement of company policy on health and safety at work, or rules forbidding discriminatory employment practices, failure to monitor the implementation of such policies or statements of intent may very well place him or her beyond the scope of the insurance policy and so personally liable to pay heavy fines or spend a period of time in one of Her Majesty's prisons. There is ample evidence to suggest that the doctrines of vicarious and personal liability will be strictly applied.

Employers' Responsibilities for Employees' Property

Many employers nowadays provide free parking space for their employees' vehicles and free locker or cloakroom facilities for articles like outer clothing or jewellery which may have to be relinquished by the employee during the working day. We turn now to the responsibility of employers in the event of such articles being stolen, damaged or destroyed.

Liability in Bailment

In some cases employers will become *bailees* of their employees' property. As such they will be answerable for any loss or damage occurring to the property unless they can prove that this did not result from their failure to take reasonable care in its safekeeping. This may necessitate providing attendants or a system of limited or supervised access to the area where the articles are kept, according to the value of the articles themselves; for articles of lesser value lesser precautions may be required.

For liability in *bailment* to arise, employees must show that their employer has voluntarily taken possession of their property; in other words, employees must temporarily have given up their own custody and control of the articles in favour of some more immediate control exerted by their employer. In a large, open-space car park, with no supervision and no physical restrictions upon employees' ability to retrieve their vehicles at will, there will normally be no bailment — no delivery of possession — and no concomitant duty on the employer's part actively to safeguard the goods. In such a case there is what the law describes as a "mere licence" to use the parking space.

Liability in Contract

Two cases since the war (one involving an actor employed as a pantomime dame and the other involving a resident hospital physician) are opposed to the suggestion that there should be an implied term in any contract of employment whereunder it is contemplated that the employee will leave personal articles upon the premises of his employer and that the employer will take care to protect them against loss by theft. Probably the same rule applies to damage or destruction, although in this event there is likely to be a remedy under one of the two preceding heads of liability.

Exclusion Clauses

Any attempt by any person, either by contract term or notice, to exclude liability for breach of a duty of reasonable care in relation to personal property is now, by the combined effect of ss.1 and 2 of the Unfair Contract Terms Act 1977, of no effect except insofar as the term of notice satisfies the statutory requirement of being reasonable as between the parties. The criteria as to what is reasonable are set out in schedule 2 to the Act and include such factors as the relative bargaining positions of the parties and the existence of alternative facilities. Since employers in effect have a monopoly over any necessary custody of their employees' belongings, the courts are unlikely to look favourably upon any attempt to exclude liability and may well hold either that it is unreasonable in the circumstances or that the revelant clause does not, on a proper interpretation, apply to the particular loss or damage sustained by the employee. To avoid the Unfair Contract Terms Act employers might endeavour to put up notices indicating that they undertake no duty with respect to employees' belongings, rather than that they merely accept no liability if any existing duty is broken but it is at least arguable that this method of evasion is prevented by the closing words of s.13(1) of the Act.

If, however, the car park is securely fenced or walled and an attendant is employed to check outgoing vehicles or to deter intruders, the law will more readily conclude that the employer is a bailee and, as such, is responsible for the safety of those vehicles while they are in his or her possession. It is all a question of degree. The irony is that the harder employers try to ensure that property belonging to their workforce is safely guarded, the more likely they are to be under a duty to take care of it.

Lockers and Cloakrooms

Similar principles apply to lockers and cloakrooms. If no attendants are provided and articles can be retrieved without supervision and at will (for example, if the only keys to the lockers are held by the employees) employers are unlikely to be liable as bailees. If, however, they exert a greater degree of control over the property in question (for example by retaining an auxiliary key to the locker or posting a porter on desk-duty near the cloakroom) a duty to safeguard that property may well arise. Likewise with rest rooms, canteens and medical centres — when an employee leaves a coat upon the back of a chair while eating in the canteen, the responsibility for seeing that it is not stolen is his or hers alone, but if it is left in a separate room provided for the purpose, or even on a rack at the end of the room, that responsibility may well shift to the employer. When workers specifically ask for care to be taken of their property (for example that it be kept in the office safe) the likelihood of a duty of care arising in the employer is even stronger.

Even when employers have taken reasonable care of articles bailed to them, they will be liable if they are stolen by any other employee or any independent contractor to whom they delegated the task of safekeeping. Whenever goods that have been made the subject of a bailment are lost, the burden is on the employer to prove that the loss did not occur in this way.

Liability in Negligence

Without a bailment, employers are only liable for losses by theft in the most exceptional circumstances (for instance where they negligently employ staff with proven criminal records in a position where they have access to employees' property). They may, however, still be liable for damage to goods left on their premises whenever this arises from the negligent conduct of employees in the course of their employment. Thus they could be answerable if negligent maintenance staff, while overhauling a central heating system, caused a flood or a fire which destroyed employees' clothing; or where a company vehicle, while leaving an open space car park, negligently collided with an employee's car. In such cases, however, the burden would normally be upon the employee to prove that these operations were conducted without reasonable care.

Occupier's Liability

Under the Occupier's Liability Act of 1957 an occupier of premises owes to all lawful visitors (including employees) a common duty of care to make premises reasonably safe. Upon modern authority it would seem, however, that this duty does not extend to the prevention of the loss of visitors' property by theft. Arguments to the contrary have been rejected in at least two decisions since the war and it now seems clear that the employee who complains (for example) of the theft of a coat from the staff cloakroom or locker room must base the claim upon some other foundation than the employer's duty as an occupier. The safer method would, of course, consist in proving that the employer was a bailee.

Again, however, there is a different rule with regard to physical destruction or damage. In this event the employer who has contravened the common duty of care as an occupier will be answerable for any resultant damage to employees' property; despite early doubts to the contrary, it now seems clear that this liability applies irrespective of whether the employee suffered personal injury on the same occasion. Thus, if an employer negligently omits to reinforce a defective ceiling, which consequently collapses causing injury and damage to employees' clothing, he or she should be liable not only to those employees who were present at the time of the collapse but also to those who had left their garments in the damaged area and were temporarily elsewhere.

Employees' Liability for the Employers' Property

Careless employees enjoy countless opportunities of endangering their employers' property: machinists may disregard instructions regarding the maintenance or functioning of their machines; sales representatives may leave merchandise or company vehicles exposed to serious risk; security officers and drivers may fall down in their surveillance of valuable consignments and personnel officers may negligently employ hardened criminals in positions of responsibility.

We now examine the various grounds on which employees can be made liable for losing or damaging their employers' property.

Can Servants Become Bailees?

As was stated on the preceding pages, delivery of possession of goods (or "bailment") may greatly increase the responsibility of the person placed in possession. If, for example, employers take possession of employees' clothing or valuables during working hours, they become responsible for anything happening to them (theft, damage, etc) unless they prove that the relevant misfortune did not result from a lack of reasonable care on their part.

If this obligation can be exacted from an employer, it might be thought that a reciprocal responsibility would be imposed, in appropriate cases, on an employee. Thus if employees were given goods for delivery and they either lost them or delivered them in a damaged state, they might be answerable for this to their employers unless they could show that it was not due to their default. English courts appear to have resisted this conclusion however, and have held that employees who gain control of their employers' property in the cause of their employment do not acquire possession but have "merely custody". The apparent result is that they cannot be liable as bailees. The rule is a total anachronism and seems to originate from the inability of slaves to own property. Logically, its status in the modern industrial context is extremely doubtful; legally, it has yet to be conclusively refuted. All one can say with certainty is that there are three situations where the rule gives way to more practical demands and allows employers to demand from their employees the duties of a bailee.

The Exceptional Cases

The exceptions arise:
   (a)   when employees are given something to be delivered to their employers; here, in the brief and perhaps non-existent interval between receipt of goods and doing something which amounts to an "appropriation" of the goods to the employer's use, the employees take them as a bailee
   (b)   when employees are allowed to take and use a chattel for a purpose unconnected with their employment, such as where an engineer is allowed to borrow tools to work on some private project at home, or a company representative uses a company car for social as opposed to professional purposes
   (c)   when there is an exceptional distance between the employer and the employee and an exceptional discretion allowed to the employee in his or her dealings with the chattel.

There is no decided case which illustrates this third exception and, in the light of authority which decides that a ship's master does not become a bailee of the ship even when it is on the high seas, its practical significance must be very limited indeed. But if employers *can* establish one of the foregoing exceptions they inherit a great advantage. They can point to the loss and require their employees to prove either that they had taken reasonable care in their handling of the property or that such failure to take reasonable care as occurred did not contribute to the loss. If the employees fail they will forthwith be liable; the employer need prove nothing more than the loss or damage itself and the fact that it occurred while the goods were in the employee's possession.

When Employees are Not Bailees

Outside these exceptions there are many instances in which, were it not for their contracts of service, the employees would normally be considered bailees. It may be that the fact of employment will eventually be considered irrelevant to their liability and that their obligations will come to be assessed in the same way as those owed by any other person who deals with goods which belong to another. Even so, there will continue to be cases in which the employees cannot possibly be classed as bailees because they acquire insufficient control of the property to justify the assertion that they are in possession. The shop assistant who carries the daily takings to the bank may well be a bailee of the money on that occasion but is unlikely to occupy the same position when it is merely in the till. What happens if property to which an employee has access, but not total overall control, is lost or damaged? The law is not altogether clear but it seems that (a) in the event of damage the employee will be answerable if and only if the employer can prove affirmatively that he or she failed to show reasonable care; and (b) in the event of theft the employer must prove additionally some sort of entrustment of the article to the employee. The position is illustrated by two cases. In the first (a Canadian decision in 1974) a driver who continued to drive a lorry after its engine had begun to knock was held not liable for the cost of the resultant deterioration because his employer could not prove, on the balance of probabilities, that the employee's conduct was careless. In the second (*Superlux v Plaisted* (1958) CA) the supervisor of a team of vacuum cleaner salesmen left 14 vacuum cleaners overnight in a car parked outside his house. He was held liable to his employers for their resultant theft.

Other Employees

Those who do not qualify as employees but are part of an organisation's extended workforce (such as directors, agents and independent contractors) are not subject to the "custody" rule and may be liable either as bailees or in simple negligence, according to whether they have gained possession of the injured property. In many cases they will also be liable for breach of their contractual duty to take reasonable care in the performance of their labour. Thus if employees of a firm of decorators negligently leave the premises unoccupied and exposed to risk (eg by failing to lock doors in their absence) their employers may well be answerable in contract for any resulting loss; likewise if they negligently employ dangerous criminals who themselves misappropriate clients' property. Technically, a similar claim may be possible against the orthodox employee; if there is an implied term in the contract of service that a company driver shall take reasonable care for the safety of other road users, there may equally be a term that he or she must take reasonable care for the safety of the employer's goods. However, no argument seems hitherto to have been raised upon these lines.

Deliberate Damage or Theft

It goes without saying that in the event of malicious or intentional mis-behaviour to chattels the employee is personally answerable to the employer, generally for trespass or conversion; he or she will also, in the majority of cases, be guilty of a breach of the criminal law.

The Practical Issues

It is often not a practical course of action to sue an employee: the company is admitting publicly that its employees have been dishonest, careless, etc and, more importantly, the company may get a reputation locally as a "bad employer" — people do not want to work for an organisation which takes its employees to court.

2 PERSONNEL ADMINISTRATION

In this chapter we examine the basic but essential factors affecting the life of personnel practitioners. What is the role of the personnel manager? What is a personnel audit and how should it be undertaken? What are the most effective ways of maintaining personnel records? Finally, we turn to the question of payroll. Even where this is not the direct responsibility of the personnel department it is inevitable that payroll questions will be directed there from time to time.

The Role of the Personnel Manager

An analysis of the role of the personnel manager in British industry today would show that personnel managers shoulder a bewildering variety of responsibilities within any given organisation. In some companies the personnel function is given high priority with individual personnel specialists having a large degree of autonomy in devising and implementing personnel policies and procedures, while in others "personnel" is viewed very much as a poor relation of the more high profile functions such as sales, production or finance.

Defining the Role

Management pundits and others have attempted to define the role of the personnel manager. For example:

"Partly a file clerk job, partly a housekeeping job, partly a social worker's job and partly fire-fighting to head off union trouble. . ." (Drucker 1955)

"The chief executive's dumping ground for unwanted tasks." (McFarland 1968)

". . . that part of management which is concerned with people at work and relationships within an enterprise. . . it seeks to bring together and develop into an effective organisation men and women who make up an enterprise. . . to enable each to make his own contribution to its success." (Institute of Personnel Management 1980)

The modern view is to encourage personnel management to be seen as part of management responsibility generally, with the task of bringing together, organising, motivating and directing people in order to maximise their performance for the good of the business. The personnel manager is therefore first and foremost a manager although the actual execution of this role will vary, depending on the degree to which the personnel function is recognised by the organisation.

It may be that the manager is restricted to an advisory role in the recruitment, training, payment, etc of staff, with the actual processes being carried out by the departmental, branch or divisional managers concerned. At the other end of the scale the personnel manager may have a highly autonomous or executive role with the authority to bypass or override line management in determining policies on how people are to be recruited, trained and managed.

Too Much Autonomy?

The latter end of the scale can, however, produce problems in identifying responsibility. Pushing too far into the executive and control field can result in the personnel manager undermining the line manager's position. Divided responsibility for human relations may lead to disagreements and eventual abdication by line managers of their responsibilities: "Oh, go and see personnel. They will sort it out ", or, even worse, "Fred really is a nuisance. You in personnel ought to sort him out".

In these circumstances employees will eventually go direct to the personnel department for help in straightening out their problems, which will result in a further erosion of the line manager's role.

When supervisors have no say in who is recruited or how induction is carried out and take no part in the disciplinary procedure, they lose authority, do not feel part of the management team and eventually become cynical about being responsible for things they cannot deliver.

Soothing the Savage Breast

The personnel function has a much more restricted role in many organisations where, typically, the manager deals with general "fire-fighting" and calming people down and lacks the status to advise the rest of the management team effectively. Here the personnel function is reduced to a routine administrative role, namely maintaining records, placing advertisements, providing secretarial support for joint consultation and observing statutory requirements.

Having a department to take care of these tasks is obviously useful to line managers, who are thereby relieved of time-consuming problems. It is a wasted opportunity, however, if this is considered to be the limit of the personnel role.

What Should Personnel Managers be Doing?

Personnel managers have a dual role: firstly, they advise the rest of the management team; secondly, they provide services for line management.

Services to line management should be given without hindering the manager's authority. Basic services may include the preliminary screening of job applicants, compiling job descriptions and personnel specifications, liaison with employment agencies, and so on. In larger organisations the role may extend into manpower planning, namely establishing forecasts for future manpower needs in relation to the organisation's corporate plan, assessing potential manpower supply both within and outside the organisation, and developing systems for monitoring manpower levels.

Training may also come within the remit of the personnel manager and involve the establishment of current and future training needs, designing and organising appropriate training or individual development courses (internally and externally), establishing systems for performance appraisal and liaising with organisations such as training boards, colleges of further education, YTS managing agents, etc.

Salary administration may be a very sophisticated operation or may consist simply of finding out the local rates of pay on offer. The personnel manager's role may include job evaluation and devising detailed pay and benefits packages. Occupational pension scheme administration is also steered towards the personnel department in many organisations.

Inevitably the personnel manager's role will involve dealing with industrial relations either in a unionised context or in individual disciplinary or grievance situations. This requires the personnel manager to understand employment law and to set up systems to ensure compliance with legal requirements. As a basic minimum this must include knowledge of creating a contractual relationship, the smooth running of that contractual relationship and its termination. In employment law terms these are the basic tools with which the personnel manager has to work — the "bottom line" from which management can adjust, accommodate and compromise in the day to day course of an employment relationship.

Very often the personnel manager's role will encompass health and safety at the workplace. Once again, the legal requirements must be understood, safety policies must be written and organisational arrangements made for dealing with accidents; clear procedures for investigating and reporting accidents at work should be laid down. The personnel manager should also ensure that changes to the legislation or codes of practice are always picked up. Additionally, the personnel manager will usually be responsible for aspects of employees' welfare, eg canteen facilities, welfare visiting, sports and social clubs.

The efficient provision of such services depends, essentially, on good administrative skills.

In-House Advisory Service

By far and away the most important aspect to the organisation of the personnel manager's role is that of advising management. This should not be seen as a neutral role: the personnel manager is not an impartial arbitrator between management and the employees — a kind of keeper of the company's conscience. Essentially the personnel manager has to work through the management team. This calls for the personnel manager to have a good knowledge of the technical problems facing the managers concerned. The human issues are invariably intertwined with the technical problems and it is impossible to advise sensibly unless there is an understanding of the context in which decisions will have to be made. The advice is better given from an informed, objective point of view than from the standpoint of a sentimental or personal interest in people. It would also be sensible for the personnel manager to emphasise strongly the need to be a part of the management team in the decision making process rather than being asked to mop up after the decisions have created problems.

This can be a difficult role to play; it involves establishing a relationship with line managers and other company managers in which the personnel manager is seen as a source of help to whom they will turn readily. One management writer, McGregor, outlines what looks like a counselling method in developing this relationship.

1. The personnel manager appraises the problem from within the line manager's viewpoint while keeping his or her own ideas in the background.
2. The personnel manager indicates his or her own view of the situation and what the personnel objective with this problem is likely to be. Additionally, information of the personnel manager's own knowledge or

experience is offered in a mutual exploration of the problem. However, the personnel manager's own solution is not voiced at this stage.

3. Together they examine possible solutions which would be mutually acceptable. The personnel manager introduces his or her own ideas, factual information, etc without forcing or imposing that solution upon the line manager. The line manager should be sufficiently confident in the relationship to think aloud without the fear of exposing weaknesses such as lack of knowledge or experience.

4. The personnel manager should support the line manager by giving self-confidence and coaching in new skills. The aim should be to develop the line manager's independence.

Key Areas of Expertise

In a nutshell, the personnel manager's role is to enable other people to do their jobs more efficiently in, and of greater benefit to, the organisation than they would do without that assistance. However, there are specific roles which personnel managers can adopt as their own and for which their specialist knowledge will be invaluable.

Employment Law Specialist

Personnel managers who specialise in employment law will quickly be able to demonstrate their worth to the company. The common law rights of individual employees engaged under contracts of employment have always been a source of concern for personnel managers, and the last decade or so has seen an unprecedented increase in the statute law governing employees' rights. Even legislative "tinkering about" often creates a more complex situation. The growth of legislation has created the need for the personnel manager to adopt a more specialist role in carrying out his or her function, not only in order to promote harmony in the workplace, but also in order to minimise the likelihood of financial losses that can result from breach of contract or unfair dismissal claims, redundancy payments, overpayment of wages, etc.

Creator of Company Policies and Procedures

The interest of outside agencies (industrial tribunals, etc) in the way companies conduct themselves has acted as a spur to greater formalisation of policies and procedures, particularly as companies respond to changing business needs. With the need to set up redundancy selection policies, relocation policies, formal disciplinary and grievance procedures, etc, the personnel manager has become a formulator of policies and procedures. The drafting of such documents in a logical and orderly way and the ability to carry out back-up research are important skills.

Communicator

The personnel manager frequently acts as the medium through which management communicates with the workforce and through whom the workforce express their views to management. This is often formalised in joint consultative arrangements such as works committees and other collective arrangements. Very often recourse to the personnel manager is one of the stages in the company's grievance procedure.

Even on an informal level the personnel manager who "walks the job" every day will often be in a unique position to assess the morale of employees generally.

Conflict Manager

The very nature of the personnel manager's role requires a degree of understanding of human behaviour and at some time or other will involve coping with conflict. Negotiations with a trade union may break down, employees may disagree with disciplinary decisions taken against them, staff may dispute the right of management to take a particular course of action. Traditionally, personnel managers were asked to pour oil on troubled water. Increasingly, nowadays, they are seizing opportunities to help management develop tactics to deal with such situations. In the longer term they will usually set about developing systems to encourage good relationships and to enable resolution of conflicts.

Personnel Policies

Having looked at the personnel manager's role, it is surprising to discover that many companies do not have a defined personnel policy. Formal statements can give a clear and consistent lead to help management in general and the personnel specialist in particular develop efficiency within the organisation. Where written policy statements exist, they usually conform to the general outline set out below.

1. Objective: the continuation of the company's existence; the stability of profit margins; the maximisation of profit margins or the growth and extension of the company, etc.
2. Policy: this section deals with general guidelines given by directors to keep management action on the path towards the objective. (The policy is not a rule or procedure, it is a guideline to be followed when managers are engaged in decision making.)

    Such a policy may well refer to the guiding standards which will be applied to the terms and conditions of employment under which employees are engaged. For instance, does the organisation intend that the general level of wages, holidays, pensions, sick pay, physical conditions of work, etc should be the best in the area or in the industry? Alternatively, does the organisation aim to provide the equivalent of the average package for the area or industry?
3. Practices/procedures: companies may put such material into the form of a procedural handbook covering all aspects from company benefits to the rules associated with conditions of employment.

The Secretary in Personnel

Secretaries are important. A muddle-headed, ill-equipped secretary can ruin a manager's career, throw a department into chaos and affect the standing of the organisation in the world outside. On the other hand, a capable secretary can provide the sound, stable pivot around which the department revolves smoothly. This is true, to a greater or lesser extent, throughout the whole organisation but nowhere more so than in the personnel department.

"Personnel" tends to be an area towards which secretaries gravitate because they believe it sounds more interesting than accounts or sales. However, as every personnel manager knows, the personnel function is not just about liking people. Large chunks of time are taken up with routine but essential administrative chores; employment legislation has to be absorbed and its implications understood; conditions of service need to be kept under review, and so on. Secretaries in a general personnel department will be involved in all these aspects of work. Consequently, it will not be sufficient for them simply to want a "people" job if they are to become valued members of the department — special personal and job-related qualities will be required.

The Right Person

In many organisations secretaries are the most accessible members of the personnel department so far as other employees are concerned. While the personnel officer is interviewing job applicants and the manager is perhaps sorting out a remuneration package for a senior executive, the secretary bears the brunt of employee inquiries and complaints. It follows from this that a welcoming manner and a willingness to listen to other people's problems are essential. On the other hand, a *too* sympathetic nature can be a drawback, allowing disgruntled employees the opportunity to take up too much of the secretary's time with lengthy descriptions of real and imaginary grievances. A balance needs to be struck and a shrewd secretary will soon learn how to differentiate the professional moaner from the employee with a genuine problem.

A firm but fair approach to employment agencies seeking business must also be developed.

It goes without saying that tact is needed by any secretary. In personnel work discretion is an absolute "must". Secretaries in personnel learn a good deal about the salaries and personal circumstances of employees at all levels, up to and including directors; they are also inevitably privy to management plans for employees' promotion (or dismissal), have advance warning of redundancy proposals and are aware of individual managers' standing within the organisation. Clearly the slightest hint or indiscreet murmur on any of these confidential matters can cause considerable damage.

51

One of the most useful tasks a secretary can perform is to "keep an ear to the ground". Secretaries tend to have a fairly sophisticated grapevine in most organisations; news spreads quickly around the secretarial network. This can be very useful to a personnel manager. A secretary who lets the manager know where trouble may be brewing, for instance, may prevent a little local difficulty from getting out of hand. This is not to say that the secretary should be seen as an "informer". It is perfectly possible to point the manager subtly in the right direction — "Why not take a trip to the fourth floor today?" — without breaking any confidences.

Basic Skills

No personnel manager would think of recruiting a secretary who did not possess adequate technical skills. Offer letters, statements of terms and conditions, and correspondence with job applicants all need to be immaculately presented.

Personnel is never "tidy". There are dozens of varying tasks to be done in the course of the day. Apart from taking all this in their stride, personnel secretaries have to maintain accuracy and attention to detail at all times. A typing error over salary in a contract can be an expensive mistake for the company. Because of the wide variety of work involved in a general personnel department, chaos will ensue if the secretary does not organise the workload in a satisfactory way. An ability to set priorities and manage time are talents well worth developing.

Increasingly, personnel departments are making use of word processors which should free secretaries for more interesting duties. The skills acquired on the word processor will be equally applicable if the personnel department decides to computerise its records and starts to use computers for longer term planning and analyses. It is unlikely that someone who is reluctant to use a computer will fit into the personnel department of the future.

When computers are used, the secretary must be made aware of the provisions of the Data Protection Act 1984 and there has to be stress on the importance of security. To comply with the Act, unauthorised access to, alteration, disclosure or destruction of personal data must be avoided by strict security measures. With this in mind the siting of the screen terminal should be given special consideration, particularly where employees from outside the department may be able to see the information displayed. Care should also be taken with print-outs which should not be left lying around on desks or in unlocked drawers; when no longer required, print-outs should be shredded rather than dumped in wastepaper bins.

The location of a secretary's desk is an important matter even when a computer is not being used. All personnel secretaries spend a proportion of their time handling confidential documents; it is inevitable that, while turning aside to answer the telephone, for instance, items will be left in the typewriter or on the desk for the inquisitive passer-by to scan. For this reason, protection of the desk by a screen in a location well away from the main office "highway" is advisable.

Where a secretary is sharing an office with others, information given over the telephone will become common knowledge, and arrangements should be made for the secretary to handle confidential calls in a private room.

Personnel Skills

Having engaged this discreet, meticulous, well organised, technically competent, sympathetic but not gullible individual, the busy personnel manager will quickly realise that the new recruit can be employed on more demanding tasks than routine secretarial duties. Indeed, one of the advantages of the personnel function from the secretary's point of view is the scope for involvement in the affairs of the department. Record keeping and recruitment are obvious areas in which a secretary can make a contribution at an early stage — provided appropriate training is given. That training should include a good grounding in the principles of employment legislation and related regulations.

The Contract

To be able to undertake administrative and other tasks concerned with recruitment successfully, the secretary needs to understand, firstly, the nature of an employment contract. Many people assume that no contract exists until a piece of paper setting out the main terms and conditions of employment is given to a new employee. Everyone involved in recruitment should clearly understand that employer and employee enter into a contractual relationship as soon as the offer of employment is accepted — whether the offer and acceptance are in writing or not. Thus, if a job is offered by telephone, it should be made subject to satisfactory references, medical, etc, if that is the intention.

Otherwise, it can happen that someone in the personnel department who is not aware of the implications makes an unconditional telephone offer to a job applicant who gives notice to his or her current employer. When unsatisfactory references arrive, the company will be in breach of contract if they wish to withdraw the offer and could be liable for damages in respect of the notice period — apart from the moral responsibility the personnel manager will feel towards the rejected candidate.

Recruitment

Anyone involved in the recruitment process needs to understand the law on sex and race discrimination. Under the Sex Discrimination Act 1975 and the Race Relations Act 1976 it is unlawful to publish advertisements which:

(a) indicate, or might reasonably be understood as indicating, an intention to do any act amounting to unlawful sex discrimination, unless the intended act would in fact be lawful or

(b) indicate, or might reasonably be understood as indicating, an intention to do an act of discrimination on racial grounds, unless that act would not in fact be unlawful because of a genuine occupational qualification.

Secretaries who draft and place advertisements will need to understand the meaning of "genuine occupational qualification" and be made aware of both direct and indirect discrimination. It should be stressed that, although it is the publishing of a discriminatory advertisement that is unlawful, both publisher and originator of the advertisement may be held liable.

Another job which a secretary is likely to be given is that of briefing employment agencies. Again, discrimination legislation steps in to outlaw the practice of giving instructions to an agency to discriminate — indicating, for example, that the employer requires a man, a white person or a single woman, etc for the job.

New Employees

The first day in a company for a new recruit is very important and the smoother the administration the more likely it is that the employee will settle in quickly and happily. A secretary will often be asked to organise first day induction arrangements and, to ensure that the exercise is carried out efficiently, it is sensible to draw up a checklist on the following lines:

- inform relevant departments, eg payroll, pensions and the department where the employee is to work, of the employee's impending arrival
- check that all the necessary tools, equipment, etc are ready for the new employee. This may include office furniture, stationery, uniform, safety wear or equipment, identity card, car parking space, locker, etc
- obtain the employee's P45, NI number, and SSP leaver's statement if appropriate
- check that arrangements have been made for the induction of the newcomer. Where possible, arrange for a colleague to be personally responsible for showing the new person around, taking him or her to lunch, and so on.

Record Keeping

Most personnel secretaries will be given responsibility for absence recording, whether the absence is due to sickness, holidays, unpaid leave, medical appointments, jury service or some other reason. Usually a form with special codes denoting the different kinds of absence is a handy tool for this purpose and secretaries will often wish to design their own so that it fits in with their own particular filing and recording systems.

Since the onus for paying statutory sick pay (SSP) fell to employers, additional detailed record keeping for sickness absence has been essential. It should not be assumed, however, that merely because secretaries are adept at keeping general absence records they will be able automatically to handle SSP. No one should be asked to undertake this task unless the rules relating to SSP have been fully explained. While personnel practitioners who have been operating the system for some time now are familiar with its idiosyncrasies, to the newcomer it can still be bewildering.

The main points which need to be covered are as follows:
- to be eligible for SSP an employee's absence must form a period of incapacity for work (PIW) of four complete days which may include Saturdays and Sundays. Two or more PIWs can link if they are separated by no more than 56 days
- the PIW must form a period of entitlement. The period begins on the first complete day of incapacity and may end for a number of reasons, eg the employee is fit to return to work, the employee reaches the maximum entitlement, the employment is terminated
- SSP is paid only in respect of qualifying days which must be agreed between employer and employee. The first three qualifying days in a PIW are waiting days for which no SSP is payable
- employees must notify the employer of their absence
- transfer and exclusion forms and leavers' statements must be supplied to employees where appropriate.

Maternity

Maternity rights are another subject about which personnel secretaries are likely to have to handle queries. With the change to statutory maternity pay (SMP) it is more important than ever that accurate records are maintained and that secretaries are familiar with the new rules.

So far as the right to maternity leave and the right to return are concerned, there is no change in the law: anyone who has been continuously employed for two years at the 11th week before the expected week of confinement is entitled to take maternity leave and to return to work afterwards (for those who work between eight and 16 hours per week the qualifying period is five years). The new rules on maternity pay affect eligibility for maternity pay for anyone whose baby is due on or after 21.6.87.

Personal History

The employee's personal file binds together all the threads of an individual's employment within an organisation and should be summarised by a personal history record sheet. This document, provided it is updated regularly, is of immense value to the personnel department as it shows at a glance essential personal details of the employee, career history, current salary and job title, training received and so on.

Apart from acting as an aide memoire, personal history records are extremely useful for analysis purposes. However busy the personnel secretary may be, a priority task should be to keep employees' record sheets up-to-date.

Auditing Personnel Procedures and Policies

It is always a good idea to call for "time out" amidst the hurly-burly of a busy personnel department to take stock of things. A systematic audit of personnel administration, policies and procedures could profitably be carried out to see how effective the personnel department is. Any newly appointed personnel manager will also find a personnel audit a useful way of finding out how things are done in the company and of locating the areas that need attention and to which a constructive contribution can be made.

Why Audit?

The examination of the current administrative practices in most companies is rarely carried out in a systematic way. Nobody ever has the time and there are always other things that have priority. However, someone must check that the company gives appropriate policy guidelines to its managers, that they are adhered to, and that managers follow the procedures laid down. It is also important to review these policies and procedures to ensure that they are relevant, efficient and, most importantly, conform to the ever-changing legal requirements.

Any audit must be designed to:
- identify areas that require policies, procedures, etc because of legal requirements, eg health and safety policy, medical examinations in certain industries
- identify documentary needs that are required by law, eg display of statutory notices such as extracts from the Factories Act, Offices, Shops and Railway Premises Act, Wages Orders
- establish precisely what the internal procedures are regarding the administration of personnel and industrial relations matters, eg the routine for processing new staff on to the payroll, the company's disciplinary and grievance procedures
- check the documentary procedures against actual practice to identify problem areas and to see if the administrative arrangements and policies are being followed.

The main areas that this investigation is likely to cover will vary from company to company but in most cases should include: recruitment and selection procedures; wage and payment systems; promotion and transfer arrangements; disciplinary and grievance procedures; company arrangements for appraisal, training and development; fringe benefits and their administration; health and safety arrangements; and, of course, equal opportunities policies and procedures to monitor and maintain them.

Personnel records and all other documentation should be surveyed to ensure that they are up-to-date. These might include written statements of terms and conditions of employment, employee handbooks, union agreements, procedural manuals and any written material that has found its way on to the company's notice board which perhaps varies the company's normal administrative practices or announces new arrangements.

Carrying Out Audits

Auditing the company's procedures can be a sensitive matter and it is not unknown for companies to bring in outside consultants to carry out such an exercise, in order to ensure that the auditor is impartial and works without any preconceived ideas. However, this takes away a valuable opportunity for the personnel manager to assess the effectiveness of the department and the company's needs in a changing environment. For new personnel managers this will offer a chance to familiarise themselves with company procedures, check out how they work and see whether people are keeping to them. From this action plans can be worked out to cover gaps and to update and train managers in the use of such procedures. The effectiveness of the audit will depend on the questions the manager asks.

Recruitment and Selection

The main areas of interest are as follows.

Job descriptions: are they adequate (in particular, do they specify performance standards) and up-to-date? Is there a system for requesting recruitment of replacements or increasing manning levels? Is every request carefully scrutinised and authorised?

Application forms: are they appropriately drafted (care is needed regarding sex and race discrimination) and is all the necessary information collected by the form to allow sensible screening of the applicant? Do all applicants complete a form? Are short lists prepared for vacancies? How are unsuccessful applicants informed?

Job applicants: are job applicants carefully screened regarding their previous employment history? Are references requested and do the reference letters request specific information? Is a telephone check of these references carried out? Is an offer or engagement letter sent and is a formal probationary or trial period stipulated? Is the employee properly appraised at the end of the trial period and a letter of confirmation sent? Is the offer of employment conditional upon receipt of suitable references and a satisfactory medical? Does the successful applicant receive details of all the company's terms and conditions of employment before accepting the job?

New employees: does the successful applicant receive proper joining instructions and is there a formal induction policy to introduce the new employee to the company?

Statements of Terms

The law requires all employees to have a written statement of their main terms and conditions of employment. (More senior or technical employees may have detailed service contracts.) The law also requires them to be up-to-date and accurate. These statements are a major source of company policy and operating rules which may change from time to time. They also frequently incorporate or refer to other documents which require updating, eg staff handbooks, employee manuals. Another source of information that is frequently incorporated is national and local collective agreements between employers and trade unions which are usually renegotiated yearly. In any event, changes to the way pay, for instance, is calculated or changes to the pattern of hours worked may be made by agreement over time while the documents remain unamended. Additionally, Parliament introduces or changes legislation on an almost continuous basis and this can also require the statement to be updated.

Although it is an extremely time-consuming exercise, reviewing statements of terms is perhaps a central task to auditing because it ranges right across the scope of employing people in the business. Of course, company handbooks will need a thorough revision as well.

Along with this documentary check, it is essential to audit the individual personnel records kept by the company, whether they are held on computer or in manual files. Are the forms well designed and do they contain appropriate information, especially covering areas such as engagement, changes to terms and conditions, and termination of employment? Are files arranged in alphabetical order and neatly assembled? Good housekeeping can save hours of time. Who has access to these files?

Provision of Information

This is an area of increasing interest to personnel managers and can range from sophisticated consultation machinery, such as works councils, to the humble company notice board.

In particular:
- are the statutory notices properly displayed? Are fire evacuation procedures displayed? Are bulletins changed regularly? What efforts are made

to ensure that the notice board contains interesting and important information which attracts employees' attention?
- who has responsibility for maintaining the notice board, tidying up and ensuring that non-company information is removed?
- does the company keep employees informed about the business, eg company plans, acquisitions, production levels and new products? If so, by what means, eg company newspaper, magazine, broad sheet?
- does the company provide an easily understandable company report for employees?
- are employees told when they have been the subject of written or oral praise from satisfied customers?
- do managers and/or the directors of the company regularly talk to groups of individual employees, eg briefing groups, departmental staff meetings?
- are employees regularly appraised to explain how they stand, the progress made, the strengths and weaknesses of their job performance?

Finally, where the company has granted recognition to a trade union it is important to check that records of minutes of meetings are kept. Agreements should be reduced to writing where they affect the terms and conditions of employment and regulate the relationship between the management and union. The points to consider in particular are:
- is there a written recognition agreement? Are substantive issues such as pay, holiday, etc covered by the agreement as well as procedural aspects? Can the agreement be terminated by either side giving notice?
- is there a formal procedural agreement covering the resolution of collective disputes?
- are there agreements to cover collective matters such as check-off, time off for trade union duties/activities, facilities for trade union representatives?
- how regularly do management and union meet?
- what is the procedure for calling such meetings?
- are all the company's managers aware of the procedures?
- who forms the management negotiating team and have they received training in negotiating skills?
- are industrial relations staff and the management negotiating team aware of recent changes to collective labour law and the practical effects these may have on the way they deal with collective issues?
- are there adequate records kept of past agreements, negotiations and meetings for reference purposes.

Discipline and Grievances

The most commonly understood "procedure" that any company has is the disciplinary procedure. However, what is contained in writing is usually greatly fleshed out in practice. It is important to establish whether the procedure as written down is in fact workable and that it is followed stringently by the managers responsible for its operation.

1. Are the company rules governing employees' conduct drafted in a positive and inspiring way rather than as a litany of what thou shalt not do! Are these rules communicated to employees?
2. Do employees know the procedure that the company will adopt if rules are broken or if job performance is poor?
3. Does the disciplinary procedure take account of the special needs of the company, eg are acts of gross misconduct specified, do special rules govern groups such as shiftworkers when members of senior management may not be available?
4. Check the quality of warning letters issued. Do they have all the necessary ingredients, ie offence/complaint specified in detail, details of employee's defence/excuses, reasons for deciding to discipline, remedial action if appropriate, period of review to see if conduct/capability improves?
5. Do supervisors and managers require instruction on interpretation of rules and disciplinary procedure?
6. Is the appeal procedure against disciplinary action ever used? Are there any useful lessons to draw from this?

Grievance procedures should be drafted to ensure that grievances are handled quickly and not "sat on". Are there time scales for each stage? How many employees use the formal grievance procedure? Are employees encouraged to use the procedure?

Company Policies

Most companies collect together in one place the documentation of their company policies and very often this is formalised into a procedural manual for, for instance, branch managers and other senior managers. The areas covered might include:
- health and safety (this should be disseminated to all employees)
- advertising and recruitment
- equal opportunities
- clothing/uniform
- time off work
- job security
- company cars
- removal and relocation
- expenses and allowances.

Job Security/Training

Finally, another important area to audit is that of the company's job security policy. If the company has a history of unsteady work with lay-offs and redundancies, what attempts have been made to stabilise employment? Has the company retained the contractual right to lay off or put employees on short time working? Other points to consider include:

(a) are there agreed criteria for redundancy selection or is it governed by custom and practice?

(b) does the company try to give as much advance notice of lay-off, short time working or redundancy as possible? Does the company consult with recognised trade unions and have severance pay agreements been reached in the past?

(c) does the company try to train and develop the potential of its employees and are employees given information about the opportunities for advancement in the company?

(d) what potential is there for part time working in the company and what is the company's policy towards using casual, temporary and agency workers?

If there is any time left over, the personnel manager might check that the maternity leave provisions are working properly; that the company takes part in MSC employment schemes where this is sensible; that the company provides booklets covering the company pension plan, bonus and incentive schemes, company insurance and health insurance plans, etc; that union agreements and meetings are properly documented and minuted. There really are not enough hours in the day!

Something for the Record

Personnel records have always made demands on employers' time and energy, whether self-imposed or as required by various government departments. Recently they have been attracting more attention than ever, what with the advent of statutory sick pay, statutory maternity pay, more comprehensive sex and ethnic monitoring and, for those with computerised records, the provisions of the Data Protection Act.

Legal Obligations

The amount of recorded information held varies considerably from employer to employer. They will all hold at least some information about their individual employees; some will supplement that with various forms requesting, authorising, assisting or confirming action to be taken in respect of employees; those with the most comprehensive personnel records will keep statistical information about trends within the workforce. Whatever the case, however, even the most reluctant record keeping employer must gather and keep certain information by law.

The Inland Revenue is probably the most demanding when it comes to keeping records, and employers will be familiar with many of the multitude of forms which that body produces. One point to note about the Inland Revenue's requirements is that, for their purposes, a "higher-paid employee" is currently one whose earnings are £8500 pa or more, or a director, and that full details must be provided of the pay and fringe benefits of such employees.

Other pay-related records which must be kept by law include wage-deduction forms; wages records, and overtime control records for young people. Much of this information is also needed by employers to comply with another statutory obligation on records, that of giving employees itemised pay statements. S.8 of the Employment Protection (Consolidation) Act 1978 gives employees the right to receive, on or before pay day, an itemised statement of pay containing:
– gross amount of wages or salary
– net amount of wages or salary
– variable deductions and the reasons for them
– fixed deductions and the reasons for them
– where different parts of the net pay are paid in different ways, the amount and method of each payment.

The statement of fixed deductions can be replaced by a standing statement which can be amended by notice in writing and which must be updated and reissued every 12 months. (Employees who work between eight and 16 hours per week are only entitled to an itemised pay statement after five years' continuous service.)

Accident Records

The Health and Safety Executive (HSE) is another body which lays down certain requirements on record-keeping, many of which vary, depending on the industry in question. One requirement which covers all employers, however, is that concerning accident records.

When an accident occurs at work which results in the death or major injury of a person, the HSE must be informed and sent a written report. This also applies to dangerous occurrences. An accident which results in an employee being unable to work for more than three days is also a "notifiable" accident but in this case the employer merely has to supply the DHSS with information if requested. Whatever form the notifiable accident takes, a record of it must be kept at the workplace. The record must include:
– the date of the accident
– the name, sex, age and occupation of the injured person and the nature of the injury
– the place where the accident occurred
– a brief description of the circumstances.

Even if an accident is not notifiable, however, the employer should keep a record of it, in case a claim for negligence is made by the injured party.

Besides the above requirements, it should include such information as: names of witnesses; what immediate action was taken; whether the injured person should have been on the premises; and, if other employees were involved, whether they were carrying out their normal duties or acting in accordance with company rules.

Statutory Sick Pay

Although there is no prescribed form for employers to use for the purposes of SSP they must, by law, keep records showing:
- the dates of each reported period of incapacity
- details of agreed qualifying days
- details of SSP paid to each employee, broken down into weekly, monthly and yearly figures
- dates when SSP was not paid, together with the reasons.

A DHSS form (Form SSP2) is available for this purpose but is not obligatory. SSP forms which are obligatory, however, are SSP1(E) — which must be completed for an employee who is ill but is excluded from the right to receive SSP, SSP1(T) — for employees whose entitlement to SSP is almost exhausted and SSPI(L) — leavers' statements.

Another important record related to SSP is that of the evidence of an employee's incapacity. This will probably be either a self-certificate or a medical certificate. Again there is a DHSS self-certificate which employers can make use of. Alternatively they might design their own and include further details related to the employee's absence, such as whether medical advice was sought. It is particularly important on such forms to ask for the first day of sickness — as opposed to absence — so that periods of incapacity can be ascertained accurately, and to include a statement to the effect that if the employee provides inaccurate or false information about the absence it may be treated as gross misconduct and so result in summary dismissal. Any evidence of an employee's illness must be kept in case a DHSS inspector asks to see it.

Sex and Ethnic Monitoring

A wide range of forms is used by companies for in-house purposes. A recent addition to this category for some employers has been that of records used in connection with sex and ethnic monitoring. Both the Code of Practice on race relations and the one published by the EOC on sex discrimination recommend that employers should adopt, implement and monitor an equal opportunity policy to ensure that there is no unlawful discrimination and that equal opportunity is genuinely available.

Monitoring such a policy involves making an initial analysis of the workforce and regularly checking the application of the policy by such means as analyses of the sex, marital status and ethnic origins of both the current workforce and job applicants. This means that it is no longer taboo to include questions about an applicant's ethnic origin in forms such as the application form. It is, however, advisable to include a statement setting out the company's equal opportunities policy and explaining that the information is being sought for, and will be used solely to assist in, the monitoring of that policy, otherwise the applicant may not be willing to co-operate. This also applies to questions about an applicant's sex and/or marital status.

Data Protection Implications

How complex and comprehensive a company's records are and how much detail is contained in individual personal files is often dictated by the method of storage and available space. Many employers operate manual record systems: envelope or manilla files are often used, with part of the employee's information sometimes written on the outside for easy access; alternatively index record cards may be used.

Increasingly, companies are switching to computerised records to overcome storage problems and to lighten the administrative burden and facilitate statistical analysis. Of course, what they must now have regard to is the Data Protection Act which will come into full effect in 1987. The key to the Act is the following eight data protection principles.

1. The information to be contained in personal data shall be obtained, and personal data shall be processed, fairly and lawfully.
2. Personal data shall be held only for one or more specified and lawful purposes.
3. Personal data held for any purpose or purposes shall not be used or disclosed in any manner incompatible with that purpose or those purposes.
4. Personal data held for any purpose or purposes shall be adequate, relevant and not excessive in relation to that purpose or those purposes.
5. Personal data shall be accurate and, where necessary, kept up-to-date.
6. Personal data held for any purpose or purposes shall not be kept for longer than is necessary for that purpose or those purposes.
7. An individual shall be entitled:
   (a) at reasonable intervals and without undue delay or expense:
      (i) to be informed by any data user whether he holds personal data of which that individual is the subject and
      (ii) to have access to any such data held by a data user and
   (b) where appropriate, to have such data corrected or erased.
8. Appropriate security measures shall be taken against unauthorised access to, or alteration, disclosure or destruction of, personal data and against accidental loss or destruction of personal data.

Although those employers who operate manual record systems might be heartily glad that the Act does not apply to them, they might do well to follow some of the general principles — particularly keeping information up-to-date!

Form Design and Use

The written statement of terms and conditions of employment is, of course, another record which employers are obliged by law to provide for their employees. As with many other records used by employers on a day to day basis, there is no obligatory form on which to set out the details. It is often something which the employers would rather design to suit their own needs.

When designing forms or records there are a few points that should always be borne in mind:
1. Short sentences are much more easily understood than longer ones; active sentences are better than passive ones, eg "include your birth certificate with the application form" is better than"your birth certificate should be included with the application form".
2. Use words with which the reader is likely to be familiar, ie "pay" rather than"emoluments", etc.
3. Only ask one question at a time; the form may be longer as a result but it should at least be clear and accurate.
4. Leave adequate space for answers.
5. If you have a list of questions requiring tick-box answers, make sure the gap between question and answer is not too wide, otherwise those completing the form might not align the ticks to the right questions.
6. Where a lot of detailed information is being given, break it down into paragraphs and, where appropriate, use sub-headings to divide sections of information.

Off the Record?

Whichever record keeping system an employer uses, storage is a perennial problem, and "How long do we keep them?" is a question to which there is no single answer. Bearing in mind that the statutes of limitation allow civil actions to be taken through the courts up to six years from the date the action complained of took place, the following is a guide to the length of time records should be kept:

Accident book reports	7 years
Attendance records	7 years
Clock cards	3 years
Employment application forms	1 year
Medical records	7 years
Overtime records	3 years
Pension fund records	Permanently

Personnel files (after termination)	7 years
Personnel records (summaries)	10 years
Trade union agreements and/or associated documents	10 years
Tax and national insurance returns	7 years
Wage/salary schedules	10 years

Payroll in Perspective

In recent years, and certainly with the advent of specialised computer systems, payroll has tended to become sectioned off from the personnel function, often within a separate department. However, there is some merit in recognising that there are certain common interests in the two areas and personnel managers should certainly be familiar with the basics of payroll administration and be aware of the workings of their systems, if only to be equipped for routine enquiries from employees.

We aim to dispel some of the mysteries surrounding payroll, consider details of the current trend in legislation requiring employers to make State benefits payable through the payroll and look at how the information contained in simple payroll systems can be used to the benefit of the personnel department without investment in expensive and complex personnel systems.

The Basics

An efficient, smooth-running payroll system is a must for any organisation. The subject of pay — how, when and where it is paid — is obviously close to the hearts of all employees and an error leading to miscalculation, delay, over-deduction of tax, etc can cause anguish for the individual concerned and annoyance to the harassed payroll/personnel department trying to explain away the mistake! However, with the increasing complexity of running payrolls, the large numbers of different functions to perform, varying payments, intervals and deductions for different employees, etc the room for error is obviously greater. Manual payroll calculation is becoming less common, even for small companies, as the complexity of the operations to be performed makes payroll an obvious priority area for mechanisation.

A computerised payroll system is, therefore, the first choice for many organisations. It is obviously essential that such a system can perform effectively all the operations required of it, which may be many and varied. The minimum requirement is for a payroll system which can facilitate statutory deductions from gross pay (ie income tax and national insurance) and can calculate basic pay, with the operator adding in variables such as overtime, bonuses, commission and any fixed deductions. It may also be necessary to have the facility for pay to be calculated at varying pay intervals for different groups of employees, as when weekly and monthly payrolls are on one system.

It can reasonably be assumed that any computerised payroll system package will contain the basic elements for calculating pay, deducting tax and national insurance and paying statutory sick pay. There are, however, other ideal requirements which the system should be able to provide.

Other Requirements

The following considerations apply when looking at what an ideal payroll system would include.

1. First and foremost the system should be able to pay the correct amounts of money at the right time and in the right place. Most computerised systems will be concerned with "cashless" pay direct into an employee's bank account, although it is obviously still possible to calculate pay on a computer, print out pay-slips and actually pay in cash. In order to ensure that as few mistakes as possible are made, the payroll system should involve a number of different checks, preferably by different people, to guard against incorrect data being entered and processed.

2. The system should be accessible, easily understood by operators and readily updated. Payroll is subject to numerous routine alterations and amendments throughout the pay period and it is essential that such changes can easily be entered into the system with the minimum of disruption. Very inflexible systems which require all information, changes, deletions, etc to be completed very early on before the payroll is processed are not at all helpful when new employees are unexpectedly taken on shortly before pay day and require paying or, perhaps more crucially, someone is dismissed at very short notice and has to be taken out of the system quickly.

3. Computer forms used for entering, amending and deleting records should be as simple as possible. Also, print-outs should be readable, with as few complicated codings as can be arranged.

4. The system should ideally be able to link in to other systems, eg a personnel system.

Pay-Slip Design

Employers must, by law, give employees on or before pay day, itemised statements of pay, otherwise known as pay-slips, containing the following details:

- gross amount of pay
- net amount of pay (ie after all deductions have been made)
- variable deductions and details of why they are being made
- fixed deductions and details of why they are being made

– where parts of the net payment are paid in different ways, the amount and method of each part payment.

Employers can satisfy the requirement to give details of fixed deductions on every pay-slip if they issue a cumulative standing statement of fixed deductions which sets out the amount of the deduction, intervals at which it is made and the purpose for which it is made.

The basic principle behind this statutory requirement is that employees should be able to work out for themselves how their net pay is arrived at. Bearing this in mind, it is obviously important that the pay-slip contains sufficient information for individuals to be able to do this. A clear lay-out for the pay-slip is important, with a logical sequence of information so that, for example, cumulative deductions (tax and NI paid to date) are not confused with monthly or weekly deductions.

Some organisations have the facility to include messages on pay-slips, pointing out any specific changes to pay which might occur, eg as a result of tax codes altering or national insurance bands increasing. Once again this has the useful effect of reducing queries as to why pay has decreased, increased or stayed the same in a particular period.

Methods of Payment

Some form of "cashless" pay is probably used across the board for non-manual workers owing to the greater security of such forms of payment. With the recent repeal of the Truck Acts, manual workers no longer have the statutory right to be paid in current coin of the realm, and so it seems likely that they, too, will be encouraged to have wages paid direct into bank or building society accounts.

With such payments there is usually a choice between credit transfer, whereby the payroll department has to credit each account individually with the money involving the exchange of paper bank giro credit forms, and payment via electronic funds transfer on magnetic tape.

The latter form of payment is becoming increasingly popular through the services of Bankers' Automated Clearing Services Ltd (BACS). This is an organisation owned by the five major clearing banks which was formed to provide a highly efficient and labour-saving means of transferring funds though the British banking system. The BACS system uses magnetic tapes rather than paper vouchers, thus eliminating the time and effort involved in handling giro credits. Employers prepare a tape detailing pay amounts, which is then processed by BACS and passed on to destination banks. The banks receiving money, credit employees' accounts and debit the employer's account through their computer system.

State Payments Through the Payroll

Payroll systems will need in future to have the flexibility to cope with a large number of changes as a result of legislative requirements which mean that responsibility for the payment of more State benefits is given to employers.

The first State payment to be paid through the payroll was statutory sick pay (SSP), introduced in April 1983. For the first time employers were responsible for paying what was, effectively, the first eight weeks of State sickness benefit. The relative success of this scheme (in the Government's view) has led to an extension of the SSP scheme, involving an increase from eight to 28 weeks' worth of payment and other changes which effectively involve the replacement of State sickness benefit entitlement altogether for employed people from April 1986. It has also led to proposals for other State benefits to be paid by employers through the payroll and reclaimed once again from monthly payments to the DHSS and Inland Revenue.

Maternity allowance: from April 1987 the responsibility for paying maternity allowance to employed women was taken over by employers. Statutory maternity pay (SMP) is paid through the payroll (and hence is taxable) to those women who qualify and is reclaimed by the same means as SSP. One implication of this change is that employers are required to pay SMP weekly for a period of up to 18 weeks while the employee is on maternity leave. This means that, for the first time, payment must carry on during such leave, which may cause problems for those organisations which transfer women to a "waiting" payroll or issue P45s when employees go on maternity leave.

Family credit: from April 1988 the Government proposes to replace family income supplement with a new benefit paid through the payroll to the main wage earner in a family. This proposal has been promoted as the first step towards the integration of the tax and social security systems. Calculation will be by the DHSS, after it has sought confirmation of earnings from employers. The amount payable will be calculated on the basis of a maximum credit, paid when the family's net income is at or below a threshold figure, based on the amount of a married couple's personal allowance from income support (due to replace supplementary benefit). If the family's net income is above the threshold the maximum credit will be reduced on a sliding scale.

The DHSS will inform employers and employees of the amount to be paid and of the period of payment. The amount will then have to be added to net pay and shown separately on the pay-slip. It should be paid in accordance with normal payroll arrangements, whether monthly or weekly. Reimbursement will again be via monthly payments of NI and PAYE.

The Government is apparently anxious to minimise administration and avoid cash-flow problems for employers and intends to consult further on the details of the scheme. One drawback which has been noted is the perhaps unwelcome intrusion into an employee's personal affairs as, for the first time, employers will be aware that individuals are in receipt of a poverty-relieving welfare benefit. Some concern has also been expressed at the difficulties of liaison with a hard-pressed DHSS, which may not produce information on time or correctly. It could be that payroll departments will be forced to deal with complaints about delayed and disallowed claims, which are not really their concern.

Since 6.10.85 employers have been able to reclaim compensation for payment of national insurance contributions on SSP through their monthly returns. It is proposed that a similar form of compensation will be offered with statutory maternity pay. If this trend continues it is possible to foresee a situation where monthly payments to the DHSS and Inland Revenue will be completely offset and possibly retrospectively claimed. This could lead to cash-flow problems for employers and will add a burden to the payroll.

Payroll Statistics

Many organisations have a computerised payroll but manual personnel records. They may well be considering computerising the latter, perhaps by buying a costly and sophisticated package. However, many payroll systems have facilities for analysis and statistics which are underused and it is well worth examining the potential of the payroll alone before embarking on a new system which may well duplicate resources already available.

Computerised payroll programs have facilities for storing and making use of areas of information which are extremely useful to the personnel practitioner. The database which is used for running the payroll can have countless other uses.

Most systems will have some form of report-generating facility which can produce print-out statistics in many variations according to personal specifications. A payroll system can be used to generate regular labour turnover reports, giving detailed breakdowns of the number of employees leaving in particular areas and classifying them by age, sex and salary level. The system will probably also have a field for job title, reason for leaving codes and space for ethnic monitoring. These can be used to produce salary comparison reports, age profiles, and sex and ethnic distribution. Absence reports can be produced from SSP material and manpower planning can be aided by breakdowns of ages, salary levels and career patterns in particular departments.

Data Protection

It is worth noting that if the personnel department intends to make use of payroll material for report generating, the exemption from registering under

the Data Protection Act 1984 will not apply. The exemption for payroll and accounts is a very narrow one and applies only where the data is used *solely* for the following purposes:
- calculating pay and pensions, making the payments and calculating deductions from pay
- keeping business accounts, records of sales and purchases, paying bills or
- making financial forecasts.

The Data Protection Registrar has suggested how narrowly this might be interpreted by indicating that payroll data may not be within the exemption if the home address of an employee is held on computer and his or her salary is always paid direct to a bank account.

3 PERSONNEL PROCEDURES

All personnel departments need to have procedures governing the way that some personnel policies will be implemented. In this chapter we look at some fairly basic areas including workforce communications (together with the statutory duty to produce Employment Involvement Reports), counselling, grievances, policies and procedures on employees' appearance and job security agreements.

Workforce Communications

If employers are to establish a good rapport with employees, there is no substitute for talking to them. The purpose of communication between managers and subordinates is to initiate action or influence behaviour, to change or influence attitudes and to increase understanding and knowledge. It should, of course, be a two-way process.

We turn now to some of the oral and written methods of communication commonly used, including the institutionalising of these methods by setting up works councils.

Oral Communication

In the first instance, employees are normally trained and instructed in their duties orally to operate machinery, use company procedures, complete company documentation, etc. Implicit in these instructions is the setting of goals and standards that must be achieved. Employees also need to know how they are doing and how they are regarded by their employer.

Every manager should have in his repertoire the ability to carry out appraisal and counselling interviews (see below), to give a lecture or presentation, and to take part in working parties and formally-run committees.

Written Communication

Written sources of communication with employees include many mundane forms and action documents. (Badly designed, poorly expressed, abrupt or excessively complicated forms seem to beset such collections.) Such documents might include:
- letters or forms used in relation to engagement, termination, transfers, etc
- formal documents such as contracts of employment, written warnings, etc
- employee handbooks or house-magazines which have limited value in communicating important messages because of the time intervals between issues, cost and usually patchy readership. However, they are useful when "in depth" coverage is needed and will serve to foster the company image and corporate spirit
- noticeboards: a necessity for statutorily required notices, eg abstracts of the Factories Act 1961, Wages Council Orders, Offices, Shops and Railway Premises Act 1963. They are useful for urgent notices and displaying other essential information
- slips in pay packets are frequently used to communicate changes of a personal nature, eg rates of pay, etc. This method should not be used to communicate dismissal for redundancy or any other reason
- organisation charts and job descriptions provide important information to employees, giving greater understanding of their role, especially if the job descriptions are written so that they contain performance targets, timetables, etc
- procedure manuals containing company policies and procedures.

The Communications Vehicle

Many employers are aware of the need to encourage and find a permanent "vehicle" for their company's communications. Where trade union membership is patchy, employers often feel that there is a need for a formal vehicle through which all employees can express their views and be involved in management decision making. In some companies, requests for trade union recognition have had the same effect but with the intention of keeping the unions out, whilst allowing a platform for vociferous employees.

The anticipation of the eventual enactment in the United Kingdom of legislation inspired by the Fifth Directive on Company Law has also made employers think. However, British employers are largely hostile to the idea of worker directors, especially if they are only to be appointed by recognised trade unions rather than the workforce as a whole.

An idea now gaining support is that of works councils/committees elected by all employees, although trade unions are generally opposed to such moves. However, there do seem to be more employers seeking to build joint consultation machinery involving all their employees, consisting of works councils, productivity committes, suggestion scheme committees, disciplinary committees, absence committees, health and safety committees, etc.

Works Councils: Advantages and Disadvantages

The use of works councils and various sub-committees has both advantages and disadvantages.

Advantages

1. In smaller companies, committees provide a useful training function, giving managers a broader view of the work carried on in the company as a whole as well as direct contact with workforce views.
2. People voted onto the committee can gain a great deal of expertise in, for instance, handling absence or safety problems.
3. Committee members can often provide a greater variety of experience on the problem under discussion.
4. Ideas to tackle problems can arise spontaneously as a result of discussion.
5. All employees can feel more in touch with those who make the decisions through the efforts of their elected members, and management can test out reactions to policies, etc. A two-way flow of ideas at the formative stages of the introduction of new technology, work methods, procedures, etc, must always be valuable.
6. Finally, an elected representative will ensure that the interests of employees are represented in the decision making process.

Disadvantages

1. Committees tend to shelve the making of decisions, indeed the committee may be split, making agreement impossible.
2. The mechanics of giving notice of meetings may mean that meetings are held too late, held after the decisions have been taken, or that decisions are delayed.
3. Time can be wasted in irrelevant discussion causing members not to bother attending.
4. A dominant or very knowledgeable chairman can exercise almost dictatorial powers, although it can be equally disastrous if a committee is chaired in a weak manner.

It is a commonsense exercise for any manager to obtain some experience before becoming involved in a committee or works council. Committee experience in clubs, religious organisations, political groups, professional bodies, etc can fill the training gap. Unfortunately, it is still the case that few companies think that this sort of training is necessary and so a little private enterprise in this respect is useful.

Forming a Works Council

It does sound rather pedantic but it really is sensible to have a properly drafted constitution and the "rules of play" clearly outlined for any works council. It does mean that:
- circumstances that might affect the work of the council are considered and allowed for in the rules
- the scope of the council's powers and interests are defined
- the frequency of meetings and the way the council gives feedback information may be determined.
A written constitution does give the impression of permanency as well as facilitating the practical work of the council.

Works councils will not just happen and become overnight successes. They do involve a great deal of management leadership, commitment and willingness to discuss and listen to the views of employee council members, even if they are poorly articulated at times.

Drafting Constitutions

The first section of the written constitution should deal with the objectives or intention of the body, for example:
"The company and its employees agree to establish a Consultative Committee with the object of providing a regular means for promoting communication between management and employees to ensure the efficiency, profitability and long term prosperity of the company".

It is, of course, possible to extend the function of such a council to enable it to carry out negotiations for pay and conditions, etc, for example:
"The college and elected staff representatives recognise the interdependence of all parties and that matters affecting the interests of management and staff shall be considered jointly by consultation and if necessary by negotiation through the negotiating sub-committee".

Care should be taken to indicate which topics are for consultation only and which ones are negotiable. The function of employee representatives and management representatives could be defined, for example:
"Worker representatives will represent the views of employees to the management body; make suggestions as to methods of working, products, terms and conditions of employment, health and safety, etc, discuss management proposals and monitor the views of employees after communicating all decisions, proposals and other issues to employees for comment and discussion".

What the Council Does

A clause defining the topics to be handled by the council may state:
"The Council will:
  (i) discuss major matters affecting the operating efficiency of the company or the interests of the employees
  (ii) receive and consider relevant information on the company's trading position, finances, plans and prospects together with information necessary for effective consultation
  (iii) consider and promote schemes for the benefit of employees and their dependants".

Other important issues involve membership, elections and the constituencies to be applied.

Checklist

1. How many members will the council have? Anything above seven or eight will be unwieldy.
2. Will the council have the power to co-opt people for special purposes or when their special expertise is relevant?
3. Will limits be set regarding length of service, age, etc for employees seeking election?
4. Ensure that candidates are proposed and seconded and that they give their consent to nomination.
5. Define the constituencies for worker members.
6. Will management members be appointed by directors? Will the directors be eligible for appointment?
7. What will the split be viz a viz management and worker representatives?
8. Who will chair the meetings, eg:
   "A management representative shall act as chairman for the first six months. Afterwards the Consultative Committee shall appoint, if they wish, two chairmen, one appointed by the management and one by the staff, who will take the chair at alternate meetings. They shall hold office for one year but shall be eligible for re-election".
   Can the chairman vote? Does he or she have a casting vote?
9. What happens to members if they transfer out of their constituency or cease to be an employee of the company?
10. Should there be a regular date for meeting, ie the last Friday of the month; what is the quorum; can members vote by proxy.
11. How will the ballot for elected members be carried out? Who acts as returning officer, scrutinises ballot papers, etc?
12. What happens if a member retires, etc? In what circumstances can the member be asked to stand down?

Other Useful Hints

The constitution ought to deal with loss of income caused by attendance at meetings or handling grievances, etc. Some consideration should be given to whether or not the worker members should hold a meeting to discuss agendas in advance. It is also essential that the constitution deals with how the workforce will receive feedback from the council meetings.

Very often a council will want to appoint a sub-committee for the purpose of dealing with a particular matter. Sub-committees usually consist of an equal number of elected staff and management representatives, unless otherwise agreed. Finally, the draft constitution should contain clauses that allow alterations to the constitution.

It should not be forgotten that, as with all things, works council constitutions should contain the seeds of their own dissolution, for example:
"The Works Council may be dissolved if:
(i)   the intention to propose the dissolution of the council is made when the agenda is drawn up
(ii)   the proposal is supported by 75% of members and
(iii) this intention is communicated to the entire workforce and put to the ballot and
(iv)   at least 75% of the workforce vote for dissolution.
    The Council shall then be considered dissolved as from the time that the workforce voted for its dissolution".

Employee Involvement Reports

S.1 of the Employment Act 1982 requires companies to include a statement on employee involvement in their annual directors' report. This requirement applies to reports relating to financial years beginning on or after 1.1.83.

The Legal Requirement

Under the provisions of the Employment Act 1982, the directors' report, in the case of relevant companies, is required to contain a statement describing the action that has been taken during the financial year to introduce, maintain or develop arrangements aimed at:
(a) providing employees systematically with information on matters of concern to them as employees
(b) consulting employees or their representatives on a regular basis so that the views of employees can be taken into account in making decisions which are likely to affect their interests
(c) encouraging the involvement of employees in the company's perfor-

mance through an employee share scheme or by some other means

(d) achieving a common awareness on the part of all employees of the financial and economic factors affecting the performance of the company.

Relevant Companies

It was in s.157 of the Companies Act 1948 that the basic requirement to produce an annual directors' report was laid down. It must be sent to the shareholders and, in most cases, must also be filed with the Registrar of Companies, where it is available for public inspection. S.16 of the Companies Act 1967 extended the information which is to be included in the annual report, and it is as an amendment to that section that the provision relating to employee involvement statements has its legal standing — despite the fact that its entry onto the statute books was via the Employment Act 1982. (The relevant section of the Companies Act 1985, which consolidated all previous legislation, is s.235.)

As such, therefore, the obligation to report on employee involvement applies to all registered companies, whether public or private, including wholly owned subsidiaries who are also obliged to produce a directors' report. A parent company may make a statement about its own employee involvement arrangements, or a general statement about the policy of the group as a whole.

What the legislation does do, however, is to limit the application of the employee involvement provision to companies employing more than 250 people on average, and these are the "relevant companies" referred to above. Employees who work wholly or mainly outside the United Kingdom should not be included in the figure and, if the number of employees fluctuates above and below 250 during the year, a formula is included in the legislative provision to enable companies to identify whether they fall within the category covered or not. To ascertain the average number of employees, for each week in the financial year identify the number who were employed under contracts of service (whether throughout the week or not), total them up and divide by the number of weeks in the financial year. Companies who employ less than 250 are not obliged by law to report on employee involvement but they may decide to make a voluntary statement.

Action not Policy

Comparisons have already been made between the employee involvement report and the statement relating to the disabled, which must also be included in the directors' report of companies employing more than 250 people. However, the emphasis on what must be included is rather different in each case. In respect of the disabled, the statement must describe the policy the company has applied during the year, whereas the employee involvement statement is required to report on action taken. A company may not have a particular policy relating to employee involvement, but may be able to cite plenty of examples of action taken during the year and this would satisfy the requirement. If nothing new has been introduced or developed since the last report, the statement can include details of action that has been taken to maintain existing arrangements for employee involvement. In this way, companies whose arrangements are already working satisfactorily need not make a "nil return" just because there were no changes to report.

Since the requirement is to report action taken, there is no need to include details of future policy or arrangements. Similarly, if no action has been taken at all in respect of employee involvement, it is perfectly permissible to make a statement to this effect in the directors' report. In fact, such a "nil return" is preferable to no statement at all. The legal requirement is one of reporting, rather than a substantive obligation to actually make arrangements for employee involvement, so that whilst non-compliance with the reporting requirement in the Companies Act can lead to legal penalties, a nil return cannot.

However, just because a nil return is not unlawful it does not mean that is is advisable. Questions may be asked by shareholders, employees and other interested parties as to why there is nothing to report and pressure may be exerted for a more active response. Likewise, companies who in practice do little, if anything, but who describe elaborate employee involvement arrangements in their report, are not likely to remain unchallenged for long. In particular, employees who have difficulty in equating the described arrangements with their practical experience of employee involvement might take up the cause.

Analysis of Current Practice

In order to do justice in their statements to the action they do take in respect of employee involvement, companies will first have to assess and analyse their arrangements. For some it may be the first time this has been done on any kind of systematic or thorough basis and that in itself may be no bad thing. Companies who felt that their employee involvement arrangements were fairly comprehensive might find, on analysis, that they are fairly thin on the ground; whilst others, who wonder what there is to include in the directors' report, might be pleasantly surprised at the extent of their arrangements in practice.

Since the employee involvement arrangements are divided into four categories in the legislative provision, it is probably easiest to deal with them on that basis, although there is quite likely to be some overlap between categories.

Provision of information: under this heading, arrangements which exist over and above the statutory requirement to disclose information for collective bargaining purposes should be included. For example, written and other formal methods of communication such as: in-house newspapers, company noticeboards, news and information bulletins, briefing groups, regular management- addressed meetings, etc. Something which is often overlooked but which is nevertheless as systematic and valuable as formal communications structures (if not more so) is the informal system. So, for the purposes of the statement, account should also be taken of face to face everyday communication between supervisors, managers and employees, and of informal yet regular meetings such as those of the canteen committee, etc. Communications training and studies or reviews of the effectiveness of the company's methods of disseminating information could be referred to under this heading as well.

Consultation: again, the action that should be reported here is that taken outside the statutory requirement to consult in redundancy situations, etc. The legal provision refers to account being taken of the employees' views so that reference under this heading should be to arrangements which provide for a two-way flow of information, eg works committees, regular meetings with trade union or other employee representatives, safety committees, joint consultation arrangements, suggestion schemes, etc.

Involvement in company performance: the example given in the statute is that of an employees' share scheme, so that the emphasis under this heading could be interpreted as involvement through financial participation. Other examples might include profit-sharing or value added schemes. However, this might also be the appropriate section in which to include information on any productivity schemes, quality circles or joint working parties which operate within the company.

Financial and economic awareness: in many companies itemisation of action taken under this heading might well overlap with that listed under *Provision of information*. However, extra arrangements might include a report to employees on the company's annual accounts, special presentations of particular aspects of the company's financial position, or financial training for managers, employee representatives, etc.

How Much or How Little

The result of an analysis of employee involvement arrangements along the lines outlined above could well be a sizeable amount of information. In this case, the company must then decide in what sort of detail it is to be included in the directors' report. There may even be a conflict of interest between, say, the company secretary who is drafting the report and other members of management. The former may be concerned to keep the statement as brief as possible within what is essentially a legal record of the company's operation. The latter may wish the statement to be comprehensive and informative enough to be a true reflection of the company's arrangements, particularly where they feel it will enhance its public image.

Some compromise solutions to the problem might be: a brief statement in general terms outlining the company's main employee involvement arrangements, with reference to a more comprehensive account in another document which is available on request; or a detailed statement under one of the employee involvement headings with a shorter account under the other three, each one being considered in detail on a rotating basis in successive years.

Whatever the form of statement finally decided on, it is obviously hoped that, as a result of reviewing their own arrangements, companies will identify areas for improvement and act accordingly. The Government would like to be able to point to the success of such voluntary arrangements for employee involvement as part of its defence against the European Community proposals for legislation to enforce worker participation.

Counselling Employees

Often without being aware of it, personnel managers find themselves involved in counselling employees. While they may see themselves as industrial relations specialists, recruitment officers or administrators, all personnel people at some time are approached by members of the workforce with problems they are unable to sort out for themselves.

The range of problems brought to the personnel department can be vast — from "tug-of-love" kidnappings or an employee's impending bankruptcy to lack of career direction or reluctance to retire. Whether the difficulties are work-related or otherwise, any problem preying on that person's mind is almost bound to affect performance at work. It is therefore vital from the organisation's point of view, as well as from the human angle, that the personnel manager possesses counselling skills.

What is Counselling?

The objective of counselling is to assist an employee to sort out a problem or to come to a decision. This is achieved by "working through" the situation with the individual in a sympathetic and understanding manner, shedding light on obscure areas, and helping the employee to look at matters from a different angle so that an apparently intractable problem may appear soluble after all.

Counselling should never be regarded as an exercise in imposing solutions or making decisions for other people. The counselling session should be designed to facilitate an easy exchange of views and comments. It obviously follows from this that a successful counsellor requires considerable patience and tact.

Counselling Skills

If people are to be expected to divulge their private fears or personal problems it is essential that an atmosphere of total trust and confidence is established. This can be difficult to achieve between, say, a junior clerk and an experienced personnel manager where the disparity in position can lead to suspicion as to the motives behind a counselling session. Perhaps the hardest barrier to overcome, however, is that between an interviewer and employees of a peer group or more senior employees. These are the people who will be most reluctant to share their problems because of "loss of face" and it will take the utmost diplomacy on the part of the counsellor to build up a satisfactory rapport and establish credibility.

An ability and a willingness to listen effectively are prerequisites for successful counselling. These mean *really* listening: paying full attention and not being distracted. Any indication that the counsellor's mind is wandering will ruin a counselling interview. Once the facts have been elicited, as far as possible, basic counselling often requires little more than the application of common sense to a situation in which the employee, because he or she is so close to the problem, is "unable to see the wood for the trees".

Work-Related Counselling

Straightforward difficulties in performing a job adequately or in not knowing what is required should be handled by the line manager. However, matters do arise in the course of employment which an employee is unwilling to take up with a supervisor. For example, personality clashes or difficulties in getting along with the supervisor can be the cause of genuine unhappiness in the workplace and employees may well turn to the personnel manager in such a situation.

Here an employee should be encouraged to analyse why and when clashes are occurring with a view to identifying potential flashpoints, which may then be avoided in future. By diagnosing the problem and looking at it from the other person's viewpoint, the employee may succeed in working out a *modus vivendi* which will alleviate some of the strains.

With regard to the job itself, many employees feel from time to time that they have reached a plateau and see no prospect of advancing further or, alternatively, lose their direction in terms of where they are going in the organisation, perhaps after applying unsuccessfully for a promotion. Here the personnel manager's broader view of the entire operation and professional knowledge of career development can assist an employee in coming to a realistic assessment of what the future is likely to hold.

When the Link is Severed

The need for support, help and guidance is not confined to mid-career crises; it becomes even more acute when employees are made redundant or face retirement.

Sadly, companies continue to experience the need to make people redundant. For the affected employees this is a shattering experience but a well-prepared personnel manager can do a great deal to lessen the impact. Because of the stressful situation in which redundant employees find themselves, it is difficult for them to find out the basic information they need to understand their exact position. The immediate role of the personnel representative is to explain to redundant employees what their entitlements are from the company and what their individual position will be as regards State benefits. Beyond this, further counselling is desirable in terms of advising employees how to obtain other employment, presentation of CVs, liaison with job-centres, and so on. It is important, when morale is at its lowest ebb, for people to realise that positive support and guidance are available.

For those who are unprepared for it, retirement can be as much a shock to the system as redundancy. This is why pre-retirement counselling is vital if ex-employees are to make the most of their newly acquired leisure time. Particularly valuable is an understanding of retirement finance and the assistance available from the social services.

Personal Problems

Difficulties at home affect everyone's outlook and consequently their work performance. Some employees guard their privacy fiercely and do not welcome outside advice; however, if their work becomes adversely affected, the personnel manager may have to take the initiative in starting a dialogue. Some situations, such as bereavement or family illness, call for a sympathetic ear and strong moral support with the offer of practical help where applicable. Compassionate leave or a temporary adjustment to hours may be offered to sort out pressing needs. Increasingly, however, personnel departments are drawn into looking at serious contemporary problems such as debt or drugs. In these circumstances outside specialist advice should be sought.

Counselling Techniques

The techniques of counselling are intended to give employees a perspective on the particular problem(s) that are impairing their usefulness to the company. They help employees to recognise the causes of problems that lie within themselves and can only be resolved by changes in their thinking and behaviour. Clearly, this requires the counsellor to have or to acquire important social skills. One researcher, Argyle, has listed the following as being important to the counsellor:

- a warm and friendly manner
- treating the person as an equal
- achieving a smooth, easy pattern of interaction; asking short, open-ended questions like "why don't you tell me what's on your mind" or just"tell me about it", to get the maximum amount of conversation from the employee
- finding some interest, experience or other bond held in common
- showing a keen, sympathetic interest in giving the employee full attention and listening carefully to what the employee has to say
- adopting the employee's terminology, conventions and generally meeting him or her on his or her own ground.

The Structure of Counselling

Broadly speaking, the interview should be planned and structured as follows — although no two situations are ever the same and it pays to be flexible. The counsellor should:

(a) encourage employees to talk about the problem(s), put them at ease and listen carefully. Depending on the circumstances, the employees should be told the purpose of the meeting or should be encouraged to put forward the nature of the discussion they want to have

(b) encourage the employees, through discussion, to gain a fuller understanding of their problem(s), eg why other employees react to their brusqueness or sarcasm; were they aware of the effect their manner was having; what are the possible solutions (and their advantages and disadvantages); what is the best solution, its implications and how should it be implemented. The employees must make their own decisions having worked through this counselling process

(c) end the interview by summarising the progress made, checking over plans for implementing the decision and, above all, arranging another interview to check progress.

Obviously, arranging and (passively) controlling these interviews can be time-consuming and difficult, very much at variance with the manager's natural inclination to direct action to what he or she thinks ought to be done. Self-control is important.

The careful tactician will always ensure that he or she has adequate information about the employee before starting the encounter, ie:
- age and length of service with company
- how long in the current job, and what the performance has been, eg check appraisal forms, selection interview findings
- any indications of outside problems affecting work and any informal comments from the superior
- what is the employee's sickness record like and has he or she been working a olot of overtime?

The Counsellor: Listening

Managers do not always believe that they have the necessary skills of reflection, clarification and the ability to summarise and listen that will make them good counsellors. However, listening is an attainable skill and the following will aid effectiveness: look at the employee and maintain eye contact; don't doodle or fold up paper clips in a thousand contortions; keep an open mind, you may have heard it all before and know all the ins and outs of the employee concerned, but there may be some important change of view or fact that comes to light. Try to spot the main point of the problem — as the employee sees it.

Listen with the "third ear" to sense the unspoken meanings, feelings, beliefs and prejudices that may be behind what the employee is saying. This underlying problem has been termed "the hidden agenda" that the employee will not articulate until he or she sees how the counsellor reacts to the other things that have been said. If the employee feels that trust has been established and the counsellor is trying to be helpful rather than censorious, the real problem will be brought into the open.

Very often this does not happen until the end of the interview. The employee may be trying to avoid a full discussion of the issue, while still wanting the counsellor to know of the problem. Consequently, the matter is brought up late in the day when there may be little time for further discussion. Perhaps a further interview can be arranged or, if appropriate, the employee can be advised to take specialist or professional assistance if the matter is outside the counsellor's competence.

Another listening skill is tolerance and understanding of the silences. They can mean that the employee is embarrassed or irritated but may also mean that the employee is about to go forward with new insight into his problems.

Clarification and Summarising

It is important that the employee realises that the counsellor is not going to "take over" his or her problems, but wishes to help the employee find his or her own solution. Clarifying remarks do help to illuminate the problem for the employee, but statements that attack the employee's self image are counter-productive, eg "It's because you are so immature and emotional that you can't handle it".

When the problem has been ventilated it is useful to summarise in a non-critical way so that the employee will agree that the summary is a true reflection of the situation.

Decision Making

The counsellor cannot control the actual decisions made by the employee; sets of ready-made alternatives should not be presented to the employee;

rather the counsellor, using his or her greater experience, knowledge, or sheer common sense, should give clues and nudges in the right direction.

Alternative solutions can be considered and the one adopted will depend on the employee's level of aspirations and needs — eg independence, freedom from debt — and ability based on age, experience, training and academic ability.

If the employee decides on a course of action, he or she may need assistance to work out a plan of campaign systematically and sort out a timetable that is realistic in the light of the pressures and demands being experienced. If possible, a further meeting(s) should be planned to allow for more discussion, encouragement and support.

How to Learn the Skills

Counselling skills are social skills and are mostly learnt through practice. Sometimes courses in sensitivity training for example, can assist but some form of monitoring counselling performance is also useful. A counselling checklist (to be answered truthfully) may be helpful if formal training is not available.

1. Did I put the employee at ease?
2. How did I cope with anxiety or hostility?
3. Did I listen effectively and encourage the employee to talk?
4. Did I see the problem from the employee's point of view?
5. Did I try to understand the employee's silences?
6. Did I go at the employee's own speed?
7. Did I provide relevant factual information at the appropriate times?
8. Did I clarify confused ideas?
9. Did I give the interview a pattern or framework?
10. Did I discuss with the employee what the meeting was intended to achieve and how it would be carried out?
11. Did I impose insights or did I encourage them?

Grievance Procedures

During the course of their employment, employees may wish to air grievances arising out of pay and conditions, the application of company rules or issues relating to colleagues. These grievances are often raised informally, even obliquely; on the other hand, employees may make use of more formal procedures that are set out in their terms and conditions statement or elsewhere.

Grievance: A Right?

It is quite clear that those who drafted the Industrial Relations Code of Practice, which is still in force, regarded the raising of grievances through appropriate channels as an employee's right:

"120. All employees have a right to seek redress for grievances relating to their employment. Each employee must be told how he can do so.

121. Management should establish, with employee representatives or trade unions concerned, arrangements under which individual employees can raise grievances and have them settled fairly and promptly. There should be a formal procedure, except in very small establishments where there is close personal contact between the employer and his employees".

Rapid Results

Furthermore, the code goes on to say that such a procedure should aim to settle grievances fairly and as near as possible to their point of origin. It should be simple and rapid in operation. The procedure should be in writing and provide for:

(a) grievances normally to be discussed between the employee and immediate superior
(b) a further stage involving a more senior manager where an employee can be accompanied by a colleague or union steward if he or she wishes
(c) a right of appeal against the decision.

The code also refers to collective disputes and recommends that where unions are recognised there should be a separate collective disputes procedure for such matters.

Such a disputes procedure frequently has more stages including the provision for bringing in a full time union official at "works conference" level. If the matter is not resolved there is often provision under a national agreement for further external stages, as in the National Engineering Agreement for example. There may be a final conciliation or arbitration stage, with a clause in the procedure such as:

"If this procedure is exhausted without agreement being reached then the parties will request ACAS to conciliate.

If agreement is not reached discussions will take place between the parties concerned to establish terms of reference for the matter to be referred to agreed independent arbitration. The arbitrator's finding or award will be binding on the parties".

There is also a requirement in the Employment Protection (Consolidation) Act 1978 for the statement of terms and conditions of employment to name a person to whom the employee can address a grievance.

Handling Grievances

The right to raise a grievance means that in practice the supervisor or manager to whom the grievance is addressed should:
- respond by welcoming the grievance rather than by reacting negatively or defensively
- listen carefully to the grievance so that the substance of the complaint is clearly understood and the "facts" as believed by the employee are clarified. Probe to see if this is the real grievance or whether there is something else, eg complaints about canteen meals can be a cover for a real grievance over washing time or other terms and conditions of employment
- postpone making a decision so that the facts of the matter can be established with other people involved or with another interested party. This provides an opportunity to check the appropriate company policy or custom and practice, or find out if the issue involved has surfaced before, etc
- make a decision, if he or she has the necessary authority, otherwise the matter should be referred, with recommendations, to the appropriate level of authority. Sometimes it is sensible to submit a written report
- finally, communicate the decision and the reasons for it in detail, eg the reasons behind the adoption of a particular company policy.

It should be noted that successful resolution does not mean that employees always get their own way or, for that matter, that management always "squash" grievances flat. Most grievances are resolved by compromise.

The Buck Stops?

If employees are still unhappy about the way their grievances have been resolved, an appeal stage should be made available for the whole issue to be looked at again by a senior manager or director of the company. At the end of the day this decision should be final. Some individual grievance procedures have a final conciliation or arbitration stage but this is not recommended by the Code of Practice except for collective disputes procedures.

One practical consideration in framing a grievance procedure is the addition of a time scale so that matters are taken quickly through procedures.

Example grievance procedure:

"The Company's policy is to encourage free interchange and communication between managers and the staff they manage. This ensures that questions and problems can be aired and resolved quickly.
1. If you have a grievance arising out of your employment you should raise the matter with your immediate superior in the first instance. If the matter is not resolved after five working days, you may put your grievance, in writing, to your Departmental Manager.

2. If the matter remains unresolved at this level after five working days you may request that the matter is referred for the decision of the appropriate Director, whose decision is final.
3. You may consider some requests or complaints too personal to discuss with your immediate Supervisor or Manager. With these matters you have the right to go to the Personnel Manager after first receiving permission from your Manager or Supervisor to do so.

We wish to ensure than any employee problem or grievance is dealt with effectively and speedily. Your co-operation is sought in bringing such matters to your Supervisor's or Manager's attention as they arise."

Employees' Appearance

Most employers expect their staff to maintain a certain standard of dress and appearance during their employment, usually to project a particular company image or to adhere to specific rules on health and safety. Case law has established that an employer generally has a large measure of discretion in insisting on a reasonable standard of clothing and in controlling the overall appearance of his staff. However, it is important that employers remain aware that the general test of reasonableness will still apply, not only in justifying particular rules, but also in determining appropriate action to be taken against erring employees.

Rules on Appearance

Particular standards of appearance are generally either specified in the employer's written disciplinary rules or embodied in custom and practice within the company. It is generally preferable that rules are written and clearly drafted if the employer is to rely on them in taking disciplinary action against employees who do not observe particular requirements. Also, it is often a good idea for the employer's reasons for the rule to be incorporated into any statement so that employees are made aware of the rule's purpose. Whatever the case, rules must be reasonable and employers are well-advised to ensure that there is adequate justification for them to avoid falling foul of tribunals. In *Talbot v Hugh M Fulton* [1975] IRLR 52, an industrial tribual held that a rule, specifying that employees should have short hair, was not justifiable on safety grounds in the case of an apprentice who, in the course of his duties, was not exposed to any particular hazard such as moving machinery in which his long hair was liable to become caught. It therefore follows that it is not enough for the employer to justify a dismissal on the sole ground that a rule has been broken if the rule is unreasonable in the first place.

Discriminatory Requirements

As well as being reasonable, rules must also remain free from discrimination. A single rule which requires only women to wear overalls will be directly discriminatory in itself if no rules governing the appearance of men are in force. Similarly, direct racial discrimination can result from rules which are confined purely to one racial group and not to others. Indirect sex and racial discrimination can occur where an unjustifiable requirement for a particular appearance is applied to all employees, but only a small number of people from one group can satisfy the requirement. One example of this occurred in *Malik v BHS* COIT 987/12 where the company's rule that female staff should wear an overall over a skirt was found to be indirectly discriminatory against Miss Malik, a muslim girl whose religion decreed that she had to wear trousers. The tribunal in this case held that the detriment suffered by Miss Malik was not justifiable on the grounds of commercial necessity in portraying a particular company image.

Generally, however, where discrimination claims arise about rules on appearance, tribunals tend to take a fairly broad approach. In *Schmidt v Austick Bookshops* [1977] IRLR 360, the EAT held that where rules were in force restricting both the appearance of men and women, it did not necessarily constitute discrimination if the rules in each case were not identical. Here, Miss Schmidt had claimed sex discrimination on the grounds that women employees were not permitted to wear trousers at work when dealing with customers. Upholding the industrial tribunal's decision, the EAT confirmed that Miss Schmidt had not suffered less favourable treatment as no direct comparison could be made between men and women as regards this rule. While trousers for women are acceptable in many situations men do not have the same choice as regards skirts. The EAT noted that there were in force restrictions on men forbidding the wearing of tee-shirts and they preferred to adopt the broader view that both sexes were subject to a restriction that a certain garment could not be worn. Therefore there was no less favourable treatment of Miss Schmidt.

Promoting Company Image

The projection of a particular company image is a major consideration for some employers and this is often the reason that particular standards of dress and appearance are required. This is especially common in certain service industries such as retailing, advertising, public relations, etc, and can, of course, be the justification behind particular rules. However, the promotion of a particular image must be kept within a reasonable context. In *Eales v Halfords* COIT 1179/51, the company operated specific dress rules for employees in their store. Mr Eales was required to wear a collar and tie, dark trousers and sensible shoes. After minor transgressions with clothing, Mr Eales dyed his hair yellow and was dismissed. The tribunal held that the level of smartness required by the company for employment in a bicycle shop had been over-estimated. However, in *Roberts v Sutcliffe Catering* COIT 24663/77/D a tribunal decided that the employee's dismissal for her persistent refusal on superstitious grounds to wear a uniform which included the colour green was reasonable. The tribunal took the view that it was important for the company to present a consistent image in their various locations and the appearance of the staff created an image which complemented the clients of the business.

Customer and Employee Objections

The risk of giving offence to customers and other staff will often influence the employer in formulating standards of appearance and taking action against employees who do not observe them. In *Boychuck v H J Symons Holdings* [1977] IRLR 395 an employee was fairly dismissed, after appropriate warnings, for persistently refusing to stop wearing badges proclaiming that she was a lesbian. The EAT ruled that it is within an employer's discretion to instruct an employee not to wear a sign or symbol that could be offensive to fellow employees or customers, though they did point out that an employer would not, of course, be at liberty to impose a restriction if there were unreasonable grounds for believing that offence would be given. It is therefore important that employers can identify a real risk or show evidence that customers or other employees have, in fact, complained about an individual's personal attire.

Maintaining Health and Safety

Particular requirements which can be justified on grounds of health and safety will almost always be reasonable. It makes sense to prohibit the wearing of particular adornments that could become tangled in dangerous machinery or to insist on protective eye goggles or ear defenders where flying splinters of material or excessive noise are particular hazards. The employer's general duty under the Health and Safety at Work, etc Act 1974 to take reasonable care for employees' health, safety and welfare is clear justification for prohibiting particular attire as long as requirements are reasonable and employees who flout safety rules on appearance can be fairly dismissed. In *Frizzell v Fladers & others t/a P J Contracting* COIT 847/232, a safety rule was in force whereby employees engaged in the cleaning of particular fuel tanks had to wear gas masks. Mr Frizzell was seen working with his mask slung over his shoulder and his subsequent dismissal was upheld as fair by the tribunal, as he admitted he had a "fair idea" that he was putting his job in jeopardy by not wearing the mask.

However, the employer must make sure that complaints about the standard of safety wear are fully investigated. In *Mayhew v Anderson (Stoke Newington) Ltd* [1978] IRLR 101, the dismissal of an employee who refused to wear eye goggles which irritated her eyes was unfair as the employers had refused to consider providing her with more suitable eye wear, and in *British Aircraft Corporation Ltd v Austin* [1978] IRLR 332, the EAT ruled that a failure to investigate an employee's valid complaint, again about protective eyewear, amounted to a breach of contract entitling the employee to resign and claim constructive dismissal.

Dismissal Procedures

Even where an employer provides clear justification for rules on dress and appearance it is important that a fair procedure is followed in carrying out dismissals. Failure to comply with a dress requirement will not generally be considered as gross misconduct warranting summary dismissal. It is therefore important that employees are informed quite clearly of the employer's position, given an opportunity to state any reasons for not observing the rule, and are issued with appropriate warnings before any decision to dismiss is finally taken. Obviously any particular objections to the rule should be fully investigated to make sure that the rule itself is fully justified in the circumstances.

Provision of Clothing and Equipment

In many cases, the employer is bound to provide clothing and equipment to employees under statutory health and safety legislation. Specific regulations made under the Factories Act 1961 apply in factories involving certain processes where protective clothing must be provided and worn, eg work involving use of asbestos, preparation of certain foods, etc. Generally, however, the most widely applicable piece of legislation is again the employer's general duty under s.2 of the Health and Safety at Work, etc Act to "ensure, so far as is reasonably practicable, the health, safety and welfare of his employees". This in itself means that if protective clothing or equipment is necessary to ensure that an employer complies with this duty, it must be provided free of charge to all relevant employees. S.9 of the Act forbids employers to charge employees for safety equipment and clothing that has to be provided to comply with their statutory duty.

The question of what is "reasonably practicable" in such circumstances was considered in *Associated Dairies Ltd v Hartley* [1979] IRLR 171. Here the employees used hydraulic trolley jacks (roller trucks) to handle and transport goods around their warehouses. At one particular site an employee suffered an injury when a truck rolled over his foot. The injury would not have occurred if he had been wearing protective footwear. At the time, the employers operated a facility whereby employees could purchase suitable safety footwear at cost price for use in the warehouse. The factory inspector, Mr Hartley, issued an improvement notice requiring the employer to provide "free" safety footwear to all employees operating roller trucks. The company appealed against this to an industrial tribunal. The tribunal unanimously agreed that it was practicable to provide free footwear but the majority held that it was not reasonable to do so, as the expense in providing free safety shoes was disproportionate to the risk involved. The company had a well publicised safety policy which drew attention to the need for protective footwear when operating roller trucks and there was no evidence that free footwear would ensure the use of safety shoes any more than mere availability under the current scheme. The tribunal concluded that as it had not been shown that greater safety would result from free equipment the improvement notice should be cancelled.

However, where an employer is shown to be in breach of his or her duty of care in failing to provide adequate protection the result can be expensive. In *Pentney v Anglian Water Authority* (1983) ICR 464, the employee was blinded in one eye when the wrench he was using to loosen a rusty nut slipped and shattered a lens of his glasses. His claim that the employer's negligence in not providing safety glasses had caused the accident was upheld by the High Court, who noted that the employee had repeatedly requested protective eyewear for some time prior to the accident although none was provided. The court held that it was reasonably foreseeable that such an accident could occur and awarded the employee a total of £11,600 compensation.

Clothing Accommodation

Employers covered by the Factories Act 1961 and the Offices, Shops and Railway Premises Act 1963 are under an express duty to provide suitable accommodation for clothing not worn during working hours and for the storage during out-of-work hours of clothing required to carry out the work. Specific orders extend these requirements in certain industries. Also, s.2 of the Health and Safety at Work, etc Act 1974 is sufficiently wide to impose a similar duty on all employers.

In some cases where employers have voluntarily taken over custody of clothing from employees they can, in law, become "bailees" of the articles, which means that they will be answerable for loss or damage to property unless they can show that they took reasonable care for its safe-keeping. For liability in bailment to arise employees must show that they temporarily gave up their own control over the articles in favour of more immediate control by the employer. If, for example, an employee leaves a coat on a chair whilst going out to lunch, the responsibility for the article will normally rest with the employee. However, if it is left in a separate cloakroom specifically provided for the purpose or in a locker to which the employer retains a key, liability can shift to the employer in bailment, if it can be shown that the degree of control over the property has transferred. Ironically, the harder the employer tries to protect the property of his or her employees, the more likely that liability in bailment for its safe-keeping will increase.

Conclusion

Clearly, matters concerning the dress and appearance of employees are full of potential pitfalls for the unwary employer. It is therefore important that in seeking to comply with the relevant legislation, employers bear in mind the overriding test of reasonableness which will be applied by the courts in virtually all circumstances in assessing employers' particular actions as regards their employees.

Job Security Agreements

The foremost ambition of working people in the first part of the 20th century was to achieve a secure job with a good pension. The gold watch, awarded for many years of loyal service to a firm, was a familiar part of the industrial scene. Then it all changed. With more affluent times young people began to spread their wings; jobs were there for the taking and to remain too long in one place was considered decidedly dull.

In the heady days of the 1960s the Japanese concept of a job for life within one company was regarded as something alien to our culture and it was assumed that — in time — Japanese employees themselves would become more Westernised and break away from what, to Western eyes, was a rigid system. It is somewhat ironic, given this background, that security of employment has once again become an issue of fundamental importance for employees and their representatives.

Since mass redundancies began in the 60s and the full horror was appreciated of putting large numbers of people in a community out of work, managements, together with trade unions, have been looking at ways of minimising the impact of redundancies on the workforce. One way of doing this is to plan ahead as far as possible and to draw up a procedure, well-known to all concerned, on how redundancies will be dealt with if the occasion arises. Going one stage further are companies which negotiate "job security agreements".

Good Practice

The 1971 Industrial Relations Code of Practice advocates that a "policy for dealing with reductions in the workforce, if they become necessary, should be worked out in advance so far as practicable and should form part of the undertaking's employment policies".

While the following of the code of practice is not mandatory, a court can take into account compliance or otherwise with its recommendations and so managements are well advised to look carefully at their policies and procedures in this area. A job security agreement, however, goes further than a mere policy. The aim is that, by taking a positive, continuing look at forward planning, both redundancies and their impact will be minimised in the future.

Potential Disadvantages

One of the major problems a company is likely to encounter when introducing the idea of a job security agreement is the suspicion of the workforce. The thought is likely to go through employees' minds that the reason for drawing up the new scheme is that the company is planning a redundancy programme. Such a reaction will provoke the very outcome the agreement is designed to avoid: anxiety and unrest. It has been the pattern in the past to conclude such agreements following particularly painful redundancy exercises when workforce, unions and management have jointly recognised the need to avoid a repetition if at all possible. Nonetheless, in most industries rapid change has meant that employees nowadays are very aware that reductions in manning can affect any business and, given careful consultation, most people may be persuaded of the benefits which a job security agreement can bring.

Another difficulty foreseen by companies, which induces reluctance to commit themselves to an agreement, is that of being locked into a particular procedure with no room for flexibility in what may be a volatile situation. Obviously this could create great problems for the company and it is therefore essential that room for manoeuvre is built into any agreement reached.

The Benefits

A rumour-ridden, anxious and insecure workforce can cause a good deal of damage to a company. When morale is at a low ebb, efficiency tumbles, valuable people begin looking elsewhere for jobs and commitment disappears. Such a scenario is likely to bring about redundancies which might possibly otherwise have been averted. While a straightforward redundancy procedure will simply mean that people know the probable method of selection and how much compensation they are likely to receive in the event of redundancy, a job security agreement will reassure employees that planning, consultation and fair procedures will make enforced redundancies less likely and, should they come about, will mean that they are carried out fairly.

When procedures are demonstrably made public, the company grapevine which feeds on rumour and suspicion becomes less of a threat. A more open approach to the whole topic reveals a caring attitude on the part of the company to which the workforce is likely to respond positively.

A major advantage for employers in concluding job security agreements is in enabling them to cost their future plans on an accurate basis.

Compiling an Agreement

The contents and length of a job security agreement are likely to vary considerably depending on the nature and size of the undertaking.

Most agreements begin with an introductory scene-setting statement which explains the objectives with phrases such as:

"The policy is to provide staff, as far as is practicable, with security of employment. To this end the company will plan its manpower requirements as far in advance as possible. It is recognised that this policy has to be consistent with operational efficiency and the success of the business".

Further sections normally set out agreed procedures for manpower reviews, early warning of potential redundancies, consultation, measures the company will take to avoid redundancies occurring and terms of severance.

Manpower Plans

Companies sometimes plan their manpower requirements in terms of numbers likely to be needed but do not go further and look at the distribution of the workforce in terms of age, skills, etc. When the commitment to effective manpower planning becomes enshrined in a job security agreement, it is likely that machinery for jointly reviewing staffing requirements will need to be established or overhauled. Where joint consultative committees are already in existence it may be appropriate to extend their scope to cover manpower reviews, perhaps on a regular basis two or three times a year. It is obviously necessary to co-ordinate such reviews at the highest level. Where the industrial relations climate is such that manpower plans can be drawn up and agreed jointly by management and unions this will consolidate the co-operative approach.

Consultation

It is normal to include a section in a job security agreement on consultation arrangements. Under the Employment Protection Act 1975 (s.99) employers are required to consult with representatives of recognised trade unions *at the earliest opportunity* if they are proposing to dismiss employees on the grounds of redundancy. In any event, such consultations must begin:

- at least 90 days before the first dismissal takes effect if the employer proposes to dismiss as redundant 100 or more employees at one establishment within 90 days or less
- at least 30 days before the first dismissal takes effect if the employer proposes to dismiss as redundant 10 or more employees within 30 days or less.

Since these are statutory minimum requirements, unions will seek to negotiate improvements on this in any job security agreement. For example, a deal on a six months' minimum consultation or notice period is not uncommon. Indeed, under the terms of a job security agreement concluded early in 1986, the Automobile Association undertook to give 12 months' notification of redundancies, although the arrangement does allow for a shorter notification period if operational circumstances make it necessary.

Situations can, of course, arise entirely outside the control of the company which mean that urgent pruning action must be taken if the business is to survive. For this reason a rider should be added to any otherwise total commitment to long consultation periods, allowing for departure from the agreed procedure in specified circumstances.

Preventive Measures

The core "security" item so far as employees are concerned is the section in a job security agreement which sets out the measures a company intends to take to minimise the need for compulsory redundancies.

In the Industrial Relations Code of Practice the following suggestions are made as means of avoiding redundancies:
– restrictions on recruitment
– retirement of employees beyond normal retiring age
– reductions in overtime
– short time working to cover temporary fluctuations in manpower needs.

Further steps which may be included are:
– consideration of diversification into new markets
– voluntary early retirement
– reduction in the use of temporary or agency staff and contractors
– voluntary redundancy.

Many of these items will need to be "fleshed out" in the document. For instance, a ban on recruitment would need to have regard to the balance of the workforce in terms of experience and skills. Details will be required of financial arrangements for early retirees or those taking voluntary redundancy.

When redeployment and/or training are involved employees will need to know what their options are. In certain cases it may be appropriate to offer an extended trial period for retraining during which time an employee could still opt for redundancy if the post proved unsuitable. Wherever possible, career counselling should be offered by the company to employees faced with the possibility of transfer.

In circumstances where employees agree to be redeployed to lower grade jobs, arrangements for protection of earnings should be specified, together with information on how future promotion will be handled. Details of the company's relocation policy in the event of a move being necessary if a person is to take up alternative employment could also be included.

Selection Issues

If compulsory redundancies become inevitable despite the action taken to prevent them, employees will want to know on what basis selection for redundancy will be made and this information is likely to be one of the elements in a job security agreement.

A section on redundancy selection is included in this book in chapter 8.

Severance Terms

Severance packages are likely to be negotiated for inclusion in job security agreements, although companies may be reluctant to be specific in their commitment because of the uncertain economic outlook. Certainly, with the withdrawal of redundancy rebate, managements will look hard in future at the feasibility of enhancing statutory payments.

Where it is vital to retain a nucleus of employees until a particular date, agreements may stipulate that people who remain in service to that time will qualify for retention pay, or a "loyalty bonus".

Payments made in addition to the statutory amounts vary between companies in the way they are calculated. Common methods used are to increase the basic amount by a certain percentage or to add on a standard number of weeks' pay, and organisations often allow for short-service employees who are outside the scope of statutory payments to receive an amount of company redundancy pay. Other supplementary payments can include pay in lieu of notice, hardship allowances and service-related payments.

Counselling Services

Another area for possible inclusion in a job security agreement is that of non-monetary assistance to redundant employees. Career guidance counselling, either provided by in-house experts or by outside specialists, can be a positive contribution towards the individual's future welfare. Similarly, assistance in financial planning may be welcomed.

Management Commitment

The making of a job security agreement is far from the end of the story. When provision is made for joint forward planning and extensive consultation a high degree of management commitment and time will be needed if the agreement is to work effectively. Once it can be seen by employees as operating to secure their employment, so far as that is possible, the organisation may expect to experience the benefits of having a stable and confident workforce.

4 TAKING ON EMPLOYEES

In this chapter we look at the practice of recruitment, including taking up references, making offers of employment and contracts of employment. The issues surrounding who is an employee and who is an "independent contractor" are dealt with in chapter 7.

Recruitment Sources

Once it has been established that a vacancy exists, the first step is to look at the sources from which employers can attract a field of candidates on which to base selection for employment.

Internal Sources

Quite often, the best starting point when looking for candidates is within the organisation itself and in most cases the internal movement of staff from job to job will occur through the promotion of individuals to take the place of those who have left or been promoted themselves. Where companies are seen to operate such a policy, it can provide an element of incentive to employees and subsequently is likely to result in lower labour turnover. In the same way, the transfer of staff from department to department or from branch to branch can also be used to good effect, particularly where certain personnel are surplus due to the recent or imminent operation of a redundancy programme. In addition, it is sometimes the case that vacancies occur at the same time as a disciplinary decision to demote an employee is made, thus obviating the need to fill the vacant job from another source — assuming, of course, that the employee's contractual rights are not infringed.

Word of Mouth Recruitment

At the bottom end of the scale of external recruitment sources is the use of "word of mouth" to advertise vacant posts. This is normally done by the employer informing existing staff (or indeed other persons) of vacancies as and when they occur and relying on them to"pass on the word" to friends or relatives that work is available. Whilst this is undoubtedly one of the cheapest methods of recruiting it is not without its drawbacks, the most important of which is that such a scheme can in fact constitute a discriminatory practice. In 1978/9 the Commission for Racial Equality undertook a formal investigation into the recruitment methods used by F Broomfield Ltd. They found that the company recruited drivers on the recommendation of staff already employed. This had resulted in a wholly white workforce because friends and relatives of existing white employees had been told of the vacancies. This effectively excluded non-white applicants from applying and was therefore indirectly discriminatory.

External Agencies

The use of external agencies in recruitment has become increasingly popular and there is now an array of sources available to the recruiter, ranging from Government employment services to specialist consultancies. Jobcentres and careers offices provide a free service but most other external agents operate on a fee-paying basis, normally calculated as a percentage of the successful applicant's commencing salary. For certain types of jobs or where the need for replacement staff is particularly pressing, the use of employment agencies can be very effective. In some cases, eg where certain specialist staff are required, the employer may decide to use the Government's Professional & Executive Recruitment Service or a private consultancy to undertake the initial recruitment exercise, including advertising and screening of candidates, to present the employer with a final shortlist from which selection can be made. Lastly, for very senior posts, the use of executive search consultants is fairly common. Such "headhunters" operate very much on personal recommendation in earmarking particular individuals for certain senior positions and approaching them with a view to obtaining their interest and consent to take up the post.

Advertising Vacancies

Employers may, however, decide not to rely on third parties for external recruitment and to advertise the vacancies themselves. This can range from putting a card in a shop window to taking a full page spread in a technical journal or national newspaper. Whilst there are no hard and fast rules in drafting the content of advertisements, certain general guidelines should be borne in mind in order to achieve the desired effect. A job advertisement should normally include the following: job title; brief details of the company; a description of the main duties and working environment; an outline of the employer's requirements — experience, qualifications, etc; details of the benefits available; directions on how to apply.

The amount of space devoted to particular issues will, however, very much depend on the type of advertisement being run — for example, where it is for an unskilled post, details of company objectives and career prospects would take a lower priority than rates of pay and working environment.

Ideally, the content of an advertisement should act as a "self-selecting" device, appealing solely to those at whom it is aimed. Therefore, attention to the description of the work involved and the employer's requirements can be crucial in order to avoid unnecessary processing of applications which plainly do not fit. Similarly, clear details of pay and benefits can assist the recruitment process by discouraging applicants who anticipate higher earnings than the employer intends to pay. Finally, any form of recruitment advertising should always specify clearly how the applicants should apply — either in person, by telephone, or by sending a completed application form, curriculum vitae, etc. The Institute of Personnel Management's voluntary recruitment code recommends this, noting that applicants frequently complain of labouring to produce a detailed letter of application only to receive a form requesting the same information, and points out that accurate instructions will again save the time of both applicant and recruiter.

Choosing where to place the advertisement is crucial. The employer should always bear in mind that the aim of the exercise is to attract suitable candidates. Therefore, it is virtually pointless to advertise for a managing director on a notice-board outside the premises and equally worthless to place an advertisement in a computer journal for a canteen assistant. Factors such as cost will always play a major role but this must be weighed against the hidden costs of the recruiter's time in sorting through hundreds of applications where a national newspaper has been used to advertise a job requiring no experience or qualifications, or, at the other end of the scale, where a small notice tucked away in the "wrong" journal has meant that the entire exercise needs to be recommenced, thus incurring unnecessary costs for the employer.

Obtaining Information from Applicants

We turn now to consider the methods of gleaning information from job applicants and to look at how these can be made more effective as tools of selection.

CVs or Application Forms?

In order to select a new member of staff from several applicants, successfully, the recruiter needs information about the candidates. The most common means of supplying this information will be either an application form or a curriculum vitae. Most job advertisements will specify which form of application is preferred and many organisations have specific reasons for requiring one rather than the other.

CVs will generally be required from more senior candidates; they are useful in that candidates can give more detail about specific work experience and achievements than would be possible in a pre-printed form. Also, because applicants draft and produce CVs themselves, the finished product gives the recruiter an opportunity to assess how the individuals present themselves in writing, and the amount of trouble taken on a CV will often give useful clues to an applicant's interest in the job and general ability. If recruiting for a position which requires an aptitude for writing or selling, a CV will often be a good tool of selection; the way in which candidates sell themselves is a good indication of how successful they will be in promoting the company's product.

Application forms in general, however, are more useful than CVs to the recruiter. Their major advantage is that the employer can ask the questions which he or she wants answered. Candidates who furnish CVs will often be selective about the personal details they supply, whereas application forms will expose any awkward gaps in career history by the use of specific questions. It is also generally easier to draw up a shortlist of candidates by comparing them on the basis of the same information requested. Many applicants will find it easier to respond to particular questions than to produce a written account of themselves; requesting CVs may even deter them from applying.

Questions to be Asked

The application form gives an employer the opportunity to request specific and crucial information about potential employees. It is, therefore, well worth spending time considering questions which need to be answered, eg are there special requirements for the organisation in terms of health or ability to drive? The form may also be used as a basis for the records kept on the applicant if he or she is appointed. Information from it will be transferred onto files and other documents, so it is worth ensuring that all necessary questions are included for these purposes.

If designing your own form there are several basic questions which should be included. The following checklist gives the major information areas which should be covered.

Identification: name; address; telephone number; date of birth; title of post applied for; recruitment source.

Education: schools attended, names and dates; examinations passed; higher education, names and dates of institutions attended; examinations passed; other qualifications and courses attended, names and dates; professional membership.

Occupation: names and addresses of all previous employers in chronological order; dates of employment (month and year); job title; synopsis of main responsibilities in each of the previous jobs; final salary; reason for leaving.

Recreation: hobbies, sports and other pastimes.

Miscellaneous: previous applications; relatives working for organisation; health record, history of illness plus attendance record in last job; driving licence/possession of own car; positions of responsibility held (at school/college/socially); foreign languages; convictions; notes in support of application.

Legislative Aspects

There are other aspects which should be borne in mind when drawing up questions for an application form. Unlawful discrimination, both racial and sexual, can creep in even unintentionally. Questions about marital status and numbers of children will not be discriminatory as long as everyone is asked them, regardless of sex. The phrasing of certain questions can be offensive and indirectly discriminatory to ethnic minorities, eg asking for "Christian" names (obviously not applicable to Hindus or Muslims) or "nationality by birth". The employer should also be wary of producing extremely complex application forms which require a greater use of written English than is actually necessary for the job. This will effectively prevent or deter some non-English speakers from completing the form.

It is obviously necessary to ask questions about an applicant's ethnic origin if the organisation is undertaking ethnic monitoring in compliance with the CRE's Code of Practice. It is sensible to use a variation of the CRE's recommended format for this: self-classification of origin by ticking boxes and indicating the purpose for questioning as being monitoring of an equal opportunities policy.

Design

The actual design of an application form should be clear and well presented making the layout inviting to complete. The form conveys an impression of the company to a job applicant so care should be taken with presentation and printing. Short sentences and familiar words are easier to respond to, as well as being less ambiguous. It is also important to ensure that adequate space is given for answers, although large areas may invite candidates to be verbose. Any parts of the form which are to be completed by the interviewer should be clearly sectioned off to avoid misunderstanding. Finally, companies should always be open to revising application forms in the light of new legislative requirements or when particular questions regularly cause confusion or result in insufficient detail being supplied.

Planning Recruitment Interviews

One job that can take up an enormous amount of the personnel manager's time is recruitment interviewing. It is always a mistake to launch into interviewing job applicants without first checking through the application form or CVs for a preliminary sort out. With no-hopers discarded because they do not match the essential criteria, a shortlist of candidates can then be created. Ideally, there should be a sensible number of around six for final selection.

Preparing for the Interview

The first requirement is to know who will interview the candidates. Is a screening interview to be held by the personnel department followed by a more specifically job-related interview with the departmental head? Is a panel of managers the chosen method of interview? Have those involved in the interview been informed of the date, venue and time, etc? Consider a meeting of those involved in interviewing the candidate beforehand to plan the interview, especially the sequence of questions.

It is also useful to explain to the candidate how the proceedings will be ordered and whether there is another interview to follow before final selection is made. Do not forget to include a map of how to get to the company's premises. Make sure the receptionist or gatekeeper knows that they are expected and where the interview will be held. Check that the interview location will be available at the time required and that interruptions will be channelled elsewhere. If literature about the company is available, ensure that candidates have the opportunity to read it if there is a waiting period before the interview.

The Physical Setting

The physical setting is also important. Consider the following:
- avoid extremes of temperature in the interview room
- ensure that the candidate is not directly facing a bright light and that noise from outside is at a minimum
- check the seating arrangements — all seats should be of the same height and comfort and of appropriate degree of formality
- provide space for the interviewee's papers, ashtray, etc
- supply tea or coffee to lubricate the proceedings.

In short, the environment in which the interview is conducted will have an important effect on the candidate's state of mind. It will either allow candidates to give their best if they are at ease or may make them take away a poor view of the company. Interviewers should always remember that they are inviting candidates into their territory and putting candidates at ease is their first duty:
- waiting time should be kept to a minimum
- see if the candidates coat, brief-case and other possessions can be moved out of the way to clear the decks for action
- guide candidates to the comfortable chair in which you want them to sit
- almost inevitably, the room will have a desk (hopefully uncluttered) and this will give a formal flavour to the proceedings; a more relaxed atmosphere can be obtained by the participants sitting around a coffee table
- explain the ground rules on smoking: "I'm a non-smoker and I would prefer that you refrained from smoking", or offer the ashtray and invite the candidate to light up
- finally, the interviewer should start off with an easy-to-answer social question such as "How did you find the journey? What lovely weather we're having", etc. The old cliches are comforting and do not intimidate. They break the ice and allow candidates to speak once they have entered the interviewer's territory.

Interviewing Props

Interview plans of the type developed by Munro Frazer (Five Fold Grading Scheme) or Professor Roger (Seven Point Plan) are attempts to improve the systematic appraisal and assessment of job candidates. There is no magic about the formulae; they are simply methods of going logically through the personal characteristics, experience, skills, etc of the candidate from the beginning to the end. Training in these methods will also encourage a more objective approach by the interviewer. Such plans ensure that conversations are brought back to cover the candidate's work history and other relevant information which may otherwise be left out of the tide of conversation.

The application form is also a useful tool to keep the interview on steady lines. The preparation carried out by the interviewer beforehand should have ensured that gaps in employment history have been picked up; possible health problems, etc, identified for specific questioning and the form should provide a space for jotting down brief notes. It is always distracting for the candidate if copious notes are written during the interview. This is best reserved for a time as soon after the interview as possible, before the memory fades. However, notes taken at the time are quite invaluable; they represent an original document which can be used in evidence in a tribunal should a complaint of race or sex discrimination be made against the interviewer. The records should represent the interviewer's assessment of suitability for the job based on legitimate criteria which have nothing to do with the sex or race of the candidate.

Effective Employment Interviewing

We go on now to look at conducting an interview and consider helpful hints on interviewing techniques and assessing candidates.

The Purpose

At all times interviewers must hold clear in their minds the purpose behind the encounter, which can be briefly summarised as follows:
- to assess candidates' past achievements and failures in order to guage their suitability for the job
- to assess whether candidates are keen to do the job
- to assess whether the candidates have personal characteristics which will enable them to fit into the organisation
- to give an opportunity for the candidates to gain a realistic view of the job and the organisation in which they have sought work.

The interviewer must retain just enough control over the meeting to guide the questioning and cover "the necessary ground" whilst not inhibiting the free flow of information from candidates. The interviewer should not forget to smile and look pleased to meet the candidate, even if it is the 10th interview that day! More often than not the candidate will be inarticulate until the ice has been broken; prising out information is often like extracting teeth, particularly so where school leavers are concerned.

It is probably better to find out about where the candidate bought her pretty dress or his Gucci sweater than to launch in on a serious attempt to obtain information! This, of course, gives conversation a chance to develop and the candidate can begin to feel more at ease. Discussion about some shared experience can get the interviewer off to a good start. Although closed questions like "You went to Southport High School didn't you" are normally considered taboo in most kinds of interviews, a few of them, for particularly nervous candidates, coupled with smiles of encouragement, will at least check out poorly written information on an application form and make them feel that they are achieving some communication. Incidentally, closed questions are an excellent way of controlling verbose candidates and obtaining shorter, more manageable, answers from them.

Suitable Work

Once candidates have "found their feet" and are maintaining eye contact with the interviewer, the open questions, the ones which can be answered with more than just "yes" and "no", come into their own. This is the chance to check the "funnies" on the application form. For instance:
- "Well, John, there appears to be a nine month gap between your employment with Briggs and J S Wilson's. What were you doing?"
- "You left J S Wilson's because you wanted more money but your job with A Forsters paid less. What happened?"
- "You don't ever appear to have been employed in factory work before. Why do you think you will like factory work?"

Whether or not the work will suit the candidate is an important question to be answered and very often it is a matter of piecing the clues together. However, it is amazing how honest candidates can be in their answers. The sales representative might describe his poorest qualities as "lacking drive and initiative". Failing that, the rapid dismissal of the candidate from a series of rep jobs for "redundancy" might amount to the same thing. Similarly, the administrative clerks who have left other jobs because they dislike dull, routine work are quite unlikely to settle into another dull, routine administrative job — no matter how nice they are.

Two-Way Process

It would be a very unbalanced and unsatisfying interview for the candidates if they were not told something about the job itself and the terms and conditions of employment. Indeed, such information, especially the bad points of the job (which should not be glossed over), will produce valuable responses. For instance, if the job involves handling meat, there are religious groups and vegetarians who might baulk at such a job. Cold, dusty or dirty working conditions should be explained and not left to the candidates to find out for themselves. If such conditions prevail, it might be sensible to take them to see where the job is performed.

Difficulties in finding shops or eating places, or poor public travel arrangements near to the place of work, might act as a disincentive to employees to stay once they are recruited. The information supplied should allow the candidate to gain a realistic assessment of the job, warts and all.

A checklist of company terms and conditions of employment and specifics of the job is a useful tool to ensure that all the relevant information is given at the interview.

Pitfalls

Some common interviewing faults are included below:
- asking multiple questions like "Tell me about your job with Briggs, what did you do, what were your responsibilities, how did you like your manager?" all in one breath merely show the interviewer's inexperience and will not get very constructive replies
- failing to listen or to concentrate on what is being said and to allow the candidate to complete remarks without interruptions. A candidate will rapidly appreciate when the interviewer's attention is elsewhere and will usually clam up
- asking questions in a disorganised, unstructured way so that communication is hindered
- making copious notes and thus distracting the candidate
- allowing approval or disapproval to creep into the interview through manner, tone of voice, or gestures adopted in relation to answers given. If candidates feel censured they will fail to give their best
- rushing the interview with indecent haste
- asking questions that might indicate an intention to discriminate on grounds of race or sex. Child care arrangements are a perfectly legitimate area to ask questions about — but don't forget to ask men as well. In this day and age men also share these responsibilities.

The latter kind of information is frequently important to see if the candidate has rationally assessed the demands of the job in relation to his or her domestic responsibilities. The important point is not to make sexist assumptions that because a woman has domestic responsibilities she will automatically have a lot of time off.

Making Offers of Employment

When a suitable candidate has been identified and an offer of the job is to be made it is important to look at the various legal and practical issues that are involved.

Offering the Job

There is nothing in law to say that a job offer has to be made in writing; it can be made orally at the end of the interview or by telephone at a later date.

However, in most cases it is more sensible to put the offer in writing so that there can be no doubt in the mind of the employer or the candidate what has been offered or the terms of the offer.

A letter which offers the job should specify the terms on which the offer is made in reasonable detail. While the law on written statements of terms and conditions of employment only provides that the statements have to be given to employees by the end of their 13th week of employment, in practice it makes good sense to send a copy of the statement with the offer letter, so there can be no doubt that the candidate, if he or she accepts the job, knows on what terms it is being offered.

This is particularly true if the terms are to include a restraint clause since, if this is not made known until after the candidate has started work, he or she will not be bound by the clause.

Formation of the Contract

The reason for this is that the contract of employment comes into force as soon as you say to a candidate: "I am offering you the position of Accounts Supervisor at a salary of £10,000 pa. Do you accept?" and the candidate does accept the job. All that is necessary for the contract to exist is the offer, and acceptance and consideration — in this case the candidate's promise to do the work in return for the salary.

If, at this stage, no terms other than the salary have been specified, it is extremely unlikely that a clause particular to your own organisation would ever be implied into the contract. In such a case, therefore, new employees would only be bound by a restraint clause, for example, if they agreed to a variation of the contract or, failing this, they were given proper notice to terminate the contract and were offered re-engagement on new terms. This, however, begs the question: what is proper notice? Again, this would not have been specified when the contract was made.

If it is considered important to make the offer during the interview — or by telephone — it should be made clear to candidates that you do not want them to accept the offer until they have received their copy of the statement of terms of employment.

What Terms?

If an offer is made and accepted orally, the terms that will be implied into the contract are those which:
- were stated in the advertisement
- were discussed during the interview
- were specified orally when the position was offered
- are so well-known and certain in your trade or industry that they will be implied automatically.

However, in practice the interview will have been the main forum for discussion of the terms and, if there is disagreement between the new employee and employer as to the terms that were agreed, the dispute can be difficult to resolve constructively.

Conditional Offers

In many cases — probably the majority — you will not want to be bound to take on the employee unless references and/or a medical examination prove to be satisfactory. In such cases it is best to make "conditional offers" of employment, which are only legally binding when the conditions are satisfied. Such an offer might be couched in the following terms:

"Further to your recent interview at these offices, I have pleasure in offering you the position of Accounts Supervisor, subject to your references and medical examination being satisfactory.

As I told you during the interview, your salary will be £10,000 pa and will be reviewed on 1st July next. The terms and conditions that will apply to the employment are set out in the enclosed statement.

I would be grateful if you would telephone me as soon as possible to let me know whether you accept, to supply me with the names and addresses of two work-related and one personal referee, and to arrange an appointment for the medical".

If the references were unsatisfactory, the offer would not stand and so no contract would be formed. Of course, there is a counterpart to the conditional offer, which is the conditional acceptance:

"Further to your letter of February 1, I accept the offer of a job as Accounts Supervisor but only on the basis that I am paid a salary of £11,000 pa, with a review on April 1".

In law, this does not count as an acceptance; it is merely a counter-offer and so no contract is formed unless or until the employer accepts the counter-offer.

Revoking the Offer

Assuming the offer was made unconditionally, the employer cannot revoke it once the candidate has accepted the job, without being in breach of contract. For instance, if someone is offered a job but the original job-holder changes his or her mind about leaving (with the company's consent) or a sudden down-turn in work occurs, in law the new recruit cannot be told that the offer is withdrawn after it has been accepted. To do so would enable the candidate to go to the County Court and bring an action for damages for breach of contract.

Similarly, if a manager agrees to special terms for a new recruit — for example agrees that someone with a difficult journey may start work at 10.00

hours, take half an hour for lunch and go home at 17.30 hours — and the personnel department does not know about this arrangement until after the job has been offered and accepted, they cannot write to the employee to change the agreement without, again, being in breach of contract. The only course of action is to try to reach agreement on hours of work or, if the arrangement cannot be allowed to stand or the offer has to be withdrawn, to pay the new employee damages equivalent to the notice to which he or she would have been entitled had they started work.

Taking up References

Most employers want to obtain references, usually from the candidate's ex-employer(s) and/or from personal referees, in order to assess the person's suitability for the job. In some cases candidates come equipped with their own copies of testimonials allegedly drafted by their former employer or friends. These "to whom it may concern" type of references are almost always couched in glowing terms and, whilst many will be genuine, the employer should be wary of accepting them at face value since they may well have been written by a friend or, indeed, by the person to whom they relate.

In most cases, therefore, it is infinitely better for employers themselves to approach the nominated referees for information. This can be done by telephoning or writing to the person concerned. Telephone references are probably the most effective in terms of eliciting frank details about the individual's character and work record, as people tend to be willing to say things over the phone that they would be wary of committing to paper. However, it is quite common practice for some organisations to refuse to give details of current or ex-employees without a written request, so the reference seeker could find that it is necessary to write to obtain information. It is far better to do this by sending a structured reference document to the referee which asks specific questions, rather than asking for an unstructured letter. The latter often results in the writer providing only information which he or she wants the employer to know and may result in relevant details about, say, absence records, details of duties, reason for leaving, etc, being omitted.

Whatever method is used to obtain information, the recruiter should always treat references as just one additional factor to be considered in the selection process, and should not rely solely on their quality or the fact that references have or have not been obtained to make the selection decision. References are notoriously unreliable in themselves. For example, an employer who is approached for a reference for an existing employee with whom he would like to part company might be tempted to provide a good reference purely to see the employee on his or her way. Additionally, the legal standing of references can to some extent discourage employers from giving any sort of testimonial at all. There is no legal obligation on employers to provide a reference but if one is supplied, care must be taken to ensure that the statement made is correct. If a reference is given negligently and without disclaiming responsibility, civil action could be taken against the writer from anyone incurring losses as a result of that negligence. Also, in some cases, an unfavourable reference might lead to claims of defamation of character by the person named: if the reference is written it could be held to be libellous, if it is oral it could constitute slander. However, this will only occur if the information supplied is given maliciously. If it is true, or the writer genuinely believes it to be true, the claim is unlikely to succeed.

Medical Examinations

Medical examinations for prospective employees are becoming more common as employers seek to predict the likelihood of poor attendance and/or to maintain health and safety standards in the workplace. Indeed in some cases medical examinations before employment or within a set period after commencement of work are a statutory requirement. For instance, the Diving Operations at Work Regulations 1981 prohibit people from being employed underwater as divers unless they have been medically examined and certified as fit for employment. Similarly, the Night Work of Male Young Persons (Medical Examinations) Regulations 1983 require that male young persons employed at night in certain specified processes including foundry work and papermaking be medically examined within 14 days of commencing employment. Additionally, the general duties of care under the Health and Safety at Work, etc Act 1974 could extend to ensuring that people are medically checked where the work is hazardous or in order to identify specific groups who may be particularly vulnerable to the risk of accidents occurring, eg crane drivers with poor eyesight.

In other cases medical examinations are often used by employers where staff benefits such as life assurance cover or occupational pension schemes are conditional upon satisfactory health standards.

Fidelity Bonding

This can best be likened to taking out an "insurance policy" against dishonesty by employees. Essentially, it involves supplying a list of employees' names and addresses to a fidelity bonder who will carry out his or her own checks on them and will report back on which employees can be accepted. There are two main drawbacks to this scheme: first, as with normal insurance policies, the small print will contain all sorts of exclusions and qualifications; second, and more important, if any employees are not accepted, the reasons will not normally be provided. This presents employers with a major dilemma — should they dismiss those people and, if so, for what reason. The dismissal may be fair — usually for "some other substantial reason" — if the employer can show that fidelity bonding is a justifiable requirement. In *Moody v Telefusion Ltd* [1978] IRLR 311, a salesman with cash collection duties agreed to terms of employment which provided for dismissal if fidelity bonding was refused. An industrial tribunal and the EAT decided that in this case it was reasonable to require fidelity insurance and to dismiss if this was rejected. However, such action could result in the loss of a good employee without good reason and, in some cases, may lead to a finding of unfair dismissal.

In practice it is usually preferable to make your own checks on employees or, if this is not practicable, to hire a reputable security consultancy to carry out the checks on your behalf. In this way you can instruct the company as to the type of check you want carried out and can insist on seeing a full report before you take action against doubtful employees.

Contracts of Employment

The cornerstone of the employment relationship is the contract of employment. Contracts of employment — in the same way as commercial contracts — are merely agreements between two parties which the law will enforce. A contract of employment comes into force as soon as a definite offer of employment has been made and accepted.

This, however, begs the question as to what terms apply if they have not been specified. In general, the terms will be drawn from three main sources.

Express Terms

These are the terms that have been expressly agreed between the employer and the applicant. The agreement might arise from the letter offering employment, from discussions at the interview, the wording of the advertisement or a combination of all three.

Implied Terms

It is usually the case that some contractual areas are not covered by express agreements, even when the successful applicant has been given a statement of terms and conditions of employment. In such cases a court would have to look to see if agreement between the parties could be implied by:

(a) the status of the employee and the type of business — for example if no notice period had been expressly agreed, the courts would consider that the more senior the employee, the longer the term of notice should be

(b) terms implied by conduct — generally known as custom and practice

(c) terms which would have been automatically included had the parties considered the matter.

Statutory Terms

Any term of a contract which aims to reduce or take away a right given by statute is automatically void and unenforceable. The statutory rights concerned are those given by the Employment Protection (Consolidation) Act 1978 — concerning medical suspension, guarantee pay, union membership and activities, maternity pay and leave and rights on termination and the equality clause which is implied into all employment contracts by virtue of the Equal Pay Act 1970 together with rights given by the Wages Act 1986.

S.1 Statements

S.1 of the EP(C)A requires employees to be given a written statement setting out the main terms and conditions of employment. The statement, which should be given within the first 13 weeks of employment, is governed by three requirements.

1. In the statement, the employer must:
   (a) identify the parties
   (b) specify the date when the period of continuous employment began (and the date of commencement of employment with a previous employer which counts towards that period).
2. The statement must contain the following particulars:
   (a) the scale or rate of remuneration, or the method of calculating remuneration
   (b) the intervals at which remuneration is paid (ie weekly, monthly or by some other period)
   (c) any terms and conditions relating to hours of work (including any terms and conditions relating to normal working hours)
   (d) any terms and conditions relating to:
      (i) entitlement to holidays, including public holidays, and holiday pay (the particulars given being sufficient to enable the employee's entitlement to be precisely calculated, including entitlement to accrued holiday pay)
      (ii) incapacity for work due to sickness or injury including any provisions for sick pay
      (iii) pensions and pension schemes
   (e) the length of notice which the employee is obliged to give and entitled to receive to terminate the contract of employment
   (f) the title of the job which the employee is employed to do.
3. Every statement given must include a note:
   (a) specifying any disciplinary rules which apply to the employee, or referring to a document which is reasonably accessible to the employee
   (b) specifying, by description or otherwise:
      (i) a person to whom the employee can apply if dissatisfied with any disciplinary decision relating to him or her
      (ii) a person to whom the employee can apply for the redress of any

grievance relating to the employment and the manner in which any such applications should be made

(c) explaining any steps where there are further stages to be taken after making such an application

(d) stating whether a contracting-out certificate is in force for the employment.

The Relationship Between Statements and Contracts

It is important to note the distinction between s.1 statements and contracts of employment: the contract comes into force as soon as an offer of employment has been made and accepted, and its terms cannot be altered simply by issuing a written statement. For instance, if the new employee was told at the interview that no overtime would be required, but the written statement included a provision to the contrary, it would not alter the basic contractual position. If the employee had accepted the offer on the basis that no overtime would be required, he or she could not be deemed to have agreed to work overtime unless that agreement was expressly made.

There are two simple ways of ensuring that there can be no conflict between contractual terms and those set out in the written statement:

– enclose a copy of the s.1 statement with the offer of the job, making it clear that acceptance of the job denotes acceptance of the employment terms and conditions set out in the statement or

– when issuing s.1 statements, ensure that employees sign a form to say that they have read the statement and agree that it reflects accurately the terms of the employment contract.

Of course, in the latter case, problems will arise if any employees refuse to sign. It would then be necessary to interview them to establish their objections and to attempt to overcome them. If there is no good reason — ie the statement was substantially the same as the previous one or, where it was the first statement, did not change the contractual position — the employer could attach a note to the personnel file stating that the s.1 statement did apply despite the employee's failure to sign, or could even take disciplinary action (for failing to respond to a reasonable instruction) if this was considered appropriate.

Effective Use of S.1 Statements

Rather than regarding the compilation of such statements as an additional chore imposed by legislation, companies would be well-advised to consider how they can use the statements to maximum effect. Many employment disputes revolve around issues which are not expressly covered by their statements or by the law. The s.1 statement can remedy this state of affairs by including provisions governing:

- when holidays can be taken, advance notice that must be given and whether additional holiday can be taken if an employee falls sick during a period of leave
- whether days off in lieu will be given if an employee is ill on a public holiday and/or whether payment will be made to employees on such days if their sick pay entitlement has been exhausted
- whether or not employees can be required to work overtime
- whether accrued holiday pay can be withheld from employees who are dismissed for gross misconduct
- flexibility of employees — ie a clause requiring them to carry out other duties (within their capabilities) when their own work is not available
- restrictions on future work undertaken by the employee on leaving the company (restrictive covenants).

When revising employment statements, it is well worth spending some time considering the difficulties that have arisen over recent years and the ways in which the statement could be amended or expanded in the future in order to eliminate such problems.

Changing the Contract

In carrying out this exercise, however, it may become apparent that the contractual terms need to be changed. It is important to bear in mind the fact that employers do not have the right to impose changes unilaterally. In general terms, the employee must agree to a variation of the contract, although in practice this does not apply to administrative changes or to those occasioned by legal measures — such as the introduction of statutory sick pay and statutory maternity pay. In these instances, employees have little option but to go along with the change.

All this, however, begs the question of what to do if the employee refuses to accept the change. If the company believes it is essential to implement it, in order to avoid the possibility of claims (in County Courts) for breach of contract, it is necessary to give the employee due notice to terminate the contract and, at the same time, offer re-engagement on the revised terms. It should be noted that merely giving employees notice of the change is not sufficient: the original contracts must be terminated and new ones offered (see the case of *Burdett-Coutts and others v Hertfordshire County Council* [1984] IRLR 91). If this is not done, the employees can recover damages in respect of any loss they have suffered as a result of the employer's action.

Employees' Rights

It will, however, be open to the employees concerned to refuse to accept the offer of re-engagement, treat themselves as dismissed (which in law would be the case) and make an unfair dismissal application to an industrial tribunal or, depending on the circumstances, a claim for redundancy pay.

If this were to occur, the employer would have to be able to show that there was a fair reason for the dismissal. This would be "some other substantial reason" in most cases, and the employer would have to be able to show that the change was necessary, rather than just convenient.

It would also be essential to show that the company had tried to implement the change in a reasonable manner: the reasons for it had been explained to the employees concerned, they had been given an opportunity to voice their objections, and all reasonable attempts had been made to overcome those objections.

Conflicting Terms

Before concluding this discussion on contracts of employment, it is necessary to focus on a particular issue that can often give rise to problems for the personnel manager — identifying the legal position where there is conflict between the sources of contract terms.

Express v Implied Terms

It has already been noted that contracts are comprised of both express and implied terms. Express terms are those that are specifically stated and agreed to by the parties either orally or in writing. Implied terms, on the other hand, are those which are left unsaid by the parties but are incorporated by the courts into the agreement in accordance with statute, by custom and practice or by the intentions and conduct of the parties throughout the employment relationship.

Where a conflict arises between an express and an implied term of the contract, the general principle in law is that the express provision will take precedence and will exclude the implied term. However, as is often the case, an implied term can be used to define the limits of an express provision or to clarify the application of particular conditions of employment. An example of this occurred in *BBC v Beckett* [1983] IRLR 43 where an express contractual right to demote an employee for a disciplinary offence was deemed to be subject to an implied term that this would be used reasonably by the employer. Thus, a decision to down-grade an employee after one offence of bad workmanship, despite his good record over a period of 14 years' service, was enough to breach the implied term of reasonableness and so to dismiss the employee constructively.

Written Statements of Terms

One of the main sources of express contract provisions is the written statement of the terms of employment issued to employees under s.1 of the EP(C)A (see above). This is not in itself conclusive of the true contractual position should conflict arise, but does provide persuasive evidence of the main contract terms, though it will be open to challenge if other evidence can be produced to show that the written terms are not correct. Where disparities between written statements themselves occur, it will normally be the most recent statement that will be valid, although this will only be the case if it can be shown that there was a revised "agreement" made between the parties. However, the mere issuing of a new statement containing changes to terms will not be enough in itself to prove that an agreement has taken place. If the employee continues to work on without objection, agreement to the variation may be implied in certain circumstances (*Jones v Associated Tunnelling Co Ltd* [1981] IRLR 477). Equally, a failure to issue a written notification of changes to terms will not mean that the original statement automatically takes precedence, as long as it can be shown that the variations have been agreed (*Parkes Classic Confectionery Ltd v Ashcroft* (1973) 7 ITR 43).

Advertisements and Offer Letters

Where contractual terms are in dispute, the courts will look to documents other than the written statement to clarify the position. In *Pedersen v London Borough of Camden* [1981] IRLR 173 the employee responded to an advertisement for a "Bar Steward/Catering Assistant" which stressed the primary function as being the bar duties. His subsequent letter of appointment was not clear as to whether there were two separate but linked jobs or one job mainly involving work in the bar. The Court of Appeal held that it was permissible to take account of the advertisement to resolve the ambiguity.

More recently, in *Robertson and Jackson v British Gas Corporation* [1983] IRLR 303, the legal standing of a letter of appointment vis-à-vis a written statement of terms has been examined. Here, the employees received letters of offers of employment in 1970 which included a statement that an incentive bonus scheme would apply to them. A subsequent statement of terms specified that the rules of the scheme would be governed by the collective agreement in force between the employer and the recognised trade union. In 1981 the collective agreement was ended by the employers and no further incentive bonuses were paid. The Court of Appeal ruled that the appointment letter took precedence over the statement of terms and that the Corporation were in breach of the term specifying that a bonus scheme would apply. Even though the collective agreement had ended, this could not preclude the contract term in the letter of offer.

Collective Agreements

The incorporation of collective agreements into contracts can also give rise to other disparities where particular agreements conflict with one another. In some cases this can be resolved where provision is made in the terms for one particular agreement to take precedence. However, if this is not expressed it is again up to the courts to look at all the evidence. In *Turriff Construction Ltd v Bryant and others* (1967) 2 KIR 659, the employees' statement of terms referred to a working rule agreement that provided for a 40 hour week. Subsequently, a local agreement was concluded between the employer and the union that provided for 51 hours and notices were posted to confirm this, although the employees never worked the greater number of hours. The Divisional Court ruled that the local arrangement had not varied the original contractual terms. There was no evidence of agreement between the employer and employees.

Works Rules

In the same way disputes can arise over works rules incorporated into contracts, normally through staff handbooks and/or notices displayed in the workplace. In *Trusthouse Forte v Adonis* EAT 788/83, the employee had been issued with a statement specifying that smoking in a no-smoking area would result in a summary dismissal. However, 10 days later he received a statement of terms incorporating the same rule on smoking but stating that breach of this would result in dismissal "after warning" and failure to improve. The EAT confirmed that the later document contained the true terms and the employee's summary dismissal had been unfair.

5 INDUSTRIAL RELATIONS

The industrial relations scene — more than any other aspect of employment law — has been subject to constant change over the last decade. Rather than look at the new rules governing trade unions and their members (which can be found in *Croner's Reference Book for Employers*), this chapter concentrates on such practical issues as consultation, check-off agreements, coping with strikes and that relatively new phenomenon, the no-strike agreement.

Employers, Unions and the Law

Arguably the most important decision employers can make as regards their relationship with their workforce, is whether or not they should recognise the right of a trade union to negotiate on behalf of their employees. This decision has far-reaching ramifications — both legal and practical. An ill-considered decision, whether for or against recognition, can result in resentment, low morale and falling productivity; a decision to recognise the union results in its gaining a host of legal rights.

To Recognise or Not to Recognise?

That is indeed the question! The answer will have far-reaching consequences and there is no simple, pre-determined formula which will produce the right answer. There are, however, some important points which employers must bear in mind when faced with a request from an independent trade union that it be recognised. The starting point must be the definition of "recognition". This is contained in s.126 of the Employment Protection Act 1975 (as amended by the Employment Act 1980): the recognition of the union by an employer, or two or more associated employers, to any extent for the purpose of collective bargaining. It follows from this that allowing a union official to represent his or her members does not, of itself, constitute recognition: the union must *bargain* on behalf of its members.

The second important consideration must be the degree of support which the union has among the relevant workers. This means taking account of: the number of employees who are members of the union; the number who would join if the union were accorded recognition; the strength of feeling of those who are against recognition; and the feelings of those who support it. It will also be necessary to give serious thought to the factor(s) which triggered the desire for union recognition. If this desire resulted from a one-off issue, is it likely that employees' commitment to the union will fade quickly once that issue has been resolved?

Whether or not recognition is granted, it will be necessary as a result, in almost every case, to review communication/consultation/bargaining methods.

It should perhaps be stressed at this point that whatever the level of support a union has, there is nothing in law that requires an employer to recognise the union — even if every single employee is a member. In such a situation the company would need to have regard only to the industrial relations consequences which would flow from a decision to withhold recognition.

Withdrawing Recognition

It must also be borne in mind that recognition of a union is not necessarily a permanent, binding arrangement. On occasions it may become necessary for a company to withdraw recognition from a particular union, perhaps as a consequence of a reorganisation or transfer of a business. Most recognition agreements acknowledge this possibility by the inclusion of a clause specifying the length of notice which must be given to terminate the agreement.

Again, there is nothing in law to prevent the employer from giving such notice, although there are some legal points to consider. Primarily, the fact that the company has withdrawn recognition from the union does not affect the employees' rights to remain members of the union and to take part in its activities (see below). It may be possible for them to remain in membership of their original union and to take out membership of another union which the employer is proposing to recognise but this, of course, will be subject to the rules of the unions concerned.

Employers should also be aware that, in respect of unions which are affiliated to the TUC, the "Bridlington Principles" will apply to transfers of union membership. These principles, which are set out in a TUC publication, *TUC Disputes Principles and Procedures*, provide that no-one who is or recently has been a member of any affiliated union should be accepted into membership of another without enquiries having been made of the original union as to whether the member:

(a) has tendered his or her resignation
(b) is up-to-date with membership subscriptions
(c) is under discipline or penalty

or whether there are any other reasons why he or she should not be accepted into membership.

Any disputes which cannot be resolved by the unions concerned should be referred to the TUC for adjudication.

A Half-Way House

In situations where there is a reasonably high level of union membership but, for whatever reasons, the employer decides not to recognise the union for collective bargaining purposes, the employer may decide to compromise by according the union representational rights. In this situation, the union would be able to represent its members in grievance or disciplinary matters, for example. As this would fall short of recognition in its legally defined sense, this would not give the union the statutory rights which are accorded to recognised trade unions.

If this course of action were to be pursued, however, it would be important to ensure that the union was not accidentally accorded full recognition. By s.126 of the Employment Protection Act 1975, collective bargaining means negotiations relating to or connected with:

(a) the terms and conditions of employment, or the physical conditions in which any workers are required to work
(b) the engagement or non-engagement, or termination or suspension of employment or the duties of employment, of one or more workers
(c) the allocation of work or the duties of employment as between workers or groups of workers
(d) matters of discipline
(e) the membership or non-membership of a trade union on the part of a worker
(f) machinery for negotiation or consultation, and other procedures, relating to any of the foregoing matters, including the recognition by employers or employers' associations of the right of a trade union to represent workers in any such negotiation or consultation or in the carrying out of such procedures.

It is not difficult to see how quickly discussions between management and a union official representing his or her members in a disciplinary situation could slip into a negotiating session!

Non-Recognition

If the company decides not to recognise a trade union, it will have none of the rights set out below. However, employees who are members of the trade union will have the right to remain in membership of the union should they so choose and will have the right to take part in its activities at "any appropriate time". Appropriate time means outside working hours or, with the permission of the employer, during working time. The employer's permission may be express or implied — ie the employer does not necessarily have to give explicit approval. For instance, if employees are allowed to talk while they work, and an employee is dismissed because he or she talks to colleagues about the benefits of union membership, that will be a breach of the employee's rights: in law, the employee will be deemed to have been dismissed for taking part in trade union activities at an appropriate time, since the employer had consented to the employees talking.

Dismissal of employees for exercising their rights in respect of trade union membership and activities is automatically unfair. Employees may also be awarded compensation by an industrial tribunal if their employer takes detrimental action against them which falls short of dismissal, eg refusing to allow them to work overtime, putting them only on work which attracts low bonus rates, refusing promotion, etc.

According Recognition

If the employer does recognise an independent trade union, major consequences will result. In addition to having to set up appropriate bargaining structures, the employer will have to prepare for the legal rights which will be accorded to the trade union, its officials and its members. These rights are described below.

Safety

The Health and Safety at Work, etc Act 1974 gives recognised trade unions the right to appoint safety representatives from among the employees. People appointed should, where reasonably practicable, have had either two years' service with the employer or at least two years' experience in similar employment. It should be noted that, while shop stewards may take on the role of safety representatives, this need not necessarily be the case.

The general function of safety representatives is to consult with the employer to promote health, safety and welfare. They also undertake the following tasks:

- investigation of potential hazards and dangerous occurrences in the workplace and examination of the causes of accidents
- investigation of complaints by employees in relation to their health, safety or welfare at work
- making representations to the employer on matters arising from the foregoing points and on general matters affecting employees' health, safety and welfare
- carrying out inspections of the workplace
- representing employees in workplace consultations with Health and Safety Executive inspectors and other enforcing authorities and receiving information from them concerning employees' health, safety and welfare.

In order to carry out their responsibilities effectively, they have the right, after giving the employer reasonable notice, to inspect and take copies of documents which the employer is required to keep by law (other than those relating to the health records of individuals) which are relevant to the workplace or to the employees they represent. They also have the right to take paid time off to carry out their functions and to undergo training.

A further right given to safety representatives is that, if they so request, the employer must establish a safety committee within three months of their request.

Information

Recognised trade unions have the right to be given information in two areas. If the employer is planning to establish an occupational pension scheme and wants to contract-out of the State second-tier scheme, the union must be given the following information:

(a) the name of the scheme
(b) the effective date of the contracting-out certificate
(c) the employment to be contracted-out
(d) the scheme benefits and employee contributions
(e) the changes to be made to scheme benefits and employee contributions to qualify for contracting-out
(f) the effect of contracting-out on State scheme benefits and contributions
(g) the date when the notice expires and the name of a person with whom the employees can discuss the scheme; the notice should explain that representations may also be made to the Occupational Pensions Board about the proposed scheme; and the notice must carry a statement that the Occupational Pensions Board may refuse a contracting-out certificate if they think there has not been proper consultation with trade unions.

The union must be consulted about the proposed contracting-out.

The second area of information relates to collective bargaining. The Employment Protection Act 1975 provides that employers must disclose to recognised unions information without which they would be impeded to a material extent in carrying on collective bargaining with the employers, and information which good industrial relations practice requires employers to disclose. There is no prescribed list of items of information which fall within these categories but the ACAS code of practice on disclosure of information to trade unions for collective bargaining purposes suggests that information on pay and benefits, conditions of service, manpower, performance statistics and certain financial information could be relevant in this respect. If an employer refuses to disclose such information, the union can lodge a claim with the Central Arbitration Committee (CAC) which, if it upholds the claim, will make a declaration specifying the information which must be disclosed.

Facilities

Employers must allow their premises to be used, if this is reasonably practicable, to carry out a ballot on such matters as:
– calling or ending a strike
– election of workplace union officials
– introducing or abolishing a political levy.

The ACAS code of practice on time off work for trade union duties and activities recommends that employers should also make available to union officials such facilities as:
– accommodation for meetings
– access to a telephone
– notice-boards
– use of office facilities where justified by the volume of the official's work.

Time Off Work

Officials of recognised trade unions — ie employees elected to represent their fellow union members — are entitled to take reasonable time off work, with pay, to undergo training (which must be approved by their own union or by the TUC) and to carry out those duties connected with industrial relations between their employer and the employees they represent.

Members of recognised trade unions are entitled to reasonable time off work, without pay, to take part in their union's activities.

Consultation

Finally, unions recognised by an employer are given the right to be consulted over issues such as business transfers and redundancies (see below).

Consultation: The Foundation Stone of Industrial Relations

The extent to which an employer consults with employees and/or their representatives is often seen as an indication of the state of industrial relations in the organisation. Many employee relations practitioners recognise that an effective consultative process is an important factor in maintaining good working relationships. Indeed, the Employment Appeal Tribunal has itself described consultation as one of the "foundation stones of modern industrial relations practice".

What is Consultation?

The term consultation is defined as follows in paragraph 65 of the Industrial Relations Code of Practice:

"Consultation means jointly examining and discussing problems of concern to both management and employees. It involves seeking mutually acceptable solutions through a genuine exchange of views and information".

So, in essence, consultation in industrial relations terms involves interaction between the employer and the workforce where proposals for a particular course of action are put forward by one party, usually the employer, and where representations, suggestions and counter-proposals from the other party or parties are discussed and considered before a final decision is taken. Consultation is not and should not be equated with negotiation. The latter implies an element of bargaining, with both parties having the power to yield or withhold consent as they seek to strike a mutually acceptable agreement. Although the code refers to the seeking of "mutually acceptable" solutions, consultation is more a system of communicating information prior to decisions being made or of detailing the reasons for particular courses of action and inviting opinion, though ultimately leaving the final decision to the employer.

Collective and Individual Consultation

The consultative process can take place both on a collective basis, whereby the employer liaises with trade union or staff association officials or other employees elected to joint consultative committees or works councils, and on a more direct individual basis, usually where decisions have a greater effect on particular members of staff. A number of statutory provisions exist which influence the conduct of consultation both collectively and individually. S.99 of the Employment Protection Act 1975 and regulations 10 and 11 of the Transfer of Undertakings Regulations 1981 give recognised trade unions consultation rights both in redundancy situations and in circumstances where there is a transfer of ownership of a business, and s.2(6) of the Health and Safety at Work, etc Act 1974 places a statutory duty on employers to consult with certain safety representatives. In addition, the statutory right of certain employees not to be unfairly dismissed has resulted in the need for individual consultation in order to ensure that certain types of dismissal remain fair.

Collective Consultation and Redundancy

The rules contained in s.99 of the Employment Protection Act 1975 specify that an employer who recognises an independent trade union and who is proposing to dismiss as redundant any employees in a group in respect of which the union is recognised, must consult with representatives of that trade union. This must be done even if the employees concerned do not belong to the union. Only independent trade unions which are recognised by the employer have the statutory right to consultation in these circumstances. Non-independent staff associations or unions which are not recognised do not have to be consulted in accordance with s.99. The question of whether a trade union is recognised can be difficult to ascertain and essentially will depend on whether it is recognised for the purposes of collective bargaining.

The obligation to consult arises only where an employer is in the position of "proposing to dismiss employees as redundant". In the case of *Association of Patternmakers and Allied Craftsmen v Kirwin* [1978] IRLR 318 the EAT held that this meant that "the employer must have formed some view as to how many are to be dismissed, when this is to take place and how it is to be arranged". Once the employer is in this position, consultation with the trade union's representatives must begin at the earliest opportunity, however many employees are to be dismissed. In any event, it must begin at least 90 days before the first dismissal takes effect where 100 or more employees are to be made redundant at one establishment within a 90 day period; and at least 30 days before 10 or more employees are to be dismissed within a period of 30 days or less. It is very important that employers note that the 90 and 30 day periods are minimum periods only. In all cases the requirement is to consult at the earliest opportunity; an employer can still be in breach of the rules if consultation does not begin at the earliest opportunity even though the 90 or 30 day period has been given.

Information and Representations

In addition to the actual requirement to consult and the stated time limits, s.99 states that collective redundancy consultation must take a particular form. Subsection (5) specifies that, for the purposes of consultation, the employer must disclose particular information in writing to trade union representatives:

(a) the reasons for the proposals
(b) the numbers and descriptions of the employees whom it is proposed to dismiss
(c) the total number of employees of each description employed by the employer at the establishment in question
(d) the proposed method of selection
(e) the proposed method of carrying out the dismissals with due regard to any agreed procedure, including the period over which the dismissals are to take effect.

When this is done, the statutory consultation is concluded. However, it should be borne in mind that such consultation must be "meaningful". It will not be valid if, for example, the employer treats the matter as a mere formality and does not consider seriously any representations made by the union. In the case of *E Green & Son (Castings) Ltd and others v ASTMS and another* [1984] IRLR 135 the employer supplied the trade union with the written information on the same day that redundancy notices were issued to the staff. The EAT held that no "meaningful" consultation could have taken place since the union had had no opportunity to discuss the proposals and make representations before notices of dismissal were dispatched. Thus it is almost always necessary for the employer to have disclosed the information and considered and replied to representations prior to any dismissal notices being issued.

Breach of Provisions

Where an employer fails in any way to comply with the rules detailed in s.99, the appropriate trade union can present a claim to an industrial tribunal. Should the tribunal find that the complaint is well-founded it can make a "protective award" — an order that the employer must continue to pay those particular employees who have been dismissed or whom it is proposed to dismiss, and for whom the trade union is recognised, for a "protected period". This is a period of time which the tribunal shall determine to be just and equitable in the circumstances having regard to the employer's default, but it is subject to certain maximum limits as follows:

– 90 days maximum where 100 or more employees are being dismissed at one establishment
– 30 days maximum where 10–99 employees are being dismissed at one establishment
– 28 days maximum where less than 10 employees are being dismissed at one establishment.

The only valid defence that employers can submit is where they can show that there were special circumstances which rendered it not reasonably practicable to comply with the requirements and that all steps towards compliance as were reasonably practicable were taken. This refers to circumstances which are out of the ordinary or exceptional — for example in *USDAW v Leancut Bacon Ltd* [1981] IRLR 295 a prospective purchaser of a business withdrew from the transaction, resulting in the company's immediate insolvency, leaving the employers with no option but to consult on the same day that notices of dismissal were issued.

Transfer of Business

Under the provisions of regulations 10 and 11 of the Transfer of Undertakings Regulations 1981, employers must follow a similar procedure where a transfer of ownership of the business as a going concern is contemplated. Regulation 10 specifies that the employer (this can mean either the vendor [transferor] or purchaser [transferee] of the business, or both) must inform representatives of recognised trade unions of:

(a) the fact that the transfer is to take place, when approximately this will be and the reasons for it
(b) the legal, economic and social implications of the transfer for the affected employees
(c) the measures which the employer envisages will be taken in relation to those employees and, if no measures will be taken, that fact
(d) where the employer is the transferor, the measures which the transferee envisages will be taken in relation to the transferring employees and, if no measures will be taken, that fact.

This information must be provided "long enough before a relevant transfer to enable consultations to take place", and where employers envisage that measures will be taken in relation to employees for whom a union is recognised, they must enter into consultations with the union. Again, in the course of consultations, employers must consider representations made by union representatives, must reply to them and, if they are rejected, must state the reasons. Similarly, where special circumstances make it not reasonably practicable to comply, the employer must take all steps towards compliance as are reasonably practicable.

Failure to comply with the provisions can result in the union presenting a complaint and, if a tribunal upholds the complaint, it can make an order for compensation to be paid to affected employees. This is limited to a maximum of two weeks' pay per employee, which can be offset against any protective award that may also have been made against the employer.

Health and Safety

Under the provisions of the Safety Representatives and Safety Committees Regulations 1977, recognised trade unions have the right to appoint representatives from the employer's workforce to undertake particular functions relating to health and safety. These include making representations to the employer on general matters affecting the health, safety or welfare of the employees in the workplace.

S.2(4) of the Health and Safety at Work, etc Act 1974 specifies that appointed safety representatives shall represent employees in consultations with the employer and subsection (6) imposes a duty on employers to consult with any such representatives with a view to making and maintaining arrangements to enable them and their employees to co-operate effectively to ensure the employees' health and safety.

Consultation and Unfair Dismissal

Consultation or lack of it is also an important consideration where industrial tribunals are determining the fairness of certain types of dismissal. Most commonly the need for consultation occurs where dismissals are for redundancy, capability and for some other substantial reason.

The Industrial Relations Code of Practice (paragraph 46) recommends that in a redundancy situation ". . . management *in consultation, as appropriate, with employees or their representatives* should give as much warning as practicable to the employees concerned . . . consider introducing schemes for voluntary redundancy, retirement, transfer to other establishments within the undertaking . . .".

However, the need for individual consultation is something that is often overlooked in a redundancy situation and this can have important implications. In *Freud v Bentalls Ltd* [1982] IRLR 443 the EAT overturned an industrial tribunal's finding that lack of individual consultation was not serious enough to make the dismissal unfair. In the particular circumstances the employee had not been consulted purely because it was not company policy to consult employees of managerial grades. However, there was evidence to show that the employee would have accepted lower grade alternative employment and this would have become apparent to the employers had they consulted. The only clear case where an employer who fails to consult can obtain a finding of fair dismissal is where it can be shown that consultation would have made no difference to the outcome (*British United Shoe Machinery Co v Clarke* [1977] IRLR 297).

Similarly, where employees are being dismissed on grounds of ill-health, consultation is highly desirable. In *East Lindsey District Council v Daubney* [1977] IRLR 181 the employee was dismissed on the basis of a report obtained from the council's medical advisor. At no stage was the employee consulted. The EAT, upholding the tribunal's finding of unfair dismissal, stated that unless there were wholly exceptional circumstances it was vital that employees were given an opportunity to make representations as "discussions and consultation will often bring to light facts which will throw new light on the problem".

Finally, in cases where dismissals are for some other substantial reason, the need to consult can again be crucial. In *Turner v Vestric* [1981] IRLR 24 the employers were found to have unfairly dismissed the employee due to a personality conflict with her manager since, among other things, no real discussion or investigation of the problem had taken place.

Check-Off Agreements

The method by which union members remit their subscriptions to the trade union concerned can vary depending on factors such as the rules of the union itself or whether the union is recognised by the member's employer. Some individuals may pay their dues directly to the union's offices; some continue to pay by the traditional method whereby local trade union officials collect the subscriptions at the workplace. However, it has become increasingly common for trade unions to seek to agree a check-off arrangement with employers in order to facilitate collection of subscriptions.

What is Check-Off

Check-off is the term given to the deduction of trade union subscriptions from employees' pay by the employer for subsequent remittance to the union. It has become a widely established practice and can have advantages for all parties: the union, the employer and the employees. For the union, obviously, it is an efficient means of ensuring that members' subscriptions are collected without the need for shop stewards to spend time chasing members for their dues and it also provides a more regular supply of income.

From the employer's point of view the chief advantage lies in the fact that the check-off system provides an indication of those employees who are or are not union members. This can be of considerable importance where, for example, a union membership agreement is in operation and the need to police the closed shop is necessary, although employers should remain wary of relying solely on check-off records to ascertain whether or not an individual is a union member. In *Tolley & others v Booths Distilleries Ltd* EAT 316/81 the EAT cast doubts on the view that, among other things, an employee's instruction to the employer to cease deduction of union duties by check-off was enough to create a resignation from the union automatically. The other benefit to an employer of a check-off arrangement is that it removes the need for workplace collections of union dues which themselves can be disruptive to normal working practices and can occasionally create disharmony between employees.

Finally, from the employees' viewpoint, deduction of union dues at source provides an easy means of keeping up subscriptions and alleviates the problem of falling into arrears.

Collective Agreements

A check-off arrangement is normally concluded as part of a formal recognition and procedural agreement made between the employer and the trade union concerned. As a collective agreement it is therefore conclusively presumed not to be legally enforceable, unless it is in writing and contains a provision which states that the parties intend it to be legally enforceable (s.18 of the Trade Union and Labour Relations Act 1974). A check-off agreement will therefore not be legally binding between the union and the management unless these conditions have been satisfied and, in practice, the vast majority of such agreements do not comply with the above provisions.

One point that should be noted is that although most check-off arrangements are normally only concluded with recognised trade unions, this does not mean that the employer is not free to agree these arrangements with non-recognised bodies, although adopting a check-off arrangement itself may have a bearing on whether the union has been granted recognition by implication.

Check-Off and the Contract

Although a collective agreement between the employer and the trade union will not itself usually have the force of law, an arrangement to deduct union dues can be enforceable vis-à-vis the individual employee's contract of employment. The employer is not at liberty to make deductions from an employee's pay unless these are specifically provided for by the terms of the contract of employment or by law. However, in the case of check-off, the authority to deduct union dues may stem from the contract itself, either where the collective agreement with the union is incorporated into the contract or where there is a separate agreement between employer and employee. Such an agreement can be made orally or in writing, although in practice employees normally complete a written authorisation to the employer to begin deducting the subscription.

Withdrawal of Agreement

The position can usually be altered by the employee withdrawing agreement to the deduction being made. Once this has been done the employer must revert to paying the entire amount of pay directly to the worker. In practice most check-off agreements and/or employee authorisations contain the facility for employees to request the cessation of deductions but some do specify particular procedures to be followed before the withdrawal of agreement is effective.

The Political Levy

Most independent trade unions retain a separate fund for expenditure on political objects and this is normally provided for by the political levy which is incorporated in and collected with union dues. The rules on the raising and retention of political funds are mainly contained in the Trade Union Acts 1913 and 1984. These Acts, although primarily directed at the trade unions, have important implications for employers who operate check-off arrangements.

S.5 of the 1913 Act lays down the rule that, where a union has adopted a resolution to hold a political fund, all members of the union (subject to some exceptions) must be notified that they have the right to be exempt from contributing to the political fund if they so wish and, in furtherance of this, trade union members may at any time give notice to the union that they object to contributing to the fund. On giving such notice (in a specified form) a union member will then be exempt from contributing to the political fund either immediately if notice is given within one month of the union's notification of adoption of a political fund, or from the first day of January following giving of the notice. Thus, in effect, union members will be liable to pay the political levy unless they expressly contract out.

S.6 of the Act provides two methods of exempting individuals from the levy where they have contracted out: either a separate subscription must be levied on those who are not exempt or, if one combined subscription is normally collected, this must be reduced accordingly by the amount of the political element. This section of the Act also provides that union members must be informed of what portion, if any, of the subscription will be used for political purposes.

As such, these provisions of the Act place certain restrictions on the payment of the political levy with which the trade unions must comply. However, the operation of these rules in the past raised an important problem in relation to check-off, since the Act itself only provides the individual member with a remedy against the union for breach of those rules. In the case of *Cleminson v Post Office Engineering Union* [1980] IRLR 1, an employer's refusal to operate a two-tier check-off system which resulted in the employee overpaying union subscriptions over a period of 12 years offered the employee no remedy other than to withdraw his consent from the check-off arrangement and seek a refund of the political element from the union. The Act could not be used to insist that the employer operate a two-tier check-off arrangement.

Trade Union Act 1984

This problem has to some degree been remedied by the provisions of the Trade Union Act 1984, which now imposes a duty on employers to operate a two-tier deduction system in certain circumstances. S.18(1) of the Act states:
"Where any person who is a member of a trade union which has a political fund has certified in writing to his employer that, or to the effect that, he:
(a) is exempt from the obligation to contribute to that fund or

(b)   has, in accordance with the 1913 Act, notified the union in writing of
       his objection to contributing to it,
the employer . . . shall ensure that no amount representing a contribution
to the political fund of the union is deducted by him from emoluments
payable to the member".

This, in effect, means that the employer operating a check-off agreement is
now placed under a duty to refrain from deducting the political levy either
where employees certify that they are exempt from paying this *or* have
commenced the procedure for gaining exemption from the levy outlined in
the 1913 Act. In practical terms this seems to indicate that employees do not
actually have to be exempt from the levy before the employer ceases deductions. All employees have to do is to certify in writing that they are exempt
and deductions must cease as soon as is reasonably practicable unless an
employee subsequently withdraws the certificate (subsection (2)). Subsection
(3) also provides that the employer must not refuse to operate check-off for
employees who certify that they are exempt, whilst continuing to operate it
for non-exempt staff.

Where an employer either continues to check-off the political levy or
operates a discriminatory system for those who are certified as exempt, the
employee can apply to the County Court for a declaration and an order to
cease the deductions or continue to operate check-off of the normal subscriptions minus the political levy.

Check-Off and Dismissals

Deduction of union dues at source can also lead the employer into the area of
unfair dismissal in certain circumstances. Where a union membership agreement or closed shop is in operation, it sometimes provides that employees
who object to union membership may make a payment to some other body,
eg a charity, in lieu of a union subscription. However, under s.58(13)(b) of the
EP(C)A as amended, where an employee is dismissed and the reason for the
dismissal is an objection to the employer checking off such a payment from
wages, the reason for dismissal is deemed to be on grounds of union
membership.

This means that such a dismissal will automatically be unfair unless there is
a valid union membership agreement in operation which has been properly
approved in a secret ballot held within a period of five years ending with the
time of dismissal (see *Croner's Reference Book for Employers* for further details of
the rules on closed shop ballots) and none of the following exceptions applies:
(a)   the employee genuinely objects on grounds of conscience or other
       deeply-held personal conviction to being a member of any trade union
       whatsoever or of a particular trade union or

(b) the employee has belonged to the class of employees covered by the agreement since before it took effect and has at no time during the operation of the agreement been a member of a specified trade union or

(c) in the case of an agreement which took effect on or after 15.8.85 and which was approved by a ballot in which the employee was entitled to take part, the employee has not at any time since the day the ballot was held been a member of a union in accordance with the agreement

(d) at the time of dismissal there was a declaration in force, or proceedings were pending, that the employee had been unreasonably excluded or expelled from the union

(e) the employee holds qualifications relevant to his employment and is subject to a written code of conduct which is in conflict with an actual or potential requirement to take part in industrial action.

Finally, the effect of check-off has also been considered in respect of action short of dismissal. In *Sakals v United Counties Omnibus Company Ltd* [1984] IRLR 475 the EAT ruled that the employer's failure to cease deductions immediately on an employee's instructions did not in itself constitute action taken to compel union membership, since the employer had demonstrated that the reason why the deductions had continued was due to the administrative procedure necessary before such check-off could cease and was not for the purposes of compelling union membership.

Strikes

Every year, when the pay-round starts in earnest, employers are faced with demands for higher pay and improvements to other conditions of employment. With this may come the exhaustion of bargaining procedures and the threat of strike action or other industrial action taken to interfere with the performance of employees' normal duties.

The personnel manager must live in the real world — if a strike is imminent he or she, as with all the other company's officers, must take steps to minimise the damage to the company. In fact, the response to strike action must be effectively managed and even prepared for within the limits set by practicality and the law.

The Right to Strike

There is no positive legal right enshrined in the (unwritten) British Constitution to permit strike action. Striking employees or groups of employees are given limited immunity from being sued or prosecuted by the Trade Union Act 1913, the Trade Union and Labour Relations Act 1974 and subsequent amendments, providing the strike action was taken "in contemplation or furtherance of a trade dispute". This is the so-called "golden formula".

The subsequent amendments to the law covering trade disputes by the Employment Acts 1980 and 1982 and the Trade Union Act 1984 add new complications. Certain secondary action is now unlawful (ie in certain circumstances, inducing or threatening a breach of or an interference with a contract of employment where the employer under that contract is not a party to the trade dispute).

Strike action must be balloted according to the provisions set out in the Trade Union Act 1984 and a majority obtained to support the action from all the trade union members who are likely to be called upon to strike or take other industrial action. If the new rules are breached by trade unions, civil actions can be taken against them by employers (or, indeed, any other affected groups or individuals) applying for injunctions to stop the union(s) from taking industrial action. In these cases the court can impose fines (which are unlimited) for contempt of court if the union fails to comply with the court's instructions.

At the same time as applying for the injunction, employers may also apply for damages caused by the industrial action of up to £250,000 depending on the number of members in the union.

Balloting

In one case a union called a ballot after a court order had been made and obtained the necessary bare majority for approval of the action. Other unions, in the face of court orders, have called off the industrial action knowing that the necessary majority would not be obtained. However, the fact that industrial action can be given the air of legitimacy by a ballot does increase pressure on employers, who may then think that such action is "legal". In fact the same range of options and sanctions are open to employers just as they were before the Employment Act 1980. The threat of injunctions and suing for damages is merely another tactic to combat strike action.

Considerations: Strike?

Many questions need to be posed by the company's negotiators when the annual wage round seems to be heading for stalemate.
1. Does the employer really have terms and conditions of employment comparable to those of others in the area/industry? Are there no more concessions that the employer can make? Which, if any, of the union's anticipated demands can the employer accept?
2. Is the employer in a position to withstand a strike and what advantages are there to the employer if a strike occurs, eg reduction of excessive stock; provision of a breathing space if sales volume and forecasts are low; radical new changes in the company's organisation? How long can the employer sit out a strike, assuming all production is substantially reduced?

3. Are the "powers that be" going to stand up and be counted when the chips are down or are substantial interest groups on the board likely to want to settle at any price once the going gets tough?
4. At what point will the employer's negotiators tell the union that the employer is prepared to face a strike? Over which issues is the employer prepared to face a strike?
5. What parts of the employer's business can be kept going during a strike? Can supplies be obtained or is "blacking" a strong possibility? How many employees will ignore the call to strike? Can they be helped to come to work or will picketing be effective? What will non-striking employees do if normal production is impossible?
6. Is lay-off or enforced holiday (with pay) for these employees inevitable? What briefing will be given to supervisors so that they are *au fait* with the company's plans and state of negotiations?

Know Your Union/Employees

Other questions that the employer's negotiators must consider concern their complete familiarity with their workforce. For instance, in the context of the employer's industrial relations history, have the employees' attitudes become more hostile? If so, why? Can these grievances be removed in the short or long term?

Do the union representatives or officials carry the membership with them or do they follow in the wake of populist concerns? Is the union going to hold a secret ballot and will the union make the strike "official"? If so, does the union grant strike pay; how much and when do payments begin? Additionally, would other unions respect the union's picket line and effectively cut off supplies?

Finally, when relationships with trade unions have been cordial in the past, is the company prepared for the inevitable change in these relationships that industrial action causes?

The Countdown Weeks

As matters develop the management team must keep many things under constant review. What is the union really after and what promises has the union made to its members? Is the strike being called for reasons other than those formally canvassed? For instance, is the strike call the result of unrest within the union? (A strike will be a proving ground for the union's leadership; hardships shared will weld the union together, etc.) Perhaps the relative failure of the union to get the small day to day problems with management resolved to their members' satisfaction may have provoked this higher level confrontation and encouraged strike action as a "show down". How long can the union hold out if a strike is called, bearing in mind that employees have to pay mortgages, rent, living expenses, etc and will only receive supplementary benefit for their dependants?

It is also important to keep testing the water so far as the management team is concerned. Issues to be checked include:
- does the employer's management believe its position to be morally right and is it really prepared to hold out when the going gets tough? Do some managers consider that if their bluff is called they will back down? How united is the management team and what shopfloor support can be expected?
- when should management's position be placed unequivocally before the workforce as a whole? Should this be done by meeting or a letter?

Planning for a Strike

Careful planning is essential for maintaining good management morale. Every department in the company will be affected by a stoppage so plans must be drawn up for them all.

Personnel and Administration

Ensure that all departments are aware of the state of the negotiations and are aware of pre-strike responsibilities; develop feasibility plans for operating the company during the strike and co-ordinate initial plans for an orderly shutdown to be implemented if the company cannot continue to operate. Coordinate the transfer of work to subcontractors or other divisions.

Draw up a confidential schedule for lay-off/enforced holidays for non-striking personnel in the event of no work being available.

A strike is a testing time for administration. An up-to-date list of employees' addresses and a list of all officers, stewards and members of the union would be useful. Start a useful contacts list, eg police, industrial relations or legal advisors, ACAS, etc. Have a sketch, drawn to scale, of the plant and premises, indicating all entrances, window locations, etc. Prepare two sets of pre-addressed mailing envelopes to all employees.

Ensure that supervisory staff know their responsibilities and how to conduct themselves during the strike, eg they should not offer provocation, and should provide information about the mood of the shopfloor.

Put together a management team to act as observers at gates to monitor picket lines, especially if some employees will attempt to come to work. All incidents should be recorded (listing date, time, names, etc).

It is essential that management selects one company representative to handle communications and act as sole spokesperson to the press, media and enquiring members of the public. Ensure that such communication does not exaggerate the facts and is in no way inflammatory.

Ensure the employer's industrial relations advisor or solicitor is regularly apprised of developments.

Manufacturing

Some actions that might be considered by the production departments are:
- make arrangements to operate departments with managerial and clerical staff support for non-striking employees or plan an orderly shut down if this is not possible and put together a painting and maintenance plan to keep non-strikers working
- inform suppliers and customers — keep them in the picture
- prepare to remove all key items from the premises, including the property of customers; prepare to locate company vehicles in a secure place so that they can be used without coming into contact with the picket lines. Perhaps use independent operators to transport goods
- ensure that equipment is not sabotaged and that the premises have adequate heating, water, food, etc.

Marketing, Sales and Purchasing

These departments must carry out a rapid review of customer contracts and especially the penalty clauses which may be invoked as a result of the industrial dispute. They might also draft telexes, etc to inform customers or suppliers in the event of a strike. Alternative warehouse facilities away from the employer's premises may ensure that the company can continue operating. Products sold in advance of delivery should be dispatched with haste.

Maintenance and Security Departments

Managers in these departments must plan to maintain services such as boilers, lighting and maintenance on an emergency basis. Perhaps outside contractors or independent operators can be brought in to help. Annual plant maintenance and safety checks should continue.

Since it is unwise to leave property unguarded when a strike is in progress, a plan should be drawn up to maintain night lighting, perimeter fencing, secure windows, etc and provide protection shields for all outside electrical transformers.

Organise security patrols of premises and yards on a 24 hour basis (arrange for outside security services if necessary). The police should be contacted to obtain a precautionary presence if a picket line appears. It might be useful to obtain telephone-message-recording equipment so that calls in relation to the strike are recorded.

Security should put together — and keep up-to-date — a list of authorised non-striking personnel; prepare parking space inside the perimeter and consider restricting access to one approved gate or door. Medical and first-aid facilities should be reviewed. Escorts should be provided for visitors and customers going to and from the premises.

Payroll/Financial Issues

Employees who take strike action are entitled to receive wages due (ie wages that they have already earned) and steps should be taken to pay these sums. Accrued holiday does not have to be paid. Files of employees away sick, on maternity leave, etc should be reviewed to ascertain the date of return to work, and payments should cease upon this expected date unless more medical certificates are received. The payments to employees who work on during the strike and put in extra hours should be co-ordinated with the personnel or salary administration departments. A petty cash system to handle increased and unplanned expenditure should be established.

The Crunch

When the 11th hour comes there must be another review of negotiating tactics. Even where a strike appears to be inevitable, negotiations in good faith for a settlement should continue. Does the employer put his or her final and best offer on the table, or should this be held back so that it can be put into play later in the form of a strike settlement? Can the offer be sweetened a little so that the union members will take the opportunity to accept and avoid losing pay by striking? Would going to arbitration offer a way out to both parties who are looking for a chance to save face? Do not, however, expect arbitration to provide a cheap way out. It invariably means increasing the offer and often leaves both parties unhappy.

The company must also decide whether or not to present its position to the press and media in an attempt to appeal to the employees over the heads of the union leadership. The set of addressed envelopes will be useful to put the company's case to employees. Finally, is it time to play the injunction card if the strike action threatened has not been balloted?

The Strike Begins

If negotiations fail and neither employer nor union have been able to reach a timely and mutually acceptable agreement, the employer will have to put contingency plans into effect.

The trade union will usually form a strike committee: the company managers should organise themselves in similar fashion. A designated person should also establish a strike log to note down incidents, facts and information. This initial period is a fact-finding time. The full effect of the strike will become apparent and vital decisions about continuing to operate either immediately or at some time in the future will have to be made in the light of what is often a rapidly changing situation. The decision to continue to operate will involve other important decisions that will have implications for the eventual outcome of the strike, ie:

(a) will management, clerical or sales employees be used to operate the plant?

(b) will employees be encouraged to cross picket lines, eg by transport being provided, etc?

(c) will replacement or temporary production employees be hired?

(d) will some departments have to close or will all operations have to be shut down?

Sometimes a combination of these options will be used, depending upon the circumstances. Obviously, the options that are chosen will have an effect upon the employees who are striking: attitudes may harden and become embittered or, in the face of determined decisions to keep the business operating, the strike might crumble. Usually, managers will be playing for high stakes and therefore are prepared to face hostile reactions.

At some stage, working employees may have to be laid off, although a halfway house such as requiring them to take their paid holiday entitlement is frequently a sensible idea. If employees are laid off they cannot claim redundancy pay by resigning in accordance with the redundancy rules contained in s.88 of the EP(C)A: this is expressly excluded by s.89(3) of the Act where lay-off or short time is the result of a strike or lock-out.

Communications

It is quite essential that departmental managers are properly apprised of their specific responsibilities, the reasons for the strike and the day to day events. This channel of communication should be a two-way process; without a conscious attempt to keep managers and supervisors properly informed rumours will fly around and might unsettle working employees if not dispelled. Make sure that affected customers and suppliers have received notification of the strike disruption and consider putting together a press release just in case the press shows an interest in the dispute.

If the company's position has not been put to the employees by letter, indicating, for instance, the outline of the negotiation, the costs of the union's demands compared to the costs of the company's final offer, etc now is the time to consider doing this.

Conduct During the Strike

Generally speaking, there are three golden rules for management to observe during a period of strike action:

(a) do not offer non-strikers rewards for their loyalty and indicate that those on strike will not receive the same rewards

(b) do not make promises of special benefits to individuals or to groups of strikers to induce them to end their strike action or to undermine the union

(c) do not threaten strikers or other employees.

Such actions do not help the management's case and can be impossible to live with later. It is surprising how frequently these guidelines are ignored during disputes.

During the strike managers should try to ensure that pickets do not block entrances and exits to strike-bound premises: police assistance might be necessary to ensure this. Those people working in, or having to deliver goods to, or who have any business at all with, the company, have a right to pass in and out freely. Every effort should be made to maintain this freedom of access for people and vehicles.

Picketing

For picketing to be lawful it must be taking place as a result of a trade dispute. It must be carried out by employees at their own place of work — flying pickets are almost always unlawful. Mass picketing is in breach of the Department of Employment's Code of Practice on Picketing which recommends six people per entrance as a maximum. Where the numbers prevent access to premises, or induce breaches of the peace, the High Court is likely to grant an injunction to stop the picketing.

Picketing must be peaceful and must be designed to obtain or communicate information or persuade the person to take part in the strike action. Violent actions, threats or intimidation are not permitted, and the carrying of clubs, weapons, knives or firearms is unlawful.

Union officials and pickets have the right to talk to people going in or out of strike-bound premises, but oral threats are not permitted. If pickets trespass or commit acts of violence or vandalism on the strike-bound premises, or to plant or machinery, or on other company employees, complaints may be filed with the police or restraining injunctions may be sought in the courts.

Management should make sure that unauthorised access to the premises is prevented; guard against attempts to organise a sit-in on the company's premises. If one does occur there might be immediate recourse to the courts to obtain an injunction for the strikers' expulsion.

Dismissing Strikers

One of the options that may be considered during the course of a strike is the dismissal of those on strike. This might be considered not as an end in itself but as a step leading to reopening negotiations and the reinstatement of the strikers who have been dismissed. Alternatively, the intention may be to dismiss the strikers and engage new staff to take their place.

In a fast moving strike situation the dismissal of strikers is fraught with legal problems. Such dismissals have to be carried out with precision, in order to take advantage of the section in the EP(C)A that removes tribunals' jurisdiction to hear unfair dismissal claims resulting from industrial action. All *the strikers taking part* in the action *at that time* in *the establishment* concerned must be dismissed.

Furthermore, if reinstatement or re-engagement is offered within three months of the dismissals, all the strikers must be made the same offer. "Picking and choosing" in either context is not allowed. Needless to say, the precise meaning of the relevant section of the Act (EP(C)A s.62 as amended by the Employment Act 1982) is subject to interpretation by tribunals.

Consequently, failure to dismiss one person taking part in the action, or the reinstatement of one of the dismissed strikers, would put the dismissals of all the other strikers within a tribunal's jurisdiction. Employees dismissed for striking have six months in which to make a tribunal claim.

Strikers may, of course, be dismissed for other reasons such as vandalism or assaulting other company employees. Such dismissals are judged by the normal criteria that are applied to misconduct dismissals if they come before an industrial tribunal.

If the decision is taken to dismiss strikers and replace them with new employees, a realistic assessment should be made of the likelihood of these new employees being willing to cross picket lines, the effect on their future trade union membership and their future employment prospects in other unionised companies, etc.

Operating the Business

It should be realised that those employees remaining at work during the strike action can be prone to the usual stress problems faced by those "under seige". This can lead to unrealistic and over-optimistic decisions being taken by the managers who are affected by the emotion of the situation. Indeed, in small companies the management team may be prone to fragment under the pressure, with one group actively trying to make accommodations with the striking employees. The need for regular meetings and good communications at all levels during a period of strike action is essential in providing group support to wavering individuals. Additionally, employees are frequently expected to work on a wider number of jobs than usual. Clerical and managerial staff will often be used on manual work to keep the business running. It is important to keep everyone busy to avoid idle speculation and rumour, but proper attention should be paid to safety when employees are doing jobs in unfamiliar surroundings and operating equipment they are not used to. Camaraderie will certainly develop, but the "them and us" attitudes should not be supported by the management team: after all, strikes do end and everyone has to live with the aftermath.

Strike Settlements

If the services of ACAS (the Advisory, Conciliation and Arbitration Service) have not yet been used, management might consider making contact with them to express a willingness to recommence bargaining when the union indicates a significant revision of its demands. Alternatively, the approach could be made directly to the union side of the negotiating committee to indicate a willingness to resume negotiations at any time, provided the meeting is called for some purpose.

The company might take the opportunity to reiterate its final position but if the union makes a change in its demands this will be a cause for negotiations to start up again promptly. If the management negotiating team has held some "goodies" in reserve to prompt a settlement, careful consideration must be given to the timing of such an offer; it will usually be made in response to some relaxation in the union position. Sometimes the involvement of the full time union officials, if they have not been involved previously, can result in a more flexible and realistic approach than that of the locally elected representative.

If the result is an impasse, both sides will have to wait to see who crumbles first when facing up to economic realities. It is perhaps more realistic to see both sides looking for some kind of way out, to settle the matter without too much loss of face. Very often this will revolve around the drafting of the words of the settlement and ACAS can be very helpful in such a situation.

Terms of the Settlement

If some agreement can be reached, any management would be well advised to set out in writing the terms of the settlement covering all aspects of the dispute. The magnitude of disputes arising out of unclear "resolutions" can be amazing to behold.

Particular attention should be given to the matters that will smooth the return to normality, especially as these are nearly always ignored or left to be thrashed out later, eg:

- changes to terms and conditions of employment agreed and the period over which the agreement is made
- if the matters above are to be applied retrospectively, what precisely are the rules?
- reinstatement terms for dismissed strikers and status of employees recruited during the strike
- the seniority and status of employees who stayed at work
- the position of strikers who have been disciplined or dismissed during the strike
- since insurance cover, pension benefits and other company benefits such as accrued holiday have probably been suspended, the resumption date

should be specified as should the question of whether the benefit is credited during the strike period.

The strikers' continuity of employment will not be broken by the strike action but the days on which they took strike action can be taken from the total period of service and consequently will affect the workers' qualification for statutory rights. Careful records of strike days should thus be kept by the personnel department.

Going Back

A smooth, quick return to work must be the aim of every manager. Production schedules should be arranged or work provided to allow little opportunity for employees to congregate to discuss the strike: they need to be welcomed back to work without any further recriminations. This may involve a letter being sent or given to every employee or a senior manager giving a speech of welcome to returning and non-striking employees; meetings ought to be held with supervisors to mould their attitudes to returning strikers, and supervisors should be instructed not to involve themselves in arguments about the strike and to quieten any hostilities between striking and non-striking employees. They should be alive to the welter of personal problems caused by the strike and be ready to advise employees who want help.

Nothing is gained by vindictiveness on the part of management or supervisors. In fact, the responsibility of maintaining good industrial relations lies with the company.

The re-establishment of service or supplies to customers must rank high in the order of priorities during the return to work and marketing departments must redouble their efforts to get the company re-established once supplies have been resumed.

"No-Strike" Agreements

A great deal of interest and controversy has been aroused in industrial relations circles with the recent increase in the operation of so-called "no-strike" agreements made between managements and certain trade unions, particularly in the electronics industry. Such agreements in effect forbid the calling of industrial action to "force" the resolution of an industrial dispute. They also contain provisions which are envisaged as sufficient to make such action unnecessary.

The Background

Agreements to restrict the taking of industrial action by the workforce and, for that matter, the instituting of a lock-out by the employer, have been part of the British industrial relations scene for a number of years. These days, most collective agreements provide some type of disputes procedure which usually precludes a lock-out, strike or other industrial action until all stages of the procedure have been exhausted and a failure to agree has been recorded. In fact, it is a specific recommendation of the Industrial Relations Code of Practice that such "peace" clauses are incorporated into a collective disputes procedure. The code itself, although originally approved under the now repealed Industrial Relations Act 1971, remains in force today and, whilst its provisions are not legally enforceable, they can be taken into account in proceedings brought before the courts. Therefore, in general terms, the principle of a"no-strike" agreement in its broadest sense is not totally new to British industrial relations.

However, the distinction between these agreements and the recent arrangements being concluded in the electronics sector really comes down to the fact that most traditional disputes agreements anticipate that the procedure may at some point become exhausted and that there will be a failure to agree. The more recent "no-strike" deals, on the other hand, are designed to ensure that the situation of a failure to agree never arises: the disputes procedure is specifically geared towards ensuring that agreement is reached, if necessary through the use of binding external arbitration. In this respect, the new type of "no-strike" deal is really an agreement which is devised to prevent industrial action arising at all, rather than providing for certain procedural steps before any such action is taken.

Features of "No-Strike" Agreements

The agreement to preclude strike action is usually incorporated into a formal recognition and procedural agreement which can also import other specific arrangements agreed between managements and the trade unions. As such, a major feature of most of the new deals being agreed is that they include a number of elements designed to enhance industrial relations in general between the employer and the employees.

Characteristically, the new agreements being concluded in the electronics area often include the following features:
– single union recognition
– harmonisation of existing terms and conditions to create a single status workforce
– facilities for employee participation
– flexible working systems
– a comprehensive disputes procedure designed to resolve differences without recourse to strike action which might incorporate a facility for conciliation or mediation and ultimately end in arbitration.

Recognition and Harmonisation

Most of the recent agreements have specified that only one trade union will be given bargaining rights for the particular group of workers involved (depending, of course, on eligibility of individuals to join that particular union). This has the advantage of limiting the problem of inter-union disputes which may in some cases have a detrimental effect on the employer's business. In most cases the electricians' union, the EETPU, has succeeded in obtaining sole recognition rights as part of the overall agreement and some other trade unions have followed suit.

Another aspect of these arrangements is that "single status" is awarded to all staff. This in effect means that the principle of common terms and conditions will apply to both manual trades, usually paid weekly in cash and in many cases entitled to shorter company sickness and holiday entitlements, and monthly salaried personnel who have traditionally enjoyed superior terms and conditions in relation to sickness, holidays, pension plans, life assurance, etc. This harmonisation of terms provides uniformity and erodes the need for the traditional arguments on comparability.

However, this has to be set against the change in attitudes needed to cope with an equalisation of terms and conditions. Some groups may feel that their status is being eroded and workers may object to changes in, for example, the form and method of payment.

Participation and Flexibility

Most trade unions view employee participation in the running of a business as of sufficient significance to warrant claims for bargaining rights on this issue. Recent "no-strike" agreements are no exception and usually incorporate provision for some arrangements for employee involvement. In a number of agreements signed in the electronics industry, consultative arrangements have been agreed which involve, amongst other things, the setting up of an advisory board or council consisting of both management and employee representatives as well as making provision for disclosure of information to the workforce.

In return for these measures, the unions involved are prepared to accept the principle of job flexibility, given that opportunities are made available for training and retraining existing workers in new skills as and when the need arises. To some degree this is an important concession on the part of the unions as it represents a shift away from the operation of traditional lines of demarcation which have been at the root of many disputes over the years. Such concessions are thus designed to limit the circumstances in which disputes of this nature can arise.

Resolving Disputes

Of course the crucial issue in a "no-strike" agreement is the disputes procedure itself which can incorporate any number of steps and usually provides for some means of conciliation or mediation along the way, often involving ACAS or some similar body. The most significant part of the agreement is the final stage of the disputes procedure. In most cases, the new-style arrangements provide that compulsory binding arbitration will operate, thus ensuring that the matter is resolved one way or the other. The choice of arbitrator is usually subject to the agreement of both parties.

Whilst arbitration is nothing new, the distinguishing factor in recent agreements is the use of what is known as "pendulum" or "final offer" arbitration. This involves the adjudicator of the dispute finding wholly in favour of the employer or wholly in favour of the union. There is no possibility of compromise by finding a middle-of-the-road solution which is often unsatisfactory to both parties. The supporters of pendulum arbitration maintain that this process encourages more realistic bargaining positions to be adopted as each side sets out to be more reasonable than the other with the aim of ensuring that the arbitrator finds in their favour. The possibility of losing at arbitration in turn often helps both parties to reach a settlement without recourse to the final stage. However, pendulum arbitration is not without its critics. The Central Arbitration Committee (CAC), whilst recognising that it is a laudable aim to encourage the two sides to settle their differences through negotiation, have recently pointed out that, if the parties cannot resolve important differences, a choice may be left between two extremes. The CAC feel that the arbitrator needs the opportunity of avoiding solutions each of which may have serious flaws.

"No-Strike" Agreements and the Law

A "no-strike" agreement made between an employer and a trade union is a collective agreement and is therefore subject to the usual rules on legal enforceability. S.18(1) of the Trade Union and Labour Relations Act 1974 provides that a collective agreement is conclusively presumed not to be legally enforceable unless it is in writing and contains a provision which states that the parties intend it to be legally enforceable. So, an agreement in itself will not be legally binding between the union and the management unless these conditions have been satisfied. In practice the vast majority of such agreements do not comply. In most cases, however, the terms of a collective agreement can become enforceable between an individual employee and the employer if they are incorporated either expressly or by implication into the worker's contract of employment. However, in the case of a "no-strike" clause in a collective agreement, this incorporation is somewhat restricted by statute. S.18(4) of TULRA provides that:

"any terms of a collective agreement . . . which prohibit or restrict the right of workers to engage in a strike or other industrial action, or have the effect of prohibiting or restricting that right, shall not form part of any contract between any worker and the person for whom he works unless the collective agreement:

(a) is in writing and
(b) contains a provision expressly stating that those terms shall or may be incorporated in such a contract and
(c) is reasonably accessible at his place of work to the worker to whom it applies and is available for him to consult during working hours and
(d) is one where each trade union which is a party to the agreement is an independent trade union

and unless the contract with that worker expressly or impliedly incorporates those terms in the contract".

Thus, in practice, unless the collective agreement complies fully with the above requirements, it will not be legally enforceable in itself or through the employees' contracts of employment. In this respect the scope of such agreements is somewhat limited when they are viewed on their own.

Strikes and the Contract

However, the foregoing restrictions are to some extent superfluous if the issue of strikes or other forms of industrial action is looked at purely and simply in terms of the individual's obligations under the contract of employment. By the very nature of a strike or other industrial action, there is almost always a breach of the contract of employment itself if workers engage in disruptive activity on a collective basis, notwithstanding the rules on the enforceability of a "no-strike" clause in a collective agreement. In this respect, there is no absolute need to incorporate such a clause into an individual's contract of employment as the contract will, by implication, already contain this term.

The individual's legal position vis-à-vis the employer will not change therefore even if a "no-strike" deal is concluded and properly imported into the contract in accordance with the rules laid down in s.18(4).

Unofficial Action

The limited enforceability of collective agreements containing "no-strike" clauses demonstrates that, in effect, the agreement itself cannot prevent individual workers from taking unofficial strike action in breach of procedure, even though this may be condemned by their own trade union. Employers are then faced with the problem of dealing with a situation which they may not have bargained for when the "no-strike" clause was agreed. In this position employers should be aware of both the legal provisions and practical methods of dealing with strike action (see above).

One important point to note is that the requirement to have a secret ballot before industrial action is taken, contained in s.11 of the Trade Union Act 1984, may not be enforceable in itself in the case of certain unofficial action. S.11 requires that before a "trade union" authorises or endorses industrial action a secret ballot must be held in order to preserve immunity from civil claims for inducing breaches of contract. The action will only be deemed to be authorised or endorsed if this has been done by:

(a) the principal executive committee
(b) any other person empowered by the rules to authorise or endorse such action
(c) the president or general secretary
(d) any other official who is an employed official
(e) any committee of the union to whom an employed official regularly reports.

However, the action will not be deemed to be authorised or endorsed if this has been done by a person who is prevented by union rules from endorsing industrial action, or where the action has been repudiated by the executive committee, president or general secretary.

So, if the above rules are not complied with, or a trade union repudiates the action, the union cannot be sued in the civil courts for inducing industrial action without a secret ballot since the ballot is only required before "a union" endorses the action. Any unofficial action which is not authorised by the union will not require a ballot but of course, like all industrial action, may render the individuals liable to dismissal.

6 PROBLEM AREAS

The one certainty on which personnel managers can rely is that there will always be problem areas. In this chapter we have selected those issues which are most likely to create problems for companies today — ranging from the management of change, through security, health problems such as possible VDU risks, stress, drink and drugs at work, to the necessary steps employers should take when employees die in service.

The Management of Change

There can be few organisations which do not have to face the challenges presented by the need to introduce changes in methods of working or organisational changes. Whether they are due to evolving technology or to economic pressures it is essential that such changes are introduced effectively.

This section reviews the extent of employers' powers to require employees to adapt to change, the ways in which they can be encouraged to accept — hopefully even welcome — new developments and the procedures which can be adopted to deal with employees who are unable or unwilling to evolve with the company. It is written largely with non-unionised companies in mind.

The Contractual Position

When implementing changes which affect employees' jobs, it is essential to ensure that the contractual position is understood — so far as possible — in order to avoid the possibility of a constructive dismissal or breach of contract claim arising.

This can be a particularly difficult area of law: by common law terms are implied into all contracts of employment accepted by employees that the employees have a duty to serve the employer and a duty to be obedient. The duty to serve, however, means to serve in accordance with the contract. The duty to be obedient extends to an obligation to obey lawful orders which are within the scope of the contract.

The question of whether particular instructions are outside the scope of the contract was examined in the case of *Cresswell and others v Board of Inland Revenue* [1984] IRLR 190. The employees were tax officers engaged in carrying out the manual administration of the PAYE system. The employer wanted to introduce a system of computer operation to facilitate the administration of PAYE which would involve a change to the method of carrying out the work. The employees sought a declaration that the instructions from the employer to operate the computer were outside the scope of their existing contracts of employment. They claimed that computerisation would mean that in effect they would be doing different work from that which they were originally engaged to perform.

The High Court ruled that the employer was not in breach of contract in requiring the operation of the computer. As long as the nature of the work remained the same there was no fundamental change to existing contracts. In this case the court was satisfied that the employer had changed only the method of carrying out the work: the employees would still be performing the duties of tax officers in administering the PAYE system. The court pointed out that employees do not have a vested right to preserve working obligations totally unchanged from when they first began work, and that employees are expected to adapt to changes in methods and techniques which do not affect the fundamental nature of the work.

The question of a job description will also be relevant in determining the duties which employees can be obliged to carry out under their contracts. If its wording is very precise, and it includes no phrase along the lines of: "to carry out such other duties as might reasonably be required", the employer will have less flexibility.

The Employer's Discretion

Courts and tribunals will usually hold that, despite being bound by the contractual terms, the employer is not in fundamental breach of contract provided the employee's basic function remains unchanged. For example, in *Saddington v Valetta Modes Ltd* EAT 280/83 Mrs Saddington was employed as an assistant in a high-class dress shop where she became well-known to the regular clientele, many of whom became dependent on her expertise and advice. The business ran into financial difficulties and it was decided that, rather than selling expensive women's dresses, it would sell men's and women's "seconds" clothing. Mrs Saddington considered her future employment with the store would be so different that she terminated her employment and claimed constructive dismissal.

The industrial tribunal held that there had been no dismissal: she was employed to sell clothes and a change in product range and quality of the clothes she was to sell did not amount to a fundamental breach of contract. The EAT agreed, pointing out that it would be unrealistic to construe a contract of employment in a way that assumed that business conditions would not change.

Similarly, it would be unrealistic to expect that an organisation's structure will never change. It follows from this that if a company decides to give special emphasis to, for example, the financial side of the business and so recruits a new finance director, employees who now have to report to that director rather than directly to the managing director will have no claim in law just because the reporting chain has lengthened. Provided that the status and responsibilities of the employees concerned have not been eroded they will be unable to make successful claims for breach of contract or constructive dismissal.

Smoothing the Way

The legal problems regarding introducing change are, of course, only half the problem. The important point is to be able to implement the changes smoothly and effectively, rather than to know whether or not employees will have a legal claim.

The key here is good communications. Rumours of impending changes to working methods will often engender feelings of hostility among the workforce, together with fears of redundancy and anxiety about not being able to cope with new machinery or other new demands.

If the company is not unionised, it will be necessary to ensure that current systems of communication are effective or, if not, to introduce new systems. These might take many forms, eg:
– a system of briefing groups
– works committees
– regular departmental meetings attended by senior management
– meetings of the whole workforce.

It is important that the fact of the changes, the reasons for them and the implications for the workforce are spelt out in detail before the company grapevine has time to work. Where possible the employees who will have to operate new machinery, for instance, should be given a demonstration, told of the company's plans for giving them full training and informed of the anticipated timescale for introducing the new methods. Ideally, employees of a similar background who have been trained on the new equipment or in the new working methods should be invited to discuss their experience with the workforce in order to allay fears of inadequacy.

There will need to be written back-up provided for employees to whatever form of communication is employed. The amount of oral information people can absorb at any one time is strictly limited and the problem is greater if the listeners are worried about the personal implications of what they are hearing. They are more likely to listen selectively and the message they receive is liable to be distorted by their fears and prejudices.

Training should begin well before the new practice has to be implemented and the method of training used should be tailored to the needs of the employees concerned.

Problem Employees

It is a truism that, regardless of the care that is taken in introducing such changes and of the training that is provided, there will often be one or two people who, at the end of the training period, will not be able to perform to an acceptable standard.

In such a case the employer should first consider, having regard to the employee's length of service, whether supervision, support or training would help to resolve the problem. If it would, a further period should be given whenever possible, its length depending on the degree of difficulty being faced by the employee and the needs of the organisation.

If it is decided that further help would not resolve the problem, before dismissing the employee the employer should look to see whether there are any alternative jobs within the organisation which the employee could perform. In looking for such jobs, the employer should be limited only by the employee's capability: jobs which are of a lower grade should be offered if the employee would be suitable to carry them out. Full written details of any changes to terms and conditions of employment that would apply if down-grading results should, of course, be given to the employee.

If there is no alternative to dismissal, it would only constitute a redundancy if the basic nature of the job had altered, as stated above.

The procedure will, of course, be different if an employee is refusing to carry out the work to an acceptable standard as a protest against the introduction of the change. In these circumstances it might be appropriate to call the employee in for a meeting which could be something of a hybrid between a counselling and disciplinary interview. If this does not succeed, the normal disciplinary procedure should be applied.

Changing the Standards

It may be that rather than wanting to change working methods, it is standards of output or of behaviour that have to be changed, perhaps as a result of the economic climate or of the recruitment of a new manager. In most cases there should be no difficulty in imposing such standards, provided they are reasonable — ie they are realistically attainable.

Where disciplinary action is to be taken against people who fail to meet the new standards, however, it is essential that all employees are informed at the outset of those standards and of the consequences of failing to achieve them. In some cases it might also be necessary to allow a transitional period — a period of time for employees to adjust to the new demands being made of them.

More difficulties might arise when such a change requires the employees to lower their standards of quality in order to complete the work within a given time. In the case of *Spencer and Griffin v Gloucestershire County Council* [1985] IRLR 393 the Court of Appeal held that cleaners, whose working hours had been reduced, had acted reasonably in rejecting an offer of alternative employment — and so were entitled to redundancy payments — because they would not have been able to achieve a satisfactory standard of work in the time available.

Again, in that case, the Court of Appeal reiterated that it was for the employer to decide on the standard of work required, but equally it was for the cleaners to decide whether they saw the new work as reasonable, given that they would be entitled to receive redundancy payments if they did not unreasonably refuse an offer of suitable alternative employment.

Promotion Problems

We are all familiar with the children's game of snakes and ladders — the frustrations of a short, sharp rise only to be followed by a long slither down a waiting snake! However, the real-life game of organisational snakes and ladders has many more serious implications for employers and employees alike.

While most personnel practitioners are aware of the problems and pitfalls that are likely to be encountered when trying to demote employees, little thought is usually given to the legal consequences of promotion; but to try to force promotion on an unwilling employee can be just as serious a breach of contract as a demotion.

Promotion

Promotion may be defined as the advancement of an employee to a job which is acknowledged to be better in terms of higher formal status and prestige, greater responsibility and a higher rate of pay and/or fringe benefits.

Upgrading is another term used in connection with promotion, meaning the movement of an employee from one grade to a higher one as part of a recognised process of improvement and development which is available to a number of staff. This may be subject to passing a test or to satisfactory performance of a job at the existing grade for a stated period of time, or to three months' probation at a higher level, at the end of which a given level of performance must be achieved. This, of course, must be distinguished from a regrading, which is the alteration of the grade and rate of pay of a job following a job evaluation exercise.

Promotion commonly occurs through filling an empty post from within the employer's organisation. Policy decisions have to be made about how widely such vacancies are to be advertised within the organisation and on the closing date for applications.

Advantages of Internal Promotions

Internal promotion has the following advantages for the company:
- it provides individual members of the company with the opportunity for advancement
- it can ensure that employees' attitudes and ideas are compatible with those of the company
- it provides a smooth transition and sound replacements when effective internal appointments are made
- recruitment and selection costs are minimal or non-existent
- skills and knowledge already acquired within the company are retained
- very often trade unions require that promotion goes to suitable existing employees before a job is advertised externally.

The Disadvantages

On the face of it, it seems sensible to encourage home-grown talent. However, there are disadvantages in promoting from within:
- employees may be too set in the company's ways and attitudes and the lack of a fresh view can be stultifying
- there is a tendency to promote a person who does the current job best — or who has been doing it the longest — rather than giving objective considera-

tion to whether or not the skills and abilities match those required in the vacant job
- the promotion of one person may set off a chain reaction of promotions which will result in inefficiency and higher training costs where people are not ready for the move
- departments which train and develop their employees may repeatedly lose their best staff to other parts of the company
- there is the eternal problem of appointing a person to supervise or manage former colleagues
- if replacements consistently come from inside, other employees will assume that no-one will ever be taken from outside and senior managers will be unaware of the talent available on the open market.

Promoting Fairly

The cornerstone of any fair promotion scheme must be that it is based on a systematic appraisal of staff which is carried out at regular intervals and which is open, ie employees should know the results of their appraisal and should be given the opportunity to make dissenting comments where necessary. Furthermore, selection procedures must give all those interested a chance of being considered.

Many large companies provide succession charts and development plans for their key management staff and this system allows the employer to concentrate on training individuals for promotion after they have been identified as possible replacements for senior or retiring staff. Such training may take the form of a temporary filling of the job or an "acting" role for the employee. When this occurs, the employer needs to be clear as to policy on pay for the period concerned. It is also essential that the employer thinks through the consequences of the employee not making the grade and makes sure that he or she is aware of the position should that happen.

Barriers to Acceptance

Why do employees accept promotion? Very often this is because they will be more independent in a more senior position, they have a chance of growing in their job, gain additional prestige and will be rewarded for services given in the past. Furthermore, salary or additional perks such as a company car are very acceptable.

On the other hand, there can be real barriers to the acceptance of promotion. Some types of promotion will involve too much struggle and responsibility for individuals who find they are not prepared to give the amount of commitment that is required. A person promoted from the shop floor to join managerial ranks may feel uncomfortable and out of place in such company. This feeling is often intensified by alienation from people who were formerly work colleagues. Alternatively, promotion may be seen to be beyond the employee's capability or not worth the effort.

The Legal Position

The legal position with regard to promotion in some respects is more complex than it may appear. If promotion is offered it does not have to be accepted; the employee is employed under a contract and, if the employer wishes to change the job that the employee does, it must be by agreement. It is conceivable that the refusal of promotion, in certain circumstances, could provide some other substantial reason for dismissal, particularly in small companies where staff are taken on with a view to promoting them into more senior positions once they have gained enough experience. This could block the normal progression of staff in the company and, in the absence of any alternative employment being available, it may provide a fair reason for dismissal. However, it should always be remembered that a unilateral attempt to change employees' terms and conditions of employment — albeit when the employer thinks the change would be to their advantage — could well give rise to a successful constructive dismissal claim.

For example, an employee who knows that he or she cannot stand pressure would have good grounds for refusing promotion to a managerial position. Similarly, an employee who works a considerable amount of (paid) overtime would have good grounds for refusing promotion to a staff job as supervisor if no bonus or overtime was payable. It is also the case that, if a reluctant employee was pressurised into accepting a promotion, subsequent dismissal on grounds of capability would almost certainly be unfair.

Unsuccessful Promotions

Cases inevitably arise where a promotion has been readily accepted by the employee but as time goes on it becomes apparent that the promotion was inadvisable. In short, the employee has been promoted beyond his or her level of competence. It is essential that companies provide support and encouragement for newly promoted managers, particularly in terms of day to day guidance. Where the employee has been pressurised into accepting promotion, a dismissal without the consideration of alternative employment being offered is very likely to be unfair. In this situation, wherever possible, the employee should be offered alternative employment (*Bevan Harris Ltd t/a Clyde Leather Co v Gair* [1981] IRLR 520) unless this is not practicable, eg if the company is too small to provide other work.

Employees are often promoted subject to a trial period, to see if they can measure up. It follows that some promotions are not confirmed and the employee may not be able to return to the old job because it has been filled. Very often a demotion from the previously held job is therefore necessary.

Such a situation arose in the case of *National Car Parks Ltd v Diamond* EAT 397/83 where a tribunal found that a dismissal in such circumstances was unfair. They found as facts that:
- Mr Diamond had not clearly understood that if he failed in his trial period he might be unable to revert to his former post and
- although the company would have been prepared to continue to pay him at the higher rate and allow him to keep his company car had he so requested, they had not informed him of this.

The message of this decision (which was upheld by the Employment Appeal Tribunal) is clear: when employees are promoted on the basis of a trial period, and their original job cannot be held open for them during this period, they should be made aware of the position. This will obviously require careful handling if employees are not to see the offer of promotion as a means of edging them out of the company. If it is not done, however, and the promotion does not work out, the company is likely to find itself on the losing side of an unfair dismissal claim.

When making a series of promotions it is sensible to promote all those in the chain on a trial period and, if it is feasible, make it clear that they can return to their old jobs if they are not found to be satisfactory or if it is necessary for one person in the promotion chain to return to his or her original job. Otherwise, it will be necessary for them all to be warned that dismissal may result if they do not reach a satisfactory standard during the trial period.

Demoting Employees

The employer may have the right in the contract of employment to employ someone to do any sort of work at any level; for instance, a contract may stipulate that a manager must also be prepared actually to carry out production procedures when not managing. However, employers do not have a general right in law to demote. An employee is employed to carry out a certain job and, if the employer wishes to demote from that position — very often to a less well paid one or to one with fewer fringe benefits — this must be done with the employee's agreement. Even demotion to a lesser job which does not involve a pay cut or disturbance of fringe benefits can be a breach of contract sufficiently fundamental to entitle the employee to leave and claim constructive dismissal. However, if the employee agrees to this course of action there is no problem. Many disciplinary procedures make provision for the demotion of employees in certain circumstances and such action will therefore usually, in that context, be fair and reasonable, even though the employee might not accept it.

Normally employers will be obliged to follow their disciplinary or capability warning procedures before insisting that the employee accepts demotion or is dismissed from the company. However, it is sensible to discuss such an option at earlier stages in the procedure if the option is a viable solution to the problem. Demotion is frequently turned down because it means that employees have to go back among the people they formerly supervised and the subsequent loss of face and status is more than they can tolerate. Sometimes the sudden reduction in pay will be a sufficient reason not to accept demotion, and many employers consider slowly returning the rate of pay to its proper level over a period of, say, six to 12 months.

The problem of people who can no longer cope in new situations and the difficulties presented by employees who have progressively lost capability as a result of age-related or attitude problems are, increasingly, nettles that employers must grasp.

Downgrading Employees

Another problem which arises not infrequently is when certain employees are downgraded following a job evaluation exercise: that is, their job does not change but in the company's eyes it is in a lower pay band than was previously the case. The traditional response in such a situation is to "red-circle" the relevant employees. In other words, their pay is not increased (or is increased to a much lesser extent than the pay of other employees) until such time as the new pay band can accommodate their wages/salary. If such a course of action is taken, it is important that the situation is explained fully to the employees concerned and that they are given the right to appeal against their downgrading — and, of course, the opportunity to apply for a higher grade job when it arises.

Merely to reduce the pay of the employees concerned to fit within their new grade band would almost certainly constitute breach of contract, so allowing the employees to make a claim for damages in the County Court (or High Court) and/or to leave and claim constructive dismissal.

If the pay of such employees is to be protected, it is important to ensure that there are no adverse equal pay consequences. For instance, if a job evaluation exercise results in male employees being downgraded and their pay levels are protected, in an equal pay claim it would be necessary to show that the pay of the men concerned was red-circled until such time as the grade bands caught up with their pay levels, and that this was not an attempt on the employer's part to perpetuate differences in pay between men and women.

Employee Inventions

Employees who make inventions from which their employer benefits are given important rights by the Patents Act 1977. All inventions made before this Act came into force (on 1.6.78) are governed by the 1949 Patents Act. Although the 1949 Act provided for an apportionment of benefit from the invention it did not operate in a particularly beneficial way for employees and the courts interpreted the Act in a restrictive way. In every contract of employment there was an implied term vesting the benefit of the employee's invention in the employer, provided the invention might be expected to be made because of the nature of the employee's job. This rule could only be overriden by a clear agreement in writing to substitute a different arrangement and an agreement to pay royalties.

The Situation Before the 1977 Act

The case of *Sterling Engineering Co Ltd v Patchett* (1955) 1 AER 369 illustrates this position. Mr Patchett, an engineer, entered into an agreement that, when he was responsible for a patentable invention concerning the manufacture of armaments between 1942 and 1944, the patent would be applied for jointly with the company and he would receive a royalty. After the war he worked on electrical appliances and for these subsequent inventions, although they were jointly patented, the company refused to pay him royalties because they were not covered by the subsisting agreement. Mr Patchett took the matter to the House of Lords where it was decided that the company did not have to pay royalties.

The Act did not apply where one of the parties was entitled, to the exclusion of the other, to the benefit arising from the patented invention and no alternative agreement existed. Thus, unless there was written agreement giving ownership to employees, they were treated as trustees of the invention for their employers' benefit. Previous cases also looked at such factors as the employee's status, skill, qualifications and the use made of the employer's facilities when assessing who owned the invention. These factors usually weighed in the employer's favour. The 1977 Patents Act was designed to change this situation.

An Invention

Not all innovations count as "inventions" for the purposes of the 1977 Act. To be patentable an invention must:
(a) be new — ie it must never have been disclosed publicly in any way
(b) involve an inventive step — which means that, when compared with what is already known, it would not be obvious to someone with a good knowledge and experience of the subject
(c) be capable of being made or used in some kind of industry — ie it must be an apparatus or a device, a product capable of industrial application.

Inventions which are excluded under the Act are those which consist only of: a discovery, scientific theory or mathematical method; a mental process; a literary, artistic or aesthetic creation; a scheme or method for performing a mental act, playing a game or doing business; the presentation of information, or a computer program.

Under the provisions of the 1977 Act, an invention made by an employee on or after 1.6.78 will only belong to the employer if:

(a) it was made in the course of employees' duties or during the course of duties specifically assigned to them and an invention might reasonably be expected to result from the carrying out of such duties

(b) the employee had a special obligation to further the interests of the employer's business.

Otherwise, the invention will belong to the employee. This sounds like the old common law position but are the scales tipped against the employee in the same way? A recent case has taken a close look at these provisions and has provided valuable guidance on their interpretation.

Recent Case Law

The case *Reiss Engineering Co Ltd v Harris* [1985] IRLR 232 involved an attempt by the company to process an application for a patent in their own name. The Superintending Examiner, acting for the Comptroller of Patents, decided that the invention belonged to Mr Harris, the employee; the company appealed to the High Court.

Mr Harris was employed as a fitter and eventually became responsible for servicing and then selling pumps as manager of a department. The valves used were Wey valves, manufactured in Switzerland by Maschinenfabrik Sidler Stalder AG. Some valves were assembled from parts made to the Swiss company's drawing, but Reiss Engineering had no research or primary design office itself. Mr Harris was involved with selling and providing after-sales service using his specialist knowledge of valves, their applications, difficulties in using them and his experience in dealing with problems after installation. Reiss Engineering did not try to solve design problems themselves but reported such problems to the Swiss manufacturer for remedy.

The Superintending Examiner concluded that Mr Harris was not employed to design or invent but was primarily concerned with obtaining sales and giving after-sales service requiring knowledge of known engineering practice or techniques. However, Mr Harris invented a new kind of valve designed to solve some of the problems found with other types, including Wey valves. Mr Harris made the invention at the beginning of August 1978 (ie after the 1977 Patents Act took effect) after he had been declared redundant and placed under six months' notice.

The High Court rejected the suggestion that they should lean heavily on previously decided cases developed in earlier authorities:

"No doubt guidance may be obtained from such previous cases as to how courts have assessed the duties of the employee in a particular case and particular circumstances; but, having regard to the clear opening words of s.39 of the 1977 Act: . . . Notwithstanding anything in any rule of law . . .

regard must be had for the law governing any employee's invention made after the appointed day (June 1, 1978)".

In effect, since the passing of the 1977 Patents Act the ownership of inventions vis-a-vis employee and employer is governed solely by the provisions of the Act.

The High Court then went on to consider whether the invention was made in the course of Mr Harris's normal duties or in the course of duties falling outside his normal duties but specifically assigned to him and, furthermore, whether the circumstances were such that an invention might reasonably be expected to result from the carrying out of these duties.

They decided that this invention was not an invention which achieved or contributed to achieving the aim or object to which Mr Harris's efforts in carrying out his duties were directed. His duties were to sell valves and provide after-sales service; he was not employed to design or invent.

"It was abundantly clear on the evidence that it was never part of (Mr Harris's) duties to apply his mind to problems arising in valves supplied to customers by or through (Reiss Engineering). During the time he was employed by them (Reiss Engineering) never took upon themselves the role of dealing with such problems. There was no evidence that they imposed on (Mr Harris) as part of his normal duties an obligation they never assumed themselves."

The High Court then looked at the second aspect, namely whether the nature of Mr Harris's duties and particular responsibilities were such that he had a special obligation to further the employer's business interests. Rubbish! said the Court. This provision depends upon the status of the employee. It envisages the position of, for instance, a managing director whose obligation is to further the interests of the business across the whole spectrum of activities of the undertaking. The particular responsibilities of a sales manager like Mr Harris were no more than to do the best he could to effect sales of the Wey valves and provide after-sales service. Beyond this Mr Harris had no special obligation to further the interests of his employer. Consequently the High Court agreed with the Superintending Examiner that Mr Harris was the owner of the patent.

Important Features of the Act

This case goes only part of the way towards illustrating the impact of the 1977 Patents Act. There are far more radical departures contained in it which are of great practical significance for the employer. In particular:
– the unenforceability of contractual clauses that assign patent rights to the employer, except where a collective agreement dealing with the ownership of inventions has been concluded with trade unions

- the ownership of an invention is no longer crucial to the employee claiming a share of the benefit. The Comptroller of Patents can make an award of compensation provided the employee can show that:
  - a patent has been granted
  - the invention was made by the employee
  - the patent is of "outstanding benefit" to the employer
  - it is "just" that an award of compensation should be made by the employer.

Even employees who own the patent and have assigned or licensed the employer to use the invention for the payment of royalties can claim additional compensation if they have sold a winner too cheaply.

Compensation Levels

The Comptroller of Patents will assess the level of compensation as a fair share of the benefit of the invention using the following criteria:
  (a) the nature of the employee's duties, remuneration and other employment advantages
  (b) the effort and skill devoted by the employee to the invention
  (c) the employer's contribution in terms of advice, facilities, development costs, managerial and commercial skills
  (d) any conditions specified in a licence granted to the employer
  (e) the extent to which the invention was made jointly with any other person.

There is no scale of compensation and there are no statutory limits to the amount which may be awarded.

Securing Your Assets

Almost every company spends a great deal of time — and money — ensuring the security of its physical assets — plant, machinery, etc. However, there are matters related to security which have a direct impact on employment law, and so on personnel managers, which are not given such attention. In particular, there are three such matters: the security (and safety) of employees who have to handle cash; the reliability of such staff, and the employer's powers — if any — to "stop and search" employees who are suspected of misappropriating property.

Safety of Employees

At present many companies still pay a substantial number of manual workers in cash every week. Even though the Truck Acts have been repealed, large sums of money still have to be handled by certain employees. This obviously means that the employer must take certain steps to ensure, so far as is practicable, the safety of those employees in order to discharge the duty of care owed by all employers to their staff.

The most obvious risk is that of theft, possibly violent theft, while cash is being taken to or from the bank. While employers do not have to go to extreme lengths to ensure the safety of employees involved in such duties, they must at least give consideration to the following points.
1. How large are the amounts involved? Obviously, the greater the sum, the more necessary it will become to consider using professional security services.
2. What instructions are given to staff regarding security precautions? As a minimum, they should be told to vary their route on each occasion, wherever possible they should avoid going at the same time each day and they should be told *not* to discuss this aspect of their job with friends or acquaintances.
3. Is it sufficient for one person to go alone? The answer to this question will be determined by factors such as the local environment: how prevalent is violent crime, mugging, etc? the amount of money involved, the transport used, etc.

In considering the precautions that can be taken most effectively, it is always sensible to discuss the problem with the Crime Prevention Officer attached to the local police station. He or she will also be able to give useful advice to the staff concerned on factors such as suspicious actions to watch for, how to avoid particular dangers and so on.

Reliable Staff

Part of the duty of care for employees' safety also requires employers to select competent staff (or to give them the necessary training) and to ensure that there is a safe system of work. Arguably, this duty requires employers to ensure that, so far as is reasonably practicable, people who work with cash are honest and trustworthy, at least to the extent that they are unlikely to hit a colleague over the head and run with the cash when returning from the bank with the weekly wages!

This may seem to be an obvious point, but references are not always checked thoroughly, particularly when employees are not employed specifically on security duties but agree to take on the collection of cash out of "helpfulness". It may well transpire that they were serving a term of imprisonment during a period when, according to their CVs, they worked for a reputable firm.

It should be noted in this context, however, that the Rehabilitation of Offenders Act 1974 does allow people to state that they have never been convicted of a criminal offence if their sentence is "spent" under the Act.

Breach of Duty

Employers in breach of their duty of care, when an employee is injured as a result, may be sued for damages by the employee in the civil courts. The normal time limit of three years is allowed for the personal injury claim to be brought.

It should be emphasised, however, that the employer is under a duty to take *reasonable* care. It is not an absolute duty to ensure employees'safety.

Similarly, the duty of care for someone employed as a security guard — whose job is to guard cash during its collection from the bank, etc — will be very different from the duty owed to a clerk who performs this function from time to time. The law accepts that some jobs involve a degree of risk of necessity and people who apply for such positions accept these risks. Equally, people who hold themselves to be experienced guards should be aware of the basic security precautions and should undertake them as a matter of routine — although this does not mean that employers in such situations can opt out of their responsibilities or liabilities.

Stop and Search

It is not uncommon for companies which handle fairly large amounts of cash or which produce small but expensive items — particularly those which can be disposed of readily and profitably — to have a clause in all employees' contracts giving them the right to stop employees on their way out of the premises and to subject them to a search. However, the validity of such a clause is questionable, particularly when it comes to body searches.

If a security guard stops an employee and asks him or her to submit to a search and the employee refuses, the security officer will be committing a criminal assault if he or she persists in the search, despite the refusal. The security guard could thus be open to prosecution.

It is more sensible to ensure that any security officers faced with such a refusal are instructed to ask the employee to wait while a member of management is summoned to deal with the situation.

When an employee does refuse to submit to a search, he or she should be interviewed by a senior manager who should attempt to establish the reason for the refusal. It is quite possible that, at this stage, the whole matter could turn into a disciplinary issue as a result of the employee's failure to obey a reasonable instruction — ie refusing to submit to a search on security grounds — rather than the underlying security issue. If this is the case, however, it is important that the disciplinary procedure is followed.

VDU Risks: Facts or Fantasies?

Many employers will have been heartily relieved by the Health and Safety Executive (HSE) Guidance Booklet on Visual Display Units (published June 1983) which seemed to dispel most fears about potential risks to employees from their use. However, since its publication there has been an increasing number of surveys, reports and studies (many commissioned or carried out by trade unions) which do not give such a comforting picture and indicate that our present state of knowledge is by no means conclusive.

Increase in Use of New Technology

VDUs are now a common feature of office equipment, whether linked to a computer or a word processor, and the rapid expansion in their use has meant that many non-computer specialists are involved in operating them. The adjustments from conventional means of writing/typing material and the often complex procedures can, in themselves, cause anxiety and strain for staff unused to new technology. Many health and safety experts believe that this is the root of the troubles VDUs have caused in the way of complaints about dermatitis, backache, eye-strain, combined with a general lack of understanding about proper design, lighting and siting of the equipment and the demands made on the operator.

Potential Health Hazards

The potential health hazards of VDUs have been watched very closely from the beginning, particularly as they are commonly used in an area which is traditionally free from major health and safety worries. The most common complaints from operators have been associated with the following problems:
- backache, headaches, eye-strain and other symptoms of bodily fatigue
- facial dermatitis, ranging from itching of the skin to actual rashes
- tenosynovitis, swelling and pain in tendons and muscles of the fingers, hands and forearms
- photosensitive epilepsy, the risk of experiencing an epileptic fit following exposure to a flickering light source (also triggered off by televisions). This will only occur amongst the very small percentage of epilepsy sufferers prone to this type of seizure
- radiation emission, causing cataracts in some operators and spontaneous miscarriages in pregnant women.

The symptoms connected to bodily fatigue and muscle swelling can be relieved by proper design and siting of equipment, adjustable chairs allowing the employee to find the most suitable operating position, for example, or placing the VDU between, rather than beneath, strip lighting panels to avoid glare. Facial dermatitis has been linked with low humidity and static elec-

167

tricity in the field of the VDU. The HSE recommends anti-static carpeting and installing humidifying devices if complaints arise.

The most serious area of concern is the potential health risk from radiation emission. VDUs work in a similar way to television screens: an electron beam is projected on to fluorescent material by the use of a high voltage energy "field". This results in the production of visible light images on the screen. In the process, however, not all the incident electrons are actually converted into visible light and wavelengths of ultra-violet and infra-red radiation can be emitted from the VDU.

A study carried out by the National Radiological Protection Board, commissioned by the HSE, concluded that the actual levels of radiation which could be detected in their research were well below national and international limits for occupational exposure. The HSE has relied upon this survey in their guidance booklet and subsequent advice in stipulating that there is no danger to operators from this particular source.

However, this has not conclusively established that there is no risk at all to operators and it must be stated that more research is needed before employers can dismiss the problem from their minds.

Statistical Evidence

The statistical evidence of potentially radiation-induced miscarriages has come mainly from the USA and Canada where there have been several reported "clusters" of women working on VDUs suffering miscarriages or the birth of malformed children. In 1980, four out of seven babies born to women working for a Toronto newspaper had birth defects. There were seven miscarriages suffered in a group of 15 pregnant women working at the Defence Logistics Agency, Atlanta in 1982 and in Sears Roebuck, Dallas, eight miscarriages occurred in an office where VDUs had recently been introduced.

Of course, it is highly unlikely that radiation from VDU screens could be responsible for all these miscarriages and deformed babies, especially as there is quite a high statistical chance of a pregnant woman suffering a miscarriage anyway. However, the official response of investigators that these particular incidences were statistical "flukes" does not seem very satisfactory.

In Britain similar problems have been reported, although not on the same scale as those in the USA. The major study which has been carried out is an investigation by the Civil Service Medical Advisory Service after women data processors working in the Department of Employment in Runcorn seemed to be suffering an unusually high rate of miscarriages.

The survey was carried out by the use of questionnaires filled out retrospectively by 800 women who had worked at the Runcorn office between 1974 and 1982. Amongst this group there were 167 pregnancies, 55 of which occurred with women working on VDUs. Analysis of the questionnaires indicated that out of the 55 pregnancies a seemingly high number (36%) had resulted in either miscarriages, stillbirths or some kind of birth defect. This compared with only 16% of abnormal results amongst the 112 employees not working on VDUs. Further analysis of the results, however, has indicated that the study cannot be seen as conclusive evidence of a causal link between radiation leaking from VDU screens and adverse pregnancy outcome. The authors of the study have made it clear that the miscarriage rate amongst the VDU users (14.5%) is in fact similar to the rate amongst the population as a whole. The surprising thing about the study, they believe, is the low rate of abnormal pregnancies amongst the control group of employees not working on VDUs.

In conclusion, the study has been labelled statistically insignificant due to its limited extent, the poor methods used and the lack of balance because personal factors relating to the medical history of the women were not taken into account. The Medical Advisory Service decided not to publish the study formally, believing that its results would mislead and disturb employees who were not aware of the unreliable nature of its conclusions.

The Union View

However, the refusal to publish the study or to take much account of its findings has caused great consternation amongst the Civil Service unions. Although spokesmen for the Council of Civil Service Unions (CCSU) have accepted that the Runcorn study is inconclusive for the reasons outlined above, they still believe enough doubt has been cast for further and more large-scale surveys to be undertaken. Indeed, Civil Service Medical Advisor, Dr Adrian Semmence, has stated that "measurement of the actual risk needs a large-scale study to disentangle the effects of VDUs from other factors"

The union position as a result of the Runcorn study is that, as long as there is any indication of potential risk which has not been disproven, all female VDU operators who wish to become pregnant should be allowed to transfer to other work, without loss of earnings or status. Informally, certain areas of Civil Service management are prepared to agree to transfers for those women who are particularly concerned.

Other unions have taken a similar line to that of the CCSU on the potential hazards of VDU work and have attempted to incorporate rights of transfer to other work in many new technology agreements. The standard view is that, while research into the problems remains inconclusive, VDU operators should be offered alternative work for the duration of their pregnancy where this is feasible.

The unions are also concerned about other potential health risks and have made recommendations about design of equipment, training and rest periods for operators. In a policy document on occupational stress published in 1983, the Association of Scientific, Technical and Managerial Staffs (ASTMS) considered the possible causes and results of stress in VDU operators. They highlighted lack of training as a major source of strain, indicating that many employers introduce VDUs without considering the need for gradual and guided adaptation from typing and clerical tasks. This can lead to depression, low concentration, headaches and general inefficiency amongst operators. The document recommends alternating VDU work with other tasks, a view shared by delegates at an international trade union conference who suggested a daily limit on the amount of time spent at a VDU.

The Association of Professional, Executive, Clerical and Computer Staff (APEX) has produced guidelines on the use of VDUs and a report based on a survey of operations amongst its members in various industries. The APEX guidelines suggest strong involvement of safety representatives when VDUs are being demonstrated prior to purchase and also monitoring of operators with regular eye-tests and flexibility towards complaints. They are especially critical of work measurement schemes (productivity comparisons between operators on the basis of the number of key depressions in each day) which can lead to extreme stress and "should be resisted at the planning stage of the introduction of new technology".

The APEX survey showed that sore eyes, backaches and headaches were commonplace amongst operators. The staff blamed non-user friendly equipment (ie bad legibility of characters, small screens and noisy printers) and badly designed furniture for most of the problems.

Unfair Dismissal

Even without union involvement, it seems that employers should be wary of relying too much upon HSE guidance that there is no need to consider transferring pregnant VDU operators.

In a tribunal case heard in Scotland (*Johnson v Highland Regional Council*, SCOIT 1480/84) a woman was found to have been unfairly dismissed after refusing to operate a VDU during pregnancy. Ms Johnson, a librarian, requested to be excused from VDU work (usually consisting of about two hours a day) as soon as she became pregnant because she believed radiation could harm her unborn child. Ms Johnson's supervisor assured her that this would not present too much difficulty as she could be moved on to other duties with very little disruption. However, senior management were not so optimistic and, after seeking advice from the council's own health and safety officers and a doctor from the HSE, they refused her request. Ms Johnson was finally dismissed for disobedience after she refused to carry out her VDU duties. She had, in the meantime, suffered a threatened miscarriage from the stress.

At the tribunal her employers reported on the advice they had received which was that there was no proven risk of any harm to a pregnant woman and they had relied on this as the basis of their decision not to rearrange Ms Johnson's duties and excuse her from VDU work. Ms Johnson was able to produce reports and articles critical of HSE guidance which convinced the tribunal that her fears were not unfounded.

In the light of this case, the message seems to be that employers should be aware of the worries of pregnant VDU operators and sufficiently flexible to consider their requests for transfer to other work if they are genuinely worried. Until further research has been carried out it is not really possible to assert conclusively that there is no risk at all from radiation emission and this potential hazard should be borne in mind, along with other health and safety factors.

The HSE have published a reading list on VDUs, *Health Effects of VDUs: A Bibliography*, which is available from St Hugh's House, Stanley Precinct, Bootle, Merseyside L20 3QY.

Stress and Mental Health

Absences due to mental ill-health and stress are responsible for a phenomenal number of working days lost and yet little has been done by employers in this country (unlike other countries) to alleviate the problem. We turn now to examine stress and its effects and to offer some thoughts on how employers can help employees and thus themselves, in dealing with this problem. We also examine the ways in which the employer can, and cannot, fairly dismiss an employee whose mental ill-health makes continuing employment undesirable or impossible.

The Dangers of Stress

The size of personal injury awards in the United States goes some way towards explaining why employers take so much more trouble over problems of stress in employees than their British counterparts. In 1956 an employee sued General Motors, his employers, for the nervous breakdown he suffered which he claimed was a result of the stress of his job. He succeeded because General Motors had taken no steps whatsoever to deal with stress brought on by the job; not unnaturally, many similar claims followed. Thus, Employee Assistance Programmes, Company Fitness Programmes, etc, virtually unheard of here, are now common in companies in America.

Obviously, some stress is necessary in any job and, if not "over the top", stress usually improves performance. However, there comes a point where healthy pressure ends and potentially damaging stress takes over. The damage that can result may not only affect the employee personally — it can, for the employer, mean reduced productivity, increased absenteeism, inefficiency, etc. Thus, the employer who feels that stress is an individual's own burden is failing to recognise the simple fact that, even if the stress arises outside work, the employee is going to cease to be a productive worker. As employees' lives revolve substantially around their jobs (approximately ⅓ of their working life is devoted to it), the employer is well placed not only to help employees whose stress arises from the job itself, but also those whose problems emanate from their personal life.

Spotting Stress

The symptoms of stress can manifest themselves in a number of ways. For example, an individual's defence mechanisms can become intensified so that denials, explanations and the habit of blaming others for one's own mistakes become urgently expressed. Behavioural changes — such as increased irritability, the inability to communicate or get on with colleagues, intense secrecy, failure to pass on office papers, a tendency to put others down or fail to listen to them, talking round a subject or using phrases such as "Sorry, I've no time to deal with you", lack of participation, etc — can best be detected by those working closest to an individual, such as an immediate superior. Changes such as poor work performance, decreased productivity, a high level of absenteeism, a high staff turnover, increased smoking, eating or drinking, physical indicators such as blood pressure, etc also point to a stress problem.

The causes of stress at work are being investigated and some events or situations clearly show up as major stress factors. Notwithstanding that stress can be caused by personal circumstances, eg difficult marriage, illness at home, etc, many stressors relate directly to work and to the employer's failure to take stress into account in running a company or business. Stress may be the result of one particular event or the result of a continuing situation, the latter being arguably more dangerous in its debilitating effect. Typical stressors are:
- changes in the job, eg in policy, procedures or nature
- increases in hours or workload (including promotion)
- reorganisation
- demotion, whether actual or in relation to others
- too little time to do the job
- decisions affecting the employee made without consultation or knowledge
- lack of confidence in management
- uncertainty over standards expected
- uncertainty over responsibilities
- new superior
- conflict with other employees, departments, etc left to work themselves out
- criticism of jobs badly done being the only feedback from management.

As can be seen, these problems are ones which employers are well able to solve themselves and thus reduce the chances of losing employees, time or money through stress.

Action on Stress

There are two distinct approaches that management can take to deal with stress. They can concentrate on the employees themselves and either help them to cope with stress when it arises or help them to equip themselves with skills and techniques in order to withstand stress successfully when it occurs. The other approach, more long term and arguably more effective, involves management tailoring its own organisation to reduce stresses and strains from the start. From the list of stressors above, two factors run through the separate items — firstly the effect of surprise on employees and secondly placing them in new and unfamiliar environments. A company which adopts a clear policy on stress can go some way towards reducing the surprise and environmental factors.

The sort of steps that can be taken by employers to reduce stress at work are:
- the provision of good and clear communications between workers and management, thus reducing a number of the problems set out above
- the control and review of the physical environment including factors such as noise and dust levels, cleanliness, etc
- maintenance of the organisation in a form conducive to ease of communication and lack of red tape
- encouraging participation
- providing effective working structures which ensure employees do not have too much (or too little) work to do
- giving consideration to using competent counselling, referral services, self-help groups, etc.

Those dealing with industrial relations or health and safety at work will find that a number of the measures suggested strike a familiar chord. This is because good industrial relations practices, health and safety procedures and stress management are all inter-related and should not be considered in isolation. Success in one area will, however, go some way towards ensuring success in others.

A word of warning to employers who do decide to deal effectively with employees with stress-related problems — do not forget the individual's behaviour can, in itself, have a bad effect on colleagues, and dealing with the former at the expense of the latter can only make the problem worse by putting others under unnecessary stress. An effective programme must also consider the problems that arise over "pet" employees allowed too much leeway.

An organisation founded to give information on "all aspects of stress in modern society and to assist in reducing harmful stress levels" exists. Employers who are concerned with the problems of stress can contact the Stress Syndrome Foundation at Cedar House, Yalding, Kent ME18 6JD.

Mental Illness

If the employee does "go over the edge" or has a past history of mental ill-health, what is the employer's position? The first important step employers must take is to distinguish between employees who suffer mental illness whilst working and those who were employed in the knowledge that there was, or still is, mental ill-health. The approach that employers should take with each is different. With the former, the employer is best advised to treat the employee as any other who is absent from work due to sickness or who is failing to work to set standards due to incapability. With the latter, however, the employer must take more care and give more allowances to such an employee as the position was known when the employee was recruited. In *W Young & Sons v Smeaton* EAT 113/82, a mentally retarded employee was dismissed from his job as a tractorman after a series of incidents. The dismissal was unfair because the employer had known he was retarded on recruitment and the employee had worked for the previous 11 years during which time he was given no more than informal warnings for similar incidents.

One way employers try to deal with mental ill-health is to avoid it altogether by screening out sufferers on recruitment. An employee who stated on his application form that he had no history of mental illness was fairly dismissed when it was discovered that he had lied (*OBrien v Prudential Assurance Co* [1979] IRLR 140). An employee may also be dismissed if his appointment is subject to a satisfactory medical report and that report discloses mental illness.

Incapacity Dismissals Generally

There are two ways in which sickness, mental or physical, can be dealt with by the employer. If the employee continues working but the standard of work performance is poor, the employer can institute disciplinary procedures with the ultimate sanction of dismissal if the employee fails to improve after oral and written warnings (always remembering that the employer has an obligation to ensure that it is the employee's incapacity that is to blame, and not the employer's failing to train, instruct, etc).

The other way in which to deal with sickness is where the employee is off work or has a bad absenteeism record due to ill-health. In the case of a lengthy absence, the EAT stated, in *East Lindsey District Council v Daubney* [1977] IRLR 181, that before an employee is dismissed "it is necessary that he should be consulted and the matter discussed with him, and that in one way or another, steps should be taken by the employer to discover the true medical position". Each case will nevertheless fall to be decided on the particular circumstances and whether or not the employer could have been expected to await the employee's return any longer. In the case of frequent absences, the dual obligation of investigation and consultation still applies, albeit in a slightly different form. It was held in *International Sports Co Ltd v Thomson* [1980] IRLR 340 that the employer must subject the attendance record and absence reasons to a fair review and give the employee appropriate warnings and the chance to explain.

Mental Illness in Particular

If an employee is dismissed by reason of mental health and claims unfair dismissal, the tribunal is going to ask a number of questions which the employer must answer satisfactorily in order to ensure that the dismissal is not found unfair. The tribunal will ask if the employer already knew of the mental illness when the employee was taken on — as stated above, the approach to such an employee will be different and the employer will be expected to act more leniently. The tribunal will want to see that the general considerations of investigation and consultation have been adopted (see below).

In *Ross Foods Ltd v Lamb* EAT 833/77 a mentally retarded employee, dismissed after warnings about the standard of his work, was held to have been unfairly dismissed because the employer had failed to talk to the Rehabilitation Officer who had helped in the past and was willing to do so again. However, the tribunal will have some sympathy where the employee's health jeopardises the business or the health and safety of colleagues and/or the public.

Investigation and Consultation

Investigation into the mental health of an employee can be difficult. An employee whose behaviour has become erratic is unlikely to react well to the employer's suggestion that a psychiatrist should be consulted. However, some investigation should be carried out or attempted. In the case of *Mackay v River Borra Board* COIT F116/220 a water bailiff was reported to be "away with the fairies" when he smashed up a suspected poacher's fishing tackle. A further report of bizarre behaviour caused the employers to call the man's father (a doctor) to take him home. This was followed by a letter of dismissal because of the employee's "nervous breakdown". The dismissal was unfair because the employers made no attempt to discover the true medical position.

Consultation with the employee is usually an important step and lack of consultation will often lead to a finding of unfair dismissal. However, if the employer can show that consultation with the employee would have made no difference to the decision to dismiss, lack of consultation will not be fatal to the employer's defence. In *Taylorplan Catering (Scotland) Ltd v McInnally* [1980] IRLR 53, the head barman in a workmen's camp at Sullam Voe, Shetland was dismissed when he developed a depressive illness in reaction to the stress of living and working in unusual environmental conditions. In finding the dismissal fair the EAT said:

> "although a measure of prior consultation is expected, it is for a specific purpose (ie so the situation can be weighed up, balancing the employer's need for the work to be done against the employee's need for time to recover his health). If it is clear that that purpose cannot be achieved, the need for a consultation which will in any view be pointless diminishes if indeed it does not disappear".

Drink and Drugs at Work

Drinking on the premises and drug-taking whether at work or elsewhere, are commonly considered to be gross misconduct offences meriting summary dismissal. Many employers will have specific company rules indicating that such misconduct will be treated very seriously. However, it can be dangerous to rely upon such rules to justify dismissal without consideration of other factors, such as the possibility that the employee may be addicted, in which case warnings not to indulge would be useless and dismissal for misconduct probably unfair.

Identifying the Problem

Drink problems with employees will probably fall into one of two categories: a one-off or even regular over-indulgence in alcohol which results in rowdy or possibly even dangerous behaviour but which is not related to an addiction to alcohol, or a deep-seated alcoholic problem which will probably come to light through other "misconduct", such as absenteeism or lateness, and which may not even be linked to drinking in its early stages. The problem for employers is to distinguish between the two: the former type of behaviour is fairly obviously a conduct problem which will merit disciplinary action or dismissal, while the latter should be seen as one of capability and ill-health, which requires different handling. This is the message which tribunals have made clear in various decisions: where an over-indulgence in alcohol affects employees' performance, employers must investigate to determine whether they are suffering from alcoholism or related illnesses, to determine how the problem should be handled.

Drinking as an Illness

The dangers of treating a capability drink problem as one of conduct can be seen in *Strathclyde Regional Council v Syme* (unreported). Mr Syme was a long-serving school janitor who had manic-depressive symptoms which were known to his employers. He also drank at work, which was treated as misconduct by the Council, finally resulting in a pressured resignation after a written warning. His (constructive) dismissal was found to be unfair at tribunal on the basis that a reasonable employer would have attempted to gain independent medical advice before dismissal. Mr Syme's problem, in their view, should have been handled differently:

"Employers nowadays are expected to be cautious in visiting such conduct with disciplinary sanctions unless or until they have no reasonable alternative in the way of trying to discover an underlying cause for the problem or of making efforts to get the individual to have it resolved".

However, in the event of establishing that drinking at work is related to personal problems, alcoholism or some other personal incapacity, employers need not necessarily endure the problem indefinitely if the employees will not help themselves.

In *Barber v Tricentrol Cars (Leeds) Ltd* (unreported) a garage electrician became an alcoholic after suffering an accident at work. His employers treated him sympathetically over a long period, giving him financial help and time off to try a cure for his drink problems. After a time, however, there was still no improvement in Mr Barber's condition and his work steadily deteriorated. He was finally dismissed after leaving his job during working hours to drink outside in a car. Although this decision was taken rather suddenly and without following proper procedures, it was still found to be a fair dismissal. The tribunal realised that the employers had reached a point where they could no longer tolerate his drunkenness. In the light of their earlier patience it was considered reasonable for them not to be prepared to put up with his behaviour.

The "golden rules" for handling a drink problem which is characterised, after investigation, as being related to personal problems or alcoholism, are as follows:

– consider the problem as an illness rather than one of misconduct
– seek independent medical advice to determine whether the employee's addiction can be treated successfully
– encourage the employee to seek help from medical experts or voluntary organisations such as Alcoholics Anonymous
– consider giving extended leave to enable the employee to undergo treatment
– investigate possible work-related causes, such as over-promotion, excessive work-load, etc and attempt to ease pressure (this may mean a transfer or demotion to less responsible work, which is a sensible alternative to dismissal and is unlikely to lead to problems of constructive dismissal)
– view the drink problem as a mitigating factor in relation to other disciplinary offences, such as poor time-keeping or lateness.

Drinking as Misconduct

There will, of course, be occasions when drunkenness at work is not related to any problems of alcoholism or illness. The seriousness of this type of misconduct and the appropriate disciplinary action will depend upon various factors: the type of work performed by the employee (if it involves driving or operating machinery the consequences of being drunk could be disastrous); the employee's seniority (not a very good advert for the company if a manager attends a business meeting in a state of intoxication!); the circumstances surrounding the incident (less serious if the employee is slightly tipsy after a birthday drink or office party); and the employer's attitude, reflected in company rules, towards such behaviour.

In *Fogarty v Austin Morris* (unreported) it was considered reasonable for a furnace operator to be dismissed for one incident of drunkenness after 21 years' service, because the consequences of such a slip-up were so grave. In such types of work it will usually be made clear through disciplinary rules that drinking at work (and possibly even possession of alcohol) is considered a serious offence meriting summary dismissal. It is important that employers ensure that such rules are well known to all employees, otherwise any subsequent dismissals may well be unfair.

In *W Brooks & Son v Skinner* [1984] IRLR 379 the employers introduced a rule that failure to work due to drunkenness after a Christmas party would lead to summary dismissal. Mr Skinner, a night storeman, became intoxicated at the party and had to be sent home. On returning to work the following day he was dismissed. At the tribunal it became apparent that the employers had not made sufficient effort to communicate the new ruling to employees, although it had been agreed with their union. Mr Skinner was truly unaware that the consequence of his misconduct would be dismissal; he believed it would mean loss of pay as had happened on previous occasions.

It is important, as with any disciplinary sanction, to apply rules about drinking consistently to all employees who are guilty of the same misconduct, otherwise it will not be reasonable to rely upon the rule to uphold a certain standard of conduct which is not observed across the board. In *Diary Produce Packers Ltd v Beverstock* [1981] IRLR 265, a delivery man was dismissed after being drunk in working hours. At the tribunal he produced evidence to the effect that three other employees who had been drunk at work or arrived smelling of drink had been warned and not dismissed. Mr Beverstock's dismissal was found unfair on the grounds that his employers had acted unreasonably in treating him differently from other employees committing the same offence.

Having clear-cut rules about drinking at work or arriving under the influence of drink does not absolve the employer from the need to investigate the circumstances fully. It is crucial to get first-hand evidence from all employees, supervisors, etc who witness the drunken employee but it is not necessary to have cast-iron medical proof that he or she was actually drunk. If it is reasonably apparent to others that the employee is intoxicated it will not be necessary to call for a blood sample! However, employers should be aware that some medical conditions, such as diabetic comas and epilepsy, mimic the effects of alcohol, as do certain prescribed drugs.

Taking Drugs at Work

It may well be that an employee who appears to be under the influence of alcohol is actually intoxicated by drugs, whether prescribed or not. This sort of misconduct is less familiar to employers and will generally be regarded even more seriously because of the illegality of the substances involved. Employees who take or sell controlled drugs, whether at work or off-duty, will be committing a criminal offence and this lends a different element to dealing with such incidents.

Two employees who were caught smoking cannabis at work were fairly dismissed, not only because of their advanced state of intoxication when working with hazardous chemicals but also because of the illegality of their actions (*Anderson and Chambers v Oak Motor Works Ltd* unreported).

Offences Outside Work

With regard to drugs offences outside work, the position is similar to that of employees charged with any criminal offence. If the offence has a bearing upon the employment, it is certainly reasonable for employers to take it into account and possibly dismiss the employee. Tribunals are sympathetic to the view that a drugs conviction, for possession or trafficking, can be a major blow to an employer's reputation and a genuine cause for concern if young people or children could be influenced by the employee concerned. In *Tabor v Mid-Glamorgan County Council* (unreported), a teacher who did not use cannabis but was convicted of cultivating it for others was fairly dismissed on the basis that he had daily contact with teenagers who might be influenced by his open views that the drug should be legalised. Another teacher, however, was unfairly dismissed after his conviction for possession of cannabis. It was established at tribunal that he had little contact with children, he disapproved of drug use and had been convicted on the basis of an isolated incident which had little bearing on his exemplary conduct and reputation (*Norfolk County Council v Bernard* [1979] IRLR 229).

The generally adverse view of drugs offences amongst the general public is also a factor which can be taken into account. In *Gunn v British Waterways Board* (unreported) a lock-keeper was fairly dismissed after a series of drug convictions which had no connection with his employment. The crucial factor taken into account was the effect these convictions could have upon the employers' reputation when they were named in a newspaper report. The Board were justified in their concern about adverse public opinion and comments from other employees and in taking these into account when making their decision to dismiss.

Dealing with Death

Unlike our Victorian predecessors, we are less familiar with coping with the experience of death whether it be amongst our family, friends or associates. It is an occurrence that brings many repercussions and not least amongst the problems is the fact that personnel managers are expected to cope with the situation in a manner befitting a company's representative. After all, no one else in the company is better fitted to pay respects to the employee's family, ensure that the administrative procedures in the company are carried out and be aware of any legal requirements.

Death at Work

The implications for the personnel manager of an employee's death will greatly depend on where it happens and in what circumstances it occurs.

If an employee dies at work it may be necessary to consider whether or not the matter should be reported to the Health and Safety Executive (HSE) or other enforcing authority. If the death is the result of an accident or dangerous occurrence an immediate phone call should be made to the HSE or environmental health officer. This applies even where the accident was not notifiable under the regulations when it originally occurred. Additionally, a written report of the accident must be sent to the HSE or other authority within seven days.

Obviously, even if the death is not connected with an accident or dangerous occurrence, it may be sensible to report it because it is the coroner's usual practice to see if the HSE or local authority know about it. This keeps the matter all square. In one case the HSE investigated the death of a workman who drowned whilst swimming in a pool after eating and drinking a substantial lunch. On the face of it there was no connection at all with a workplace accident; the accident did not even occur at the place of work.

Unfortunately, in some industries, death occurring at work by violent means is not unknown. Here the police should be involved at the earliest opportunity and the HSE or other authority notified as above. In all circumstances an ambulance should be called and relatives contacted to explain that the employee has been taken ill at work and has been transported to a named hospital. Perhaps the offer of transport to hospital would be a kind suggestion. Many personnel managers would see their role as providing support to the employee's relatives and would wish to accompany the relatives to the hospital but this depends on the strength of the welfare role adopted by the personnel manager and the time that is available.

Personnel managers should not forget that a sudden or violent death in the workplace will leave colleagues distressed and disorientated. Someone must take charge and deal sympathetically with the situation. Some employees might have to be sent home although most will probably prefer to stay and seek reassurance of the workgroup.

Death at Home

If the employee dies away from work the personnel manager's role is largely reactive, ie setting into motion the necessary administrative arrangements and responding to the needs of the employee's relatives. In circumstances where the employee has had an illness leading to the death, links may have already been created with the family by regular welfare visits. It is quite possible that the personnel manager would want to offer practical assistance in making funeral arrangements or contacting a solicitor to handle probate or providing support to a relative tackling a personal application for probate, etc.

Where an employee has no relatives or friends, the employer has no legal responsibility to arrange for burial. This obligation quite properly resides with the local authority and used to be known as a "pauper's burial". Local authorities are required by law to arrange matters at local expense. If any monies are owed by the company to the deceased they can be used to defray these costs.

Administrative Arrangements

The normal processing chain to discharge the employee from the payroll will have to be activated by the personnel manager. Payments will include pay earned to date (or until the end of the pay period) and pay in lieu of any accrued holiday entitlement. Outstanding loans or advances of salary can be deducted from monies owing provided written permission was granted by the deceased; otherwise the loan will be a debt to settle later by the executor or personal representative of the deceased.

One question frequently asked is about statutory notice pay. There would appear to be no requirement in law to make payments in lieu because the contract has been frustrated, technically ended by operation of law. However, many employers, realising the difficulties facing the family in gaining access to money assets from banks, etc, do pay a sum equivalent to pay in lieu of notice to help out.

There would appear to be no problems paying over these sums to a spouse, relative or executive of the deceased's estate, provided they sign to the effect that they have received the monies. It is also a good idea to confirm the transaction in writing.

A glance at the PAYE booklet will explain what the employer should do with the P45 in these situations. All three parts should be sent immediately to the appropriate tax office.

The necessary forms should be completed to start recovery of death in service benefits for the named beneficiary, or the trustees consulted to decide to whom the payments should be made. Similarly, the process should be triggered to organise any spouse's pension, etc, which may be payable.

It may also be necessary to terminate or adjust other company benefits such as mortgages, health insurance, etc. It is a good idea to become familiar with the rules of such schemes. Incidentally, there is an interesting aspect to rules affecting company benefits, especially death in service benefits. An employee who has been dismissed and paid in lieu of notice (without signing an acceptance of the monies in "full and final settlement of any claim that could arise from the termination of employment") could die during the notice period and the relatives would be able to sue for the death benefit that they have lost. Clearly, the pay in lieu of notice would not discharge the loss arising from the breach of contract (ie not allowing the notice to be worked). If the rules of the scheme say that cover ends upon the termination of employment, the employer may have to pay these sums without recompense from the insurer.

Recovering Property, etc

The employer will also wish to recover company property such as keys, clothing, equipment, identification badges, even, perhaps, the company car (which is usually worth its weight in gold to the family at a time like this). Given the sensitivity of the occasion it might be better to soft pedal or speak to a member of the family who is not too emotionally involved or to the Executor to remind him or her tactfully and to agree on a suitable date for recovery of the property.

Other considerations include:
– organising a collection
– writing an obituary for in-company and/or trade journals
– informing other interested parties who might have worked with the deceased in the past
– organising flowers or wreaths to be sent to the funeral, providing this is acceptable to the family.

The Law

Needless to say, the Parliamentary draftsman has been at work drafting rights given to employees' personal representatives in the event of em-

182

ployees dying in service. In particular, the following areas are quite comprehensively covered by Schedule 12 of the Employment Protection (Consolidation) Act 1978.

Redundancy payments: where notice has been given to an employee who dies during the notice period (whether or not pay in lieu of notice was given) the redundancy payment provision will apply as if the contract ended on the date of the employee's death.

Similarly, the calculation of the "relevant date" (ie when statutory notice is added on to work out the period of continuous employment) will require the date to be brought forward to the date of death.

Offers of re-engagement: where an employee dies without accepting or refusing the offer of re-engagement and the offer has not been withdrawn, a redundancy payment need not be paid if it would have been unreasonable for the employee to have refused the offer.

Trial periods: where the employee dies during a trial period (ie in a new job offered as suitable alternative employment in a redundancy situation) without having terminated or given notice to terminate the contract, the employee's relatives will not be entitled to a redundancy payment unless it would have been reasonable for the employee to have terminated the contract.

Where an employee has given notice to terminate the contract during a trial period, the notice will expire on the date of the employee's death.

Employee's counter-notice: where an employee gives counter-notice to the employer whilst under notice of redundancy, the employer has the option to refuse and say that no redundancy pay will be given. The employee will formally be asked in writing to withdraw the counter-notice. If the employee dies, however, the Parliamentary draftsman really goes to town!

"25 (1) Where in the circumstances specified in paragraphs (a) and (b) of subsection (1) of section 85 [of the EP(C)A] the employee dies before the notice given by him under paragraph (b) of that subsection is due to expire and before the employer has given him notice under subsection (3) of that section, subsection (4) of that section shall apply as if the employer had given him such notice and he had not complied with it."

In simple language, the employee is treated as having left in defiance of the employer's wishes. The employee's relatives are therefore only entitled to as much redundancy pay as an industrial tribunal feels is just and equitable. The tribunal must take into account the reasons why the employee sought to leave employment and the reasons the employer needed the employee to continue.

Lay-off or short time redundancy claim: where the employee dies, having given notice of intention to claim a redundancy payment because of lay-off or short time, there may be an entitlement to redundancy pay.

In all these circumstances the personal representative of the deceased employee can bring a claim to an industrial tribunal, which can order payment of the whole or part of the redundancy payment.

Other Legal Provisions

Schedule 11 also allows other individual rights to be pursued by the deceased employee's personal representative, ie:
- right to itemised pay statement
- written statement of reasons for dismissal
- guarantee payment
- rights involving suspension from work on medical grounds
- complaints regarding trade union membership, activities, and time off work rights
- maternity rights
- unfair dismissal
- redundancy payments and insolvency rights.

Importantly, the Act allows the deceased employee's personal representative to start tribunal actions or to continue with those already started. Where there is no personal representative the industrial tribunal has powers to appoint such a person, being either:
(a) a person authorised by the deceased to act on his or her behalf or
(b) the widower, widow, child, father, mother, brother, or sister.

Similar provisions can be found in the legislation relating to statutory sick pay so that payments can be claimed.

Observing the Proprieties

Companies commonly send someone to represent them at the funeral of an employee if the family have no objection. It is sensible to try to make this a member of the management team who knew the employee well. Anyone who attends on such an occasion should wear dark clothing. There is bound to be adverse comment about light grey suits or bright red jumpers! It is also useful to find out the customs involved in non-Christian burials before attendance. Flowers are also frequently sent or a donation made to a charity if this is the family's wish. Of course, a letter of condolence (which is almost a forgotten art form) is usually much appreciated.

Personnel managers should remember that grieving families do not want to hear about the wonderful death in service benefits that the company gives. They do not view their loss in money terms. They would rather hear of the value the company placed on the deceased for the work he or she carried out.

7 PARTICULAR EMPLOYMENTS

In addition to the general problem areas faced by most organisations, particular categories of employees can bring their own difficulties. In this chapter we look at such groups as temporary, casual and agency workers, homeworkers, apprentices, probationary employees, directors, drivers, sales representatives and disabled workers. We begin by reviewing the problems that arise in distinguishing between employees and independent contractors.

Employee or Independent Contractor

Whether a person is an employee or is self-employed has very important ramifications in the field of employment law. The main advantage to an employer of a contract with an independent contractor is that the statutory rights under the Employment Protection (Consolidation) Act 1978 do not apply to someone who is self-employed and NI contributions do not have to be paid by the employer. Thoughts of excluding liability for unfair dismissal, redundancy payments, maternity rights, etc have made an increasing number of employers look at the possibility of hiring staff on a self-employed basis.

A Question of Law

It is important to bear in mind that it is a matter of law whether the contract is a contract of employment or one with an independent contractor; the mere fact that an employer wants to hire someone as an independent contractor does not, without more, make the contract under which he or she is hired a contract for services.

The Control Test

Until recently a contract of employment was universally known as a contract of service (as distinct from a contract with an independent contractor — a contract for services). The parties to a contract of service were the master and servant. It is not surprising, therefore, that the distinction between the two types of contract rested on the degree of control which the employer had over the performance of the contract.

Mackenna J in *Ready Mix Concrete v Minister of Pensions* (1968) 1 AER 433 said:

"Control includes the power of deciding the thing to be done, the way in which it shall be done, the means employed in doing it, the time when and the place where it shall be done. All these aspects of control must be considered in deciding whether the right exists in sufficient degree to make one party the master and the other his servant".

Although the control test has, to some extent, been superseded, the degree of control exercised by the employer is still an important factor in determining the status of the parties and, in many cases, it will be unnecessary to look any further than the degree of control exercised by the employer to see that a contract is clearly one of employment.

The degree of control exercised over the work done under the contract will usually clearly distinguish an unskilled person who is working as an employee and one who is an independent contractor. It is much more difficult, however, to distinguish between an employer and a self-employed person where the job is skilled or more technically biased. The employee's skill and technical expertise mean that the employer cannot have any great degree of control over *how* the work is carried out. The inability of the control test to provide a clear solution to the question of the status of the parties where the work was more skilled meant that a new test had to be devised.

Integration Test

In *Stevenson, Jordan and Harrison Ltd v MacDonald and Evans* (1952) 1 Times Law Reports 101, Denning LJ (as he was then) suggested that the distinction between a contract of service and a contract for services was that:

". . . under a contract of service, a man is employed as part of the business, and his work is done as an integral part of the business; whereas, under a contract for services, his work, although done for the business, is not integrated into it but is only accessory to it".

By this test, it was thought, very marginal cases could be distinguished. The examples put forward by Denning LJ were the cases of a ship's master, a chauffeur and a newspaper reporter, who were all employees, as compared with a ship's pilot, a taxi-driver and a newspaper contributor who were all employed under contracts for services.

The test also has the advantage that a contract under which the contractor has employed and self-employed functions may be analysed. In this case an employee had written a book which contained some material from manuals which he had written for clients of the company and some material from lectures which he had given to universities.

It was held that he was an employee so far as the writing of the manuals was concerned, since their preparation was a part of his job. The lectures to the universities were in a different category; however helpful it might have been to the company for him to give those lectures (by the way of advertising and promoting his status) they were, nonetheless, only accessory to the contractual part of his work. That the company paid expenses for him to give the lectures only showed that the work was helpful to the company and that they considered it beneficial themselves, but it did not make the lecturing a part of his employment.

The main drawback of the integration test is that it does not take into account the diverse nature of businesses. Some companies, for example, will hire a chauffeur as an employee whilst others, in exactly the same type of business, will use taxis or hire-cars. To say that in the former case the chauffeur is an employee because his or her function is a part of the business, and that in the latter the drivers are self-employed, is obviously a very artifical distinction.

The Multiple Test

The difficulties inherent in both the control and the integration tests led the courts to look for further methods of distinguishing between employees and independent contractors on an individual basis. In the *Ready Mix Concrete* case (above) Mackenna J held that all the terms of the contract should be looked at and the court must then decide on the type of contract before them by balancing those factors which tend to show that the contract is one of employment against those tending to show that the person is self-employed.

This test does not exclude questions of control and integration which still remain important considerations in determining the type of contract. But it does mean that these are only two of the many matters which are to be taken into account in determining the status of the parties.

The other matters which the courts and tribunals take into account are outlined below.

Ownership of Equipment

A contract under which people doing the work supply their own capital equipment, or pay their own business overheads in connection with the services which they are providing, is likely to be a contract for services.

In the *Ready Mix* case the "employee" bought a concrete mixing lorry from an associated company of Ready Mix under a hire-purchase agreement. The fact that this expensive piece of equipment was supplied by him was strong evidence that the contract was one for services. In a case where the cost of the capital equipment is lower, the inference of self-employment will not be so great and, indeed, an artisan employee would normally be expected to supply the tools of his trade. Nonetheless, if a company wants to hire people as independent contractors, rather than as employees, consideration might well be given to a provision in the contract that they provide their own capital equipment. The more enterprising might even consider hiring the necessary equipment to the contractor for the contract period.

Incidental Expenses

A similar inference of self-employment occurs where contractors have to pay expenses incidental to the carrying out of their functions under the contract. In *Beloff v Pressdram Ltd* (1973) 1 AER 241, one of the factors in favour of a contract with a journalist being one of employment was the fact that the employers provided her with an office and secretarial assistance. This might be allowed for either by hiring the necessary facilities to the contractor or, in a case such as *Beloff*, by contracting for the work to be presented untyped (although obviously the greater the ancillary organisation which the contractor needs and supplies in performance of the contract, the more likely it is that he or she is working independently).

Personal Obligation

A contract of employment is a personal contract placing an obligation on a particular person to carry out the work. If contractors can, at their option, delegate the duties under the contract, the contract is not one of employment. The most obvious way of using this fact to create a contract for services is for the "employee" to become a limited company, since a company, although it has a "corporate personality" at law, cannot be an individual in the sense required by an employment contract.

A contract with a partnership would not lead to quite such a clear-cut situation since the partners themselves are individuals and it is clearly established that there can be contracts of employment which are entered into by husbands and wives together. These facts, together with the increasing incidence of job-sharing, make it unlikely that the mere fact that one of the contractual parties is a partnership will prevent the contract from being one of employment.

Exclusive Service

The personal nature of the contract of service also places on employees an obligation to work only on their employers' behalf. Thus, a contract under which the "employee" is free to work for other employers is likely to be a contract for services. This is best exemplified by the case of a sales representative who sells the employer's products as only one of a range of goods (see also *Massey v Crown Life Insurance* [1978] IRLR 31 where the contract was held to be one for services, amongst other reasons, because the contractor, an insurance agent, could, and did, take work from other companies).

Hours of Work

Where the hours of work are fixed by the contract, it is an indication that the contract is one of employment. The hours of employment may well not be fixed in one of two ways, both of which lead to the inference that the contract is one for services. In the normal case of independent contractors, they will be hired to do a particular job and, although the date by which it must be completed will usually be set, the actual times at which the work must be done are less likely to be laid down by the contract.

The second type of case in which unfixed hours show that the contract is one for services is where the contractors are not obliged to work at particular times if they do not wish to do so.

The need for definite hours in a contract of employment might also stem from the personal obligations arising out of such a contract. Employees must give exclusive service to their employer during the times at which they are contracted to work. If the times of employment are not specifically limited by the contract itself the employee might be seen as having a total obligation to serve the employer at *all* times without any adequate recompense for such service. A contract of this type would be disallowed by the courts as against public policy; the contract may be one of service, but it cannot be one of servitude (which would be the effect of such an obligation).

Payment

The method of payment is important. An employee will usually be paid a wage or a salary. An independent contractor is much more likely to be paid for the work which has actually been done.

The type of payment is far from conclusive since many employees are paid by results either on a commission basis or on piece work. Additional matters such as the time between payments are also taken into account; an independent contractor is more likely to be paid on completion of the work whereas an employee is usually paid at regular, comparatively short, intervals.

Casual Employees

The question of employment status regularly arises where an employer has contracted for additional workers to supplement the regular workforce. One of the most common means of doing this is through the use of "casual" labour, individuals who have traditionally been treated as self-employed. Case law has tended to reinforce this view though each case will be dependent on its own particular circumstances. In the landmark case of *O'Kelly and others v Trusthouse Forte* [1983] IRLR 369 the lack of obligation on the employer to provide work and the lack of commitment on the employee to accept it, were the principal factors which denoted independent contractor status for "regular" casuals employed in a hotel. However, where the term "casual" has been applied merely as a label and other factors are consistent with a contract of employment, the person will be classed as an employee. Thus in *Tate v Leeds Polytechnic Student's Union* COIT 1473/151 a "casual" catering assistant who worked regularly every week under standard terms was held to be an employee.

Casual staff have always tended to be paid "out of the till" and left to take care of their own tax. However, employers should note that under Inland Revenue rules casual staff should be treated as employees for tax purposes. Where casual staff insist that they are to be treated as self-employed and paid without deductions, employers should always seek Inland Revenue approval, otherwise they themselves may risk being liable for the worker's unpaid tax.

Guidelines for Employers

It is much better for employers to try and check for themselves whether their casuals and homeworkers are better classed as employees or self-employed rather than to wait for a tribunal or the Inland Revenue to do so. The following checklist sets out some of the most important factors to consider.

Indicating a Contract of Service
– The work is under the employer's direction and control, by whatever means
– work is done alongside other employees
– equipment and materials are provided by the company
– standard weekly hours are worked
– the nature and price of the work are not negotiable
– the rate of pay is as per other employees
– tax and national insurance contributions are deducted by the employer

190

- other benefits are payable, particularly if dependent on past service, eg holiday pay
- the worker is covered by a disciplinary and/or grievance procedure
- there is a mutual obligation to provide and to do work.

Indicating a Contract for Services
- The quality and output of work are controlled by the worker
- the worker has the right to substitute others to do the work
- the worker employs his or her own employees
- there is investment of capital or risk of financial loss carried by the worker
- premises, tools and materials are provided by the worker
- hours of work are decided by the worker
- pay rates or price for work are fixed by the worker
- the contractor pays tax and national insurance contributions as a self-employed person
- there is no provision for notice to terminate the contract
- the worker is deemed to be in business on his or her own account
- the worker considers him or herself to be his or her own boss
- there is no obligation on either party to do or to provide work
- the worker is free to work for others and does so.

Other Factors
- The label on the contract is not conclusive
- the conduct of the parties can override the written contract
- the intentions of the parties can be the deciding factor in an ambiguous situation
- custom and practice in the industry may count
- all the factors of the relationship must be balanced.

Temporary Workers and the Law

Many companies use temporaries to supplement their regular workforce for a variety of reasons. Some are employed on short fixed term contracts, while others are taken on on a seasonal basis; yet another group includes those who are considered to be no more than casual labour. The rights and employment position of such workers can be difficult to identify, and the situation has been complicated still further by case law.

What is a "Temporary"?

The term "temporary worker" is one which is widely used, but what is meant by it can vary a great deal from company to company, and will depend largely on the reason for the employer taking on such a worker. Temporaries are often used to stand in for permanent employees who are absent due to illness or for those away on maternity leave, others may be seasonal workers taken on to cover peaks and troughs in the workload; more recently, business uncertainty caused by the recession has led to the increased use of temporaries in situations where permanent employment cannot be guaranteed.

As far as the law is concerned, however, while employers can apply the label "temporary" to whichever workers they choose, it will not affect the fact that the term is not recognised by the various Acts which regulate the rights of people at work.

Statutory and Contractual Rights

One of the perceived advantages of taking on temporary employees is that they may be offered less advantageous terms and conditions of employment than permanent staff. As far as purely contractual terms are concerned, eg holiday and occupational sick pay entitlement, this is largely the case, although employers must be wary of the equal pay implications of offering less beneficial terms to predominantly female temporary workers, compared with their permanent male counterparts. Also, in industries covered by a Wages Council, the minimum pay rate set down in the order must be offered.

Employment rights laid down by statute are a different matter, however. They depend on employees having accumulated a specified period of service and apply to all those who work under contracts for at least 16 hours a week, whether temporary or permanent. (Those who work for at least eight but less than 16 hours a week receive the equivalent rights once they have been continuously employed for five years or more.) For example, a temporary worker who has already been employed for a year is entitled to guaranteed pay, medical suspension pay, statutory minimum notice, a written statement of terms and conditions of employment and written reasons for dismissal.

However, some employers only take on temporaries for 12 weeks or less, the reason being that employees employed on that basis are entitled to very few statutory rights. First of all, temporaries employed under a fixed term contract for three months or less lose the right to receive guaranteed pay and medical suspension pay; those who have been engaged to perform a specific task for three months or less lose those two rights as well as the right to statutory minimum notice. (This only applies as long as the employee does not already have three months' continuous service.) In addition, temporaries employed on contracts for three months or less are excluded from receiving SSP, unless the gap between successive contracts is less than eight weeks. Many employers also believe that written statements of terms and conditions of employment only have to be given to employees with 13 weeks' service or more. However, the law actually requires such statements to be given *not later than* the 13th week of service. In any case it is always advisable to set down in writing the terms and conditions of someone's employment. It is particularly important to do so with temporary workers whose terms and conditions differ from those of permanent staff. If there is nothing in writing to confirm their ineligibility for certain contractual benefits, it may be an implied term of the contract that they are entitled to them.

Continuous Service

The rules on calculating continuous service are very complicated and, as far as temporary workers are concerned, there are some particularly important points to bear in mind. First of all, a series of contracts with no gaps in between (even for contracts lasting only a few weeks or months) are all added together to calculate the total period of continuous service. Therefore, even if each contract is for three months or less, as long as they all run consecutively, the period of continuous employment will be increasing with each contract. This is the case even if the work done under each contract is different or if the contracts are each for a fixed term; all that matters is that the contracts are with the same or an associated employer.

In many cases the continuity of employment of temporaries is broken when a contract is terminated and not renewed immediately. However, if a pattern begins to develop whereby the employee only works, say, during the peak workloads and has no contract in between when the work drops off, a period of continuous service may still be accruing. The rules on continuous service provide that, if there is no contract because of a "temporary cessation of work", service will be continuous and the gap between the two (or more) contracts will also count.

The full implications of this rule can be seen from a case which was decided in the House of Lords —*Ford v Warwickshire County Council* [1983] IRLR 126. It was held that where there is a succession of contracts with intervals between them, continuity is not broken unless and until, looking back from the last date of expiry of a contract, there is a gap which cannot be described as temporary. (A gap which is due to something other than a cessation of work might also break continuity.) The House of Lords emphasised that all such cases must be decided on their facts, but there are obvious implications for regular temporaries, particularly those who work on a seasonal basis. In fact the Lords suggested that seasonal workers would have continuous service if the gaps between contracts are short in relation to the length of the contracts themselves. Similarly, a gap in employment will not break continuity if by custom or implied arrangement the employer considers the employee as continuing in employment for all or any purposes. An informal agreement that the employee will report for work again in a few weeks' time may be enough to imply such an arrangement.

EC Draft Directive

Although United Kingdom legislation does not recognise the term "temporary worker" the European Commission has produced a draft directive, aimed at giving temporaries the same rights as permanent employees. For the purposes of the directive, a temporary worker is defined as someone who enters into a contract of employment or an employment relationship for the purpose of carrying out an assignment. A permanent worker is someone who enters into a contract of employment of indefinite duration with an employer. The draft directive's main proposals are to provide that: contracts must be for an indefinite period or must clearly state when the employment will end (fixed term contracts); the pay, terms and conditions of temporary workers should be comparable with those of permanent staff; temporaries are to be compensated if the contract is terminated prematurely; and the operation of temporary employment agencies is to be further regulated.

Agency Workers: Your Employees?

Earlier in this chapter we looked at the legal tests that a court or a tribunal will apply to determine whether or not a worker is an employee. From these tests it can be seen that most workers obtained from an employment agency, by the very nature of their jobs, will almost always be considered to be "employees". Obvious exceptions do begin to occur at the upper end of the staffing spectrum where, for instance, specialised technical knowledge is provided by agency workers. So, if they are considered to be employees, whose employees are they? Is it the agency who supplies and pays them or the client employer who sets them to work and supervises their efforts?

Whose Employees?

This question has important implications not only for employment rights but also for tax, national insurance, statutory sick pay, statutory maternity pay and health and safety at work.

Although employment agencies are required by law to deduct income tax and national insurance contributions *as though* they were the employer, this is not conclusive evidence that the workers are the employees of the agency — the day to day control is in other hands, ie the "client" employer. The tests to find out who the employer is are, once again, multi-factor depending entirely on the realities of the individual situation.

Employment Agencies Act 1973

The Act applies to both employment agencies and employment businesses (employment agencies supply workers for permanent and temporary placement with "client" employers; employment businesses supply the services of workers to client employers).

The Act defines "employment" to include both contracts for services (self-employed) and contracts of service (employees) but does not go on to define who is the employer of the worker, ie the client employer or the supplier of the labour. However, the Act does require the employment agency to supply workers with a written statement containing full details of their terms and conditions, including a statement specifying whether or not they are employed under a contract of service or as self-employed workers. The statement should include information about the kind of work which they may be supplied to do, minimum rates of pay and any expenses payable. This statement should be given when the workers commence and must be updated in writing to take account of agreed changes. A copy of the written statement must be kept at the agency's premises for inspection.

Additionally, Regulation 9 of the Conduct of Employment Agencies and Businesses Regulations Act 1976 requires the employment agency to inform clients of the employment status of the workers they are supplying to them.

These statements do not provide conclusive evidence of the status of the workers. To do so would allow agencies to contract out of the provision of employment rights contained in the Employment Protection (Consolidation) Act 1978 and this is specifically prevented by s.140 of that Act. Consequently, although these statements are persuasive evidence of the relationship, the reality of the situation must also be considered by any adjudicating court or tribunal.

Is There a Contract?

The "client" employer exercises a day to day supervisory function over agency workers but they receive payment from the agency. In such circumstances there is no "consideration" by the client employer to the worker; the payment for the services is made to the employment agency. Thus, it is argued, there can be no contract between the "client" employer and the worker.

In *Alderton v Richard Burgon Association Ltd* QBD (1974) CLR 318 the court looked at the relationship between the worker, agency and the client employer. The agency actually paid the worker (a driver) and deducted his tax and national insurance contributions. The agency had agreed with the client employer that the driver was not to be employed by the agency but by the "client" employer on terms agreed with the worker by the agency on the "client" employers behalf. The driver committed various criminal offences and the agency was cited as the driver's employer. The case against the agency was dismissed because the court gave great weight to the contract between the "client" employer and the agency. It was not possible on the evidence to show that the written contractual arrangements were a sham.

Another case that demonstrates the importance of the written statement as persuasive evidence of the relationship is *O'Sullivan v Thompson-Coon* QBD (1973) 14 KIR 108. The worker was supplied by an employment business to work on T-C's farm as a relief worker. The employment business fixed the employee's rate of pay and other terms and conditions of employment. Thompson-Coon could not select workers or dismiss them but could return a worker to the employment business if he or she proved unsatisfactory. The worker paid her own national insurance contributions. As a result of a tractor accident which injured the worker, T-C would have been criminally liable for failure to maintain a safe tractor if the worker was found to be his employee. In the event, the Divisional Court decided that he was not the employer. The following factors swayed their decision:

- T-C had no power of selection, suspension or dismissal
- the employment business fixed the worker's remuneration, which was paid gross
- the contract between T-C and the employment business to supply the worker said that the worker was not T-C's employee.

It is far more unlikely that workers supplied by employment businesses will be considered as "employees" of the "client" employer. The situation is rather more fluid in the case of employment agencies and employers would be well-advised to ask for the terms of business under which the agency operates, especially if the agency worker is to be used exclusively for a long period of time.

Working from Home

The use of homeworkers by employers, mainly to supplement existing "in-house" production and service, has become increasingly common in a number of industries. It is a method of working which appears attractive to the employer as it generally means that overhead costs such as power, light and heat can be reduced. Also, as such workers are often considered to be self-employed, the administrative burden of income tax and NI deductions can be removed. However, the true status of homeworkers (or outworkers as they are sometimes called) is fraught with complications and court rulings in the past have lent credence to the view that homeworkers should be treated for statutory and contractual rights on the same basis as ordinary employees working within the business.

The Contractual Position

Homeworkers are often considered by the employer to be self-employed, but the question of whether a worker is an employee, engaged under a contract of service, or a self-employed contractor is one which has regularly come before tribunals and higher courts.

In establishing the type of contract in force the general tests used by the courts over the years have included examining the degree of control which the employer exerts over the way in which the work is carried out; whether the worker is integrated with the organisation; and the multiple test involving looking at all the surrounding factors to determine their consistency with the contract's nature, eg the regularity of working, method of paying income tax and national insurance, etc. The tests for determining whether or not home-workers should be classed as employees have been applied regularly to outworkers to determine their legal status and qualification for statutory rights. The tendency in the leading cases is to find that homeworkers are employees.

Controlling the Work

The element of the employer's control over the way in which the worker performs his duties was a key factor in deciding the contractual question in *Gismatic Ltd v Neal* EAT 129/83. In this case Mrs Neal worked at home as a bookkeeper for a company, having her work delivered to her and dealing with it in accordance with the employer's instructions. One of the company's directors oversaw her work by examining the books every three months and preparing a trial balance. When he was not available to do this Mrs Neal had to submit the books to an accountant. Throughout the employment she was supplied with materials by the company and in the latter part of her contract she had had PAYE deductions made from her payments. The industrial tribunal and the EAT decided that she worked at all times under the direction and control of the company and was not in business on her own account.

In an earlier case, *D'ambrogio v Human Jacobs Ltd* [1978] IRLR 236, the element of control was considered in conjunction with the regularity of the work supplied to Mrs D'ambrogio, a clothing machinist. Here the employer provided the worker with a sewing machine and each day he took material to her to be made up and to collect finished garments. Mrs D'ambrogio had no freedom to delegate her duties and she worked a regular 40 hour week. She too was held to be an employee.

A Continuing Relationship

A factor which has been decisive in establishing the legal status of a home-worker is the development of a continuing relationship between the parties over a substantial period of time. As a general rule the longer the arrangement has existed the more likely it is that the agreement is a contract of employ-ment, although, of course, subject to other tests. In *Airfix Footwear Ltd v Cope* [1978] IRLR 396, a woman worked at home making heels for shoes which were manufactured by the company. She was supplied with tools, materials and patterns and worked according to the company's instructions on a five day week basis. She was paid on piece-work rates without the deduction of tax and national insurance. The arrangement lasted for a period of seven years. In determining the preliminary point as to whether she was an employee and so entitled to claim unfair dismissal, the EAT, upholding the industrial tribunal's decision, held that over such a period of time a continuing relationship had been established which was one of a continuing contract of employment.

Obligations of the Parties

The obligation on the employer to provide work and the obligation on the employee to undertake it have been significant factors in determining the question of legal status. As a rule, mutuality of obligation is a good indicator of a contract of employment. However, in the past the EAT has ruled that it is not absolutely conclusive. In fact the case of *Nethermere (St Neots) Ltd v Gardiner & Taverna* [1983] IRLR 103 demonstrated disagreement between the majority of the EAT and the dissenting party (the legal member) over this particular question. Here the employers were manufacturers of trousers and Mrs Gardiner and Mrs Taverna were two of a number of homeworkers used regularly by the company as machinists. They had work delivered to them daily, working between four and seven hours a day on company machines and being paid according to the amount of work completed. No deductions were made from their pay and each of them was at liberty to decide the amount of work they wanted to do. The industrial tribunal found as fact that there was no obligation on Nethermere to provide work, and no obligation on the women to accept it. However, they held that the women were not performing services in business on their own account. The majority of the EAT upheld this view. Though mutuality of obligation was a factor, the economic and business reality of the situation was consistent with contracts of service. This was based on the fact that there was no freedom for the women to negotiate rates of payment or the nature of the work, and though at liberty to choose how much work was done, in reality they could not refuse to perform work which they had already accepted. There was also no question of economic risk consistent with a contract for services. The dissenting member held that the lack of obligations on the parties was a clear indication that the relationships were contracts for services and the women were in business of their own account.

Statutory Rights of Homeworkers

As stated, a homeworker who is an employee will qualify for protection against unfair dismissal, redundancy payment rights, etc, assuming of course that he or she has the requisite continuous service and is not excluded in any other way. It is also important to note that the definition of "worker" in s.26 of the Wages Act 1986 specifically includes homeworkers, whether classed as employees or self-employed. This means that employers in industries specifically covered by wages orders are bound to pay minimum levels of remuneration to homeworkers.

The Factories Act 1961 also expressly recognises out-workers. S.133 requires employers who are engaged in certain designated industries to keep particular records of homeworkers and provide the information to the factory inspector as required and to the district council. The records must include the name and address of the workers concerned. The designated employments are specified in earlier regulations including the Factories (Home Work) Orders 1911, 1912 and 1913 and the Home Work (Lampshades) Order 1929. In addition, the general duty under the Health and Safety at Work, etc Act 1974 to take reasonable care for employees' health, safety and welfare automatically extends to homeworkers with employee status. It is therefore advisable for the employer to make sure that the environment in which the homeworker operates is hazard-free and that the worker is fully trained in the safe handling of goods in undertaking his or her duties. This will be especially important in particular processes involving the handling of dangerous substances such as adhesives and particular chemicals and also where dangerous machinery is used, eg guillotines, presses, etc.

Organisation of Homeworkers

It is often considered by critics of homeworking that one of the difficulties faced by outworkers is their isolation from the business. This has tended to make some trade unions adopt a hostile attitude to homeworking as it has been seen as a threat to the organisation of labour in the employer's business and as a means of undermining existing terms and conditions of employment. However, although trade unions still see homeworking as undesirable in general, more recently the trend has been for unions to attempt to influence the conditions of homeworkers by making increased efforts to extend collective agreements to include them. The TUC policy on homeworkers includes the recommendation that unions should insist that outworkers become "employees" of the company, that union membership amongst homeworkers should be encouraged and that details on working methods of homeworkers should be kept by trade unions, as well as including them in the terms of employment negotiated for other members of the workforce.

Homeworking Trends

Until relatively recently homeworking operated mainly in the areas of manufacturing, although it was also incorporated within certain service industries. Piece-rate working is common in the production-based processes and ensures that the employer retains some measure of control over output. However, the advent of the technological revolution has meant that homeworking is becoming increasingly common in the more complex information-based sector. Developments in computerisation and telecommunications have meant that data processing functions can now be home-based with some success and some companies have extended the use of homeworking to more senior staff, who can be used as consultants working from home but kept in day to day contact with the company's resources via computer terminals.

A particular study which looked at the advantages and disadvantages of new technology homeworking showed increased productivity as well as significant reduction in overhead costs and a more flexible approach to working hours. The latter was cited as particularly important in jobs where major demands were made on data processing facilities since work could be arranged to fall in with periods when spare capacity on computers was available. The disadvantages for employers mainly lay in the area of administration of homeworking and the problems of retaining an element of control of activities of the workers and the monitoring of output. This, however, tended to be confined to work of a more senior level where output could not readily be assessed through conventional payment by results schemes.

People on Probation

Putting new employees — or those who are promoted to new positions — on to probation or a trial period can be extremely effective from a managerial point of view even though probationary periods of themselves have little legal standing.

The purpose of such periods is to ensure that the performance of new employees is monitored on a regular basis, problems are resolved at an early stage and, crucially, that employees who are incapable of meeting the requirements of the job are dealt with promptly. There are, however, some legal aspects which should be noted if probationary periods are to be effective.

How Long and for Whom?

The length of a probationary period will obviously be determined by the levels of skill and responsibility demanded by the job to a large extent, but there are other factors to take into account. For example, employees' time-keeping and absence rates and general conduct will be as important as their job performance in some cases. As a general rule, and wherever possible, the period should end in sufficient time for "no-hope" employees to be dismissed with notice before they gain protection against being unfairly dismissed. In many cases six months will be a sensible period, providing a fair opportunity for employees to settle down and demonstrate their worth to the company and for the employer to make a realistic assessment of their overall performance.

There is no reason why all new employees should not serve probationary periods: the consequences of employing an incompetent filing clerk for too long can be just as damaging as the continued employment of an incompetent manager.

The Practicalities

To be effective a probationary period requires the active participation of the employee's supervisor. Rather than the employee merely being left to his or her own devices for several months, regular meetings should be held, during which overall performance can be reviewed, problems highlighted and training needs identified.

At the end of the specified period it is important to mark successful completion formally. If it is allowed to pass by on the assumption that employees know that they have met the required standard because no action has been taken against them, it is demoralising for new staff and can well engender the view that the company has no interest in or concern for its workforce or their level of performance.

If an employee has failed to match up to the necessary standard but has shown signs of improvement, there is no reason why the probationary period should not be extended, or a new period established; indeed, this is far more sensible than going to the lengths of dismissing the employee and recruiting a replacement who may turn out to be even worse than his or her predecessor! It is important, if the period is extended, that the employee is told very clearly of the deficiencies in performance and is given the date on which the extended probation will end. It is useful to confirm this in writing but this should be done in a constructive, positive way, rather than being seen as an inevitable run-up to dismissal.

Fixed Term Probation

It is important to give thought to the way that the contractual term governing probationary periods is worded. A statement that says:
"You will be employed on a probationary period of three months initially. Thereafter your employment may be terminated by one month's notice on either side"
could be construed as a fixed term contract for three months, meaning that, even if the employee proved to be irredeemably incompetent in the first week or two of employment, the employer would have to pay the employee to the end of the three month period or face the possibility of a claim for damages for breach of contract in the civil courts.

Such a claim was made in the County Court in the case of *Dalgleish v Kew House Farm Ltd* [1982] IRLR 251. Mr Dalgleish was employed as a maintenance fitter and his letter of appointment stated:

"Your position will be probationary for a period of three months at the end of which time your performance will be reviewed and if satisfactory you will be made permanent".

In the event, his employers decided he was not satisfactory after three weeks of employment and he was dismissed with one week's pay in lieu of notice.

He claimed that this was a breach of his contract: the employers, he argued, were not entitled to terminate his employment before the end of the probationary period. However, this claim was rejected by the County Court, whose decision was upheld by the Court of Appeal. The Court held that the words "at the end of which time your performance will be reviewed" did not constitute a promise — either express or implied — that the probationary status would continue in any event for three months: the employers were entitled to dismiss him at any time during that period.

However, to avoid the possibility of such a claim being made by an employee, it is wise to specify in the offer letter the notice terms that will apply during the probationary period.

Rights of Probationers

It must be recognised that probationary periods do not constitute a one-way street for employers: they do impose rights as well as responsibilities as the case of *Inner London Education Authority v Lloyd* [1981] IRLR 394 showed. Mr Lloyd was employed as a teacher on a two year probationary period, although neither the school in which he taught nor the education authority concerned were aware of his probationary status. As a consequence, when his ability was in doubt, his colleagues felt reluctant to offer the help and guidance which a probationer would normally have received.

The fact that he was on probation came to light after 17 months, and he was eventually dismissed because of his unsatisfactory probation. He claimed that his dismissal was unfair, and this claim was upheld by the tribunal and the EAT. The ILEA appealed to the Court of Appeal which, again, affirmed the decision of the lower courts. Although Mr Lloyd was apparently incapable of carrying out the job effectively, the tribunal was not perverse in taking into account the fact that, as a probationer, he was entitled to certain advice and guidance which he had not received. It was therefore unreasonable for ILEA to treat his incompetence as a sufficient reason for dismissal as he was not given the help he should have received.

Apprenticeship and the Law

An understanding of the nature and legal effects of the relationship between employers and apprentices is important, especially if employers find that the stresses and requirements of their business during a recessionary period are not allowed for in their written contracts of apprenticeship.

Contract: In Writing

The purpose of the apprenticeship contract is that the employer agrees to instruct and teach apprentices a trade, business or profession and to maintain them, whilst the apprentices in their turn agree to serve the employer and to learn from him. It should be clear in the contractual terms whether the intention is that work is the primary object, although some teaching will be provided, or that teaching is the primary purpose with an element of service included. Such contracts are for a fixed term that can vary in length but are usually for three or four years. The agreement must be in writing if the parties wish to obtain the advantages of apprenticeship. It must be said that these advantages are largely one-sided. The employer has only limited rights of dismissal and has to carry the cost of instruction and wages which in many industries are specified by national agreement. Bearing in mind that such terms are usually being offered to immature 16 year olds, with or without much sense of vocation, it is questionable who has the best bargain. Close attention to the drafting of the written terms can pay dividends. Even if the employer uses the written terms provided by employers' federations or local stationers, depending on the particular problems that may be faced, additional changes could be made to deal with new situations.

Terms Allow for Modern Conditions

The modern apprenticeship is often a mixture of instruction from the employer and external, supplemental college courses. The contract terms should state whether or not attendance at a college course is compulsory in the apprentice's own time or in company time. Other related terms, ie payment of course fees, examination fees, travel expenses, subsistence, etc, should be covered. The effect of failing such external courses should be spelt out, especially if no further chances to pass will be given. What effect on the contract will a poor college assessment or report have? Will there be an internal system of appraisal? Perhaps the contract should contain a clause allowing the termination of the contract if the appraisals are poor during, for instance, the first six months of employment, thus allowing potentially poor performers to be weeded out.

The Effect of Modern Legislation

Apprenticeship contracts usually specify payments to be made: sick pay and holiday entitlement; and minimum rates, etc. All the relevant headings required by the Employment Protection (Consolidation) Act 1978 must be covered in the manner required by the Act. Any national agreement that regulates the main terms of employment of the apprentice should be properly incorporated into the contract. All the rights given to employees under modern legislation also apply to apprentices — including maternity rights.

When the Apprenticeship Expires

It can be extremely useful to spell out in the terms of employment that after the expiry of the apprenticeship there is no right to be retained as a skilled worker, or to spell out such procedures as may be agreed between the company and recognised trade unions. In any circumstances, the expiry of the apprenticeship will not entail the payment of redundancy pay if the employer does not re-employ the apprentice as a skilled worker (*North East Coast Shiprepairers Ltd v Secretary of State for Employment*) [1978] IRLR 149). This is the leading case where it was decided that the expiry of the apprenticeship was the reason for dismissal, not the failure to re-engage as a skilled worker because of the lack of work available.

The apprenticeship is a once in a lifetime agreement, the terms of which can never be offered again to the same employee. Similarly, a claim of unfair dismissal arising from the expiry of the apprenticeship and failure to re-engage would be treated as "some other substantial reason" of a kind such as to justify the dismissal. Some of the expenses of a fruitless tribunal hearing could be avoided if an exclusion clause is drafted to prevent claims in respect of rights for redundancy pay and unfair dismissal at the expiry of the contract. Such exclusion clauses can be agreed to apply to any fixed term contract of one or more years' duration including apprenticeship contracts (EP(C)A s.142 as amended by s.8(1) of the Employment Act 1980).

It is important to note that termination of the employment before the expiry of the fixed term will invalidate such a clause and will activate all the usual statutory rights. Thus, the reasons for terminating the contract must be allowed for in the wording of the contract, otherwise the employer will be in breach of contract. One tribunal has already said that "the circumstances in which (an apprentice is dismissed) . . . in breach of contract, even in a redundancy situation, is fair must be rare" (*J A Paviour & P Thomas v Whitton's Transport (Cullompton) Ltd* [1975] IRLR 258).

Consultation

In making any changes to the standard terms of apprenticeship the employer must consult with any recognised union if appropriate, because of their traditional interest in regulating the entrants into their trade. The suggestions contained above can usually be justified on the grounds of improving the calibre of trade entrants.

Employing Sales Representatives Effectively

Like any other employee, a travelling sales representative is engaged on specific terms and conditions, but because of the nature of the job there are particular matters that should be thoroughly thought out before the start of employment. The standard terms of employment for such employees should recognise the performance orientation of the job, the problems of control and discipline and should also cover the use of the representative's "tools of the trade": the company car, samples, etc.

Terms and Procedures

After the salary package has been sorted out, it is usually left to the personnel manager to draft the contractual terms and other employment procedures. Particular attention should be paid to:
- setting sales targets and drafting appropriate rules
- the allocation of sales territories
- commission payments and drafting appropriate rules
- the allocation of company cars and expenses
- control and administrative procedures.

Even when the salesperson leaves employment, the personnel manager must be aware of the possible commercial damage that can be done if he or she sets up in competition or joins a competitor. In fact, many of these problem areas can be clarified by framing clear contractual terms and procedures.

The Contract

All employees who work 16 hours or more each week (eight hours after five years' service) are entitled to receive a written statement of terms and conditions of employment. All the important terms must be described, such as working hours, remuneration, holiday pay, sick pay, etc.

Hours of work for the salesforce are usually described as being "dictated by the needs of the business and the requirements of individual customers", unless there is a core period that they are required to work, ie normal office hours.

Terms covering matters such as holiday pay and sick pay usually follow the same rules and entitlement as are applicable to other employees. However, some areas take on specific importance for sales representatives, particularly remuneration and sales targets.

Sales Targets

Employers frequently specify performance targets either in terms of sales turnover or sales profits. Even if the employer does not admit that targets are set, there is a tacit understanding that, for instance, the profits on the sales representative's turnover must always be at least equal to the cost of his or her direct and overhead costs; otherwise there will usually be grounds for terminating the contract. Sometimes the targets expressed may be geared to the particular needs of the employer at the time. For example, the establishment and maintenance of new customers when new territories are being developed.

Employers usually ensure that a regular review of targets takes into account changes in the trading conditions. Setting impossible targets is the best way to demotivate the salesforce: agreed and realistic sales targets set at regular intervals in consultation with employees are more effective.

The drafting of contract clauses should:

(a) give the employer the right to change targets at regular (monthly, quarterly, annual) intervals in the light of changing circumstances

(b) give a right of appeal so that employees can raise objections and these can be dealt with fairly

(c) specify the consequences of failing to meet targets if the targets are going to be used for disciplinary and/or dismissal purposes

(d) give circumstances in which targets will be reduced, ie during periods of extended sickness or leave of absence and circumstances in which no reduction will be allowed, ie training or holiday periods.

Commission Payments

Commission payment levels do not always coincide with sales targets; they are often treated as a separate matter subject to careful drafting, particularly in respect of the associated rules.

Employers should consider:

– a flexibility clause to change the rate or percentage of commission according to trading circumstances

– whether special promotions should be subject to normal commission rules or their own rules as required

– whether commission will be payable in advance or in arrears

– precisely when commission falls due to be paid, ie when the sale is reported by the sales representative; when it is confirmed by the customer; when the goods or services are provided; or when the payment is received from the customer. Similarly, if the employer does not complete the sale because of lack of stock, etc, will the employee still receive commission?

- how will cancellations or refunds affect commission payments? Will there be adjustments to future commission or a deduction made from salary?
- to what extent can the salesforce set their own prices and will this therefore affect the amount of commission received?
- what rules are attached to the paperwork the salesforce must produce in support of an order? (There is no harm in stating that only company paperwork will be accepted as proof of an order)
- what steps will the employer take to obtain evidence of the orders accepted for commission payments each pay interval and of the correct calculation of the commission?
- what procedure will be used to deal with queries or appeals relating to commission payments?
- finally, what happens to commission when the employment ends? Will payments continue until all the business placed by the sales representative is accounted for? Will a sum be agreed in lieu of outstanding payments? What will happen to repeat orders or ones that will come to fruition some months or years hence? Will commission payments and entitlement cease when the employment ends? Will the salesperson remain liable to repay commission if the order is subsequently cancelled, even if he or she is no longer an employee of the company?

These are some of the main areas for which the employer may consider drafting special rules to avoid future arguments.

Changes to Commission

Where the employer has a contractual right to make these changes employees should normally be consulted beforehand and given prior notice of the change. Where the employer has no contractual right to make changes, agreement should be sought from the salesforce. Where this fails, a unilateral change to the contract should only be pushed through where the employer has terminated the contracts of the salesforce on the grounds of business efficacy and offered re-engagement on the new terms. Before doing this, the employer should have:

(a) given the employees advance warning of the change
(b) demonstrated that there will be serious implications for the business if commission rates are not changed
(c) taken steps to explain the reasons for and effect of the changes to the employee
(d) shown that the need to make the change outweighs the loss the employees will sustain.

Another term that may be subject to change is sales territories.

Sales Territories

Once again, employers may need to keep their options open to take account of changing circumstances. Sales representatives may work from a particular base or be given a patch for which they are responsible, eg the southwest region, north London, etc. However, the employer may wish to move a representative for disciplinary reasons, to develop a new area or to change boundaries or amalgamate areas. These changes may result in a loss of commission and the employee could have valid reasons for objecting. If the employee is effectively prevented from earning commission because of the change, it may well constitute a fundamental breach of contract. Consequently, it may be sensible for employers to make clear that they intend to reserve the right to change territories or boundaries and perhaps to guarantee earnings levels for a limited period whilst efforts are made to build up the territory.

Company Cars

Employers ought to look systematically at the rules and procedures required to ensure that company cars and expenses are properly controlled.

The main points to look at when framing comprehensive rules are:
- who will pay for the Road Fund Licence and insurance for the vehicle?
- for what purposes may the car be used, eg company business, social, domestic, pleasure, etc, and in what circumstances may it not be used, eg hire or reward, driving tuition, rally driving, etc?
- who may use the car, eg other company employees, spouse or other relative, any licenced driver in an emergency, etc?
- the employee should be required to disclose to the company all material facts affecting the persons who drive the car, eg motoring offences, deterioration of health, etc
- will the employee be required to pay any insurance policy excess?
- what is the procedure for reporting accidents to the police and to the company and for giving evidence to the police, etc?
- what are the rules affecting replacement of vehicles on a temporary basis, eg must authorisation be given before a car is hired as a replacement?
- what alterations to the car are not permitted, eg fitting car radios and other accessories? Will the company exclude liability for loss or damage to personal effects?
- what will the rules be regarding foreign travel, either on business or pleasure?
- there should be detailed rules about maintenance, servicing and repair of the car. Of course, cleaning the vehicle inside and out should not be forgotten!
- it should be stated clearly who is responsible for petrol and oil payments when the vehicle is used for:

- company purposes or
- private purposes
- a decision should be made as to the necessity to provide first-aid boxes for travelling sales representatives if they are likely to work in isolated areas or be at particular risk of minor injury.

Dismissal: No Licence

Where employees must use a car in order to carry out their jobs successfully, loss of the driving licence will be sufficient reason for dismissal provided the employee:

(a)   could not carry out duties adequately, or without additional expense, by public transport or

(b)   had not made suitable alternative arrangements to be driven, by his or her spouse for instance, or in another chauffeur-driven car at personal expense or

(c)   could not undertake other duties which did not require a driving licence.

Controlling the Salesforce

The control of sales representatives' expenses is almost always a problem. It is surprising how many contracts state that the employer undertakes to reimburse expenses without any mention of the word "reasonable"! Some employers put financial limits on entertaining, hotel accommodation, meals, etc, and usually supporting documentation is required, eg receipts, bills, etc. Dismissals for "fiddling" expenses will usually be fair provided the employer carries out an adequate investigation and has reasonable grounds to believe in the guilt of the employee after hearing any defence. Another problem area lies in ensuring that sufficient work is being carried out during working hours. Hence, the existence of call sheets specifying times of calls and other details so that the movements of the salesforce can be checked. These sheets may be in the nature of planned future calls and after-call reports. Targets for calls completed can be set, for example 20 customer calls per day, depending on the employment circumstances. Evidence of this nature is important in establishing fair reasons for dismissal when an employee fails to perform to the required standard. However, this only provides evidence of industry, not effectiveness, and may provide grounds for dismissal for misconduct.

Restraint Clauses

When sales representatives leave their employer there is the potential danger that they may set up in competition or join a competing company. They may systematically store away important commercial information such as customer lists and information on prices and discounts which may be of value to a competitor. If a clause is to be drafted to protect the employer against this, it must be a reasonable one. If the geographical area is not reasonable or the period of time is too long, no court will allow the employer to enforce it. It can be difficult to draft effective restraint clauses because their reasonableness will depend on the circumstances of each individual case. For instance, a restraint clause banning a sales manager from working for a 12 month period throughout the United Kingdom was unreasonable because the company only operated in the south of England.

Refusal to agree to a restrictive covenant can be grounds for dismissal, providing this was a reasonable request by the employer in that it was necessary in order to protect business interests (*R S Components Ltd v Irwin* [1973] IRLR 239).

Discipline and the Tachograph

Employers who run fleets of lorries, or even just one lorry, have now gained considerable experience in the use of tachographs. It has been a mandatory requirement that all heavy goods vehicles be fitted with the instrument, often called "the spy in the cab", since 1.1.82. The tachograph records a variety of information about the vehicle's use. The provision of this information is a valuable management tool because it gives the employer an idea of what drivers are doing during working time.

Background

Vehicles of 3.5 tonnes gross weight must be fitted with tachographs. Drivers must operate the instrument and employers are required to examine the tachograph charts to ensure that the maximum statutory driving hours and breaks are being observed. Not only does the instrument record whether the driver was resting, doing other duties, driving, etc; it also gives additional information on speed, driving technique and distance travelled.

Tachograph Information

There are three information traces recorded on the tachograph chart. Each trace is plotted against time and the recording continues through 24 hours. The traces record whether the vehicle is moving or stationary, the distance travelled and the speed of the vehicle. Some tachographs record fuel consumption or other variables of interest to the employer. From this information it is possible to say for how long the vehicle was moving, its speed, whether breaks were taken at the right time and whether braking and accelerating have been done smoothly. It is possible to identify where delays are encountered and to calculate average speeds.

Managers using tachographs in this detailed way can find spin off benefits such as:
- re-routing to avoid traffic jams
- re-routing to save mileage on journeys
- improving mileage per hour
- improving loading times by pinpointing good drop off times
- maximising driving time as a percentage of hours of work
- improving the number of completed deliveries
- improving driving standards, resulting in less wear and tear
- improving turn-round time at drops and at depots.

These benefits are, of course, only possible if co-operation can be obtained from recognised trade unions and employees concerned. Employers who recognise a union would be well advised to conclude agreements on the use of tachographs, if this has not already been done. The two contentious areas of tachograph use — to improve productivity and to collect evidence to discipline drivers — must be covered in any agreement.

Detailed analysis may even result in fewer jobs or less overtime being necessary. A more positive approach to negotiations may be on the basis of productivity. Deals could be devised to utilise the tachograph information. For example, drivers working on a "job and finish" basis may work less than their contractual hours and could be given a heavier workload. Total journey times could be speeded up, particularly if effort is concentrated on turn-round times, ie loading and unloading. Offering incentives to drive faster is taboo and is specifically referred to in EC Regulation 3820/85 on drivers' hours which states:

"Payments to wage-earning drivers, even in the form of bonuses or wage supplements, related to distances travelled and/or the amount of goods carried shall be prohibited, unless these payments are of such a kind as not to endanger road safety".

Tachographs and Discipline

One immediate problem is when the driver tampers with the tachograph record. Sometimes this is a result of failure to instruct the driver properly on how to insert the tachograph chart, or leaving the same chart in the instrument for more than one day. Sometimes the charts reveal hand drawn lines or overlapping lines, or the trace may stop abruptly because of the insertion of a sticky piece of chewing-gum. However, as soon as the instrument is opened, a nick appears on the chart and an experienced eye can soon identify such misuse.

The tachograph is therefore difficult to cheat provided the supervisor checks the tachograph chart carefully rather than giving it a cursory glance.

Not only can false records result in prosecution, they can form the basis, after further investigation, for internal disciplinary action, since tampering with the charts may conceal-time wasting, fraudulent claims for night allowances and overtime, etc which could justify dismissal or some other disciplinary action.

Tachographs and the Courts

Of course, criminal courts use a different standard of proof from industrial tribunals. A Yorkshire court was told that a driver had opened the tachograph at 17.50 hours (revealed by the nick on the chart) and then, until 18.32 hours, the speed trace appeared to be drawn in by hand. An attempt had been made to draw in the distance trace and the trace had been deliberately smudged when it was realised it was impossible to draw it finely enough. Another of the driver's charts had been double-recorded. The traffic clerk had alerted the employer and said that he was certain that the driver in question was responsible. The driver denied altering the charts and said that the instrument did not always close properly and the warning light did not always work.

The driver's defence was that there was insufficient evidence to show that he had altered the charts and the discrepancy on the second chart could be due to simple error. The jury gave a majority verdict of not guilty.

The court had come to its verdict on criminal matters on the basis that the person had not been proved to be guilty "beyond all reasonable doubt".

Tachographs and Tribunals

If the driver had been dismissed and had claimed unfair dismissal before an industrial tribunal, the legal test would have been less onerous. The tribunal would have to decide, on the "balance of probability" whether the driver was at fault and whether the employer had carried out sufficient investigation on which to base a reasonable belief in the driver's guilt. To illustrate this point, in *Greensides v J T Ellis and Co Ltd* (unreported), the tribunal considered the following evidence: tachograph records showed that on one of the three nights when Greenside claimed a subsistence allowance he had finished work at 16.00 hours, had done around 20 minutes driving the next day, and that the overnight stay was six or seven miles away from his home. The employer concluded that, since he had not exceeded permitted driving hours, there was no reason for him not to have returned to base. The claim was, therefore, fraudulent. The transport manager interviewed Greensides and dismissed him for "stopping out for the money". Greensides, according to the company, had said that he had parked his vehicle and had gone home, collecting it the following morning. He asked for leniency because he had never made such a claim before. Later he altered his story to say that he had fallen ill and spent the night in the cab. His appeal to a director was turned down. The tribunal said that it was for employers to adopt a reasonably flexible approach when dealing with long-distance lorry drivers who stop overnight and claim subsistence allowances. This does not mean that they can stop at any time they wish and spend the night somewhere near home after finishing the day early.

The tribunal believed the employer's version of the facts and found the dismissal fair. The employer had carried out a proper investigation and had given the driver the opportunity to make representations. The driver's conduct justified dismissal and the employer's actions fell within a band of reasonableness that was to be expected from an employer of the smallish number of 70 to 80 people.

Effective Procedures

The following suggestions can be made for using tachograph evidence when taking internal disciplinary action.
1. Have systematic procedures for handling and collecting the charts, and ensure regular visual inspection of all charts, even if no use is made of the charts other than ensuring compliance with the driving hours' regulations. In some cases unions will not agree to charts being scrutinised for any purpose other than policing statutory requirements. Sometimes the charts are held by the shop steward and, after the visual check, there is no further management access to them for analysis over a period of time. It remains to be seen how long these agreed practices last.
2. Employers should give training in the operation of the tachograph, especially to new employees who may only have used different models.
3. Employers should take consistent disciplinary action against drivers submitting charts which indicate a breach of statutory duty or company rules. Employers should remember that their "O" licences need to be protected and they must be seen to be controlling their drivers. ˙
4. Breaches of the driving hours' regulations will justify disciplinary action but probably not dismissal for the first offence unless a previous warning has been given. Where fraudulent claims for payment are included, however, dismissal may be justified for the first offence.
5. Employers should ensure that clear written operational instructions exist to assist drivers in certain situations, eg procedures to adopt when it is not possible to deliver a load; stopping out overnight; breakdowns; exceeding driving hours, etc. Clear guidance should be given in the form of standing orders.
6. Employers should consider whether or not their training methods are sufficient: if tachograph data on driving techniques is used in an attempt to identify drivers who are "heavy-footed", the onus on the employer is to consider retraining before proceeding through the disciplinary procedure. Indeed, teaching defensive driving techniques to all drivers may provide

many benefits in terms of reducing accidents, saving petrol, wear and tear, etc. Fixing company maximum speeds is another way of making savings.

Disciplinary Action

Any disciplinary action against drivers who breach statutory rules, company rules, standards of driving competence, etc should follow the recommendations of the ACAS Code of Practice on discipline or the company written disciplinary procedure. Tribunals recognise the necessity of a flexible approach to drivers — management control over them can never be as complete as over a factory worker and in many cases evidence must be implied.

If employers intend to use tachograph evidence to step up their control and increase disciplinary action, when in the past they have taken no action, they should tell their employees that the "ball game" has changed.

As seen previously, a good investigation is essential to a successful defence against a claim of unfair dismissal. Perhaps traffic managers should receive a little guidance and training in how to "investigate", as opposed to jumping to conclusions. Another essential aspect of the procedure the employer must go through is to allow employees to make representations to explain their version of what happened and to present mitigating circumstances, etc before the employer comes to a decision whether to dismiss or to take some other disciplinary action.

The ACAS Code suggests that employees should be allowed to have a representative or a colleague present when disciplined and they should be told what avenues are open to them if they wish to appeal against disciplinary decisions.

Company Rules and Disciplinary Procedures

If the employer has written company rules and disciplinary procedures it is important to check that they cover drivers as an employment group. Rules should cover the following:
- loss of driving licence for whatever reason
- overloading, excessive speeding, failure to check roadworthiness of vehicle including petrol and water levels, tyre pressures, sheeting and roping, etc
- reporting convictions for driving offences or licence endorsements
- careless driving, excessive number of accidents, etc
- the use of the tachograph and care of the chart record
- reporting accidents
- use and care of despatch notes, etc and other paperwork affecting the transport of goods
- signatures of persons receiving transported goods
- carrying unauthorised passengers
- vehicle security.

The company disciplinary procedure should indicate what disciplinary offences will be treated as gross misconduct, for example:
- using company vehicles for private use without authorisation
- claiming subsistence payments without entitlement
- falsifying or neglecting tachograph records
- refusing to take a load without adequate reason
- failing to telephone the traffic office before returning to base without a load.

Obviously, different types of transport operators will view offences differently and the rules should reflect company practice.

Directors: The Employment Position

An issue highlighted by some of the more spectacular boardroom dismissals — and subsequent payoffs — is the precise status of company directors for employment protection purposes. As far as claiming compensation is concerned the entitlement, if any, is going to depend on the nature of the directorship and the terms upon which the person concerned was appointed. The word "director", it must be said, is something of a term of art because although in its strict sense it will denote someone duly appointed in accordance with the company's Articles, it is not defined in the Companies Act, and is simply expressed to include those who perform the duties of a director, regardless of the title they are given.

On the other side of the coin, there are many who are designated "director" but who have never been appointed to any such post in the understood sense. It is, for instance, quite common in the public sector for senior employees to be categorised as, say, director of a particular function, when in fact they are not, in law, company directors.

Non-Executive Directors

Dealing with company directors only, a distinction can be drawn for some purposes between what are termed non-executive directors and directors with service contracts. Both will have been appointed as laid down in the company's Articles, but the former can be removed either through the lapse of the time specified in the Articles for such appointments or by being dismissed by the directors or the company in a general meeting — again, there are no limits on what the Articles can prescribe.

So long as the proper procedures have been followed, non-executive directors will have no redress against the company if they are dismissed or, their period of office having expired, they are not reappointed, save that their fees to the point when they leave the company will be payable.

Service Contracts

The position is quite different with a director who also holds a service contract. This point arose in the case *Albert J Parsons & Sons Ltd v Parsons* [1979] IRLR 117. This was an unfair dismissal claim by one of the Parsons family who had been a director of the family firm and who had been removed from office by his brothers after a disagreement. The claim failed because he was unable to prove that he was an employee. There was no contract in existence, and the facts made it impossible to imply one, as he received fees as a director and not anything approximating a salary. Moreover, he and his fellow directors paid national insurance contributions as though they were self-employed.

A contract, express or implied, is therefore essential if directors are also to be regarded as employees of the company. As a matter of law, however, it is necessary for such service contracts either to be in writing, and a copy kept at the registered office or principal place of business or, if there is no written contract, for a written memorandum of the terms upon which they serve to be maintained (Companies Act 1985, s.318(1)).

This, in most cases, should resolve the matter fairly easily. It is not at all unusual for directors to hold contracts that are rather more generous than those likely to be in force for other employees of the firm. Leaving aside the size of their remuneration, the principal benefit enjoyed by many directors is the protection afforded by the length of their appointment. This in turn will, if they are removed from office, determine the amount of compensation.

Rights on Dismissal

As an employee a director with a service contract can, if dismissed, pursue remedies on two fronts: for unfair dismissal and for wrongful dismissal. The entitlements, however, are very different. The compensation for unfair dismissal is fixed by various criteria, but is essentially circumscribed by limitations as to overall quantum. In the event of wrongful dismissal, the question is whether or not the contractual requirements as to termination have been breached.

The Companies Act 1985 (s.319) stipulates that directors' service contracts must not be for a period greater than five years without the prior approval of the company in general meeting; further, various anti-avoidance provisions are built in to ensure that the contract is not simply topped up periodically.

This clearly restricts the claim which a director will be able to make. The Act also forbids the granting of contracts that unduly inhibit the company's right to remove directors so that, if proper cause can be shown, the assessment of compensation would duly be affected.

The grounds on which directors may be dismissed are, in essence, no different to those applicable to other employees, although they are rather more far-reaching in that directors owe special duties to the company, breach of which will warrant removal. They are also, under the Companies Act 1985 and the Insolvency Act 1985, liable to disqualification by the court, and a consequence of this must normally be the termination of their contract.

The people in whom the power to remove a director rests will usually be covered in the Articles; it may be open to the other directors, or it may require action by the shareholders. As far as the rights available under the Employment Protection (Consolidation) Act 1978 are concerned, it is necessary to observe proper procedures and to be able to substantiate the action in accordance with the statutory fair reasons for dismissal.

Dismissed directors may bring proceedings before an industrial tribunal and, if they can establish that they were employees of the company, they may be awarded reinstatement, re-engagement or compensation if the dismissal is held to be unfair. However, it must be noted that the standards of competence and conduct expected of directors are higher than those appropriate to most other categories of employee and many procedures that would be demanded in other cases — warnings, a chance to improve, appeals, etc, are clearly not always appropriate when dealing with directors.

Termination of Board Membership

Problems occasionally arise when directors lose their jobs under service contracts because their membership of the board may automatically be terminated in consequence. The position here depends on the nature of the contract and the terms of the Articles. It is not unknown for service contracts to provide that the executive responsibilities constitute a job that is capable of surviving removal as a director. Much will also depend on the provisions in the Articles governing the removal of directors. As these are impliedly incorporated into any service contract, it would be difficult to complain of breach of the service contract if they were properly invoked.

To complicate matters further in the case of managing directors, removal as a director, if merely exercised in accordance with the general powers to remove directors and not for a specified reason will, as a rule, constitute a breach of the service contract governing the appointment as managing director.

If a service contract does not specify a notice period there can be yet greater contractual complications. Should this be the case, termination of the board appointment itself, if it also signifies termination of the service contract (which is usual but not inevitable), may not amount to a breach of contract. The power to remove is impliedly incorporated into the contract and it would not therefore be open to the ex-director to complain of wrongful dismissal. Clearly, however, most appointments are under a contract which does specify the period.

Contract Renewal

Failure to renew a service contract which must by law run for not more than five years, will generally amount to a dismissal under the EP(C)A, although not to a wrongful dismissal. What is not altogether clear, however, is whether, if at the same time the director has failed to be reappointed to the Board and so is not eligible, he would have any remedy. There is an argument of some strength to the effect that, if he or she is not reappointed or is removed in accordance with a power reserved under the Articles or for reasons specified in the Articles, there can be no question of unfairness. There are, however, some defects in this argument, which does not appear to have been tested; it is safer to assert that, in those circumstances, any dismissal would come within the category of "some other substantial reason".

Grounds for Disqualification

Certain difficulties arise from the liability of directors to be disqualified from holding office in prescribed circumstances. Bankruptcy does not automatically lead to vacation of office unless the Articles so provide; invariably they do and it would be usual to find a similar provision in any service contract. The position of someone in that situation would seem to be that the contract terminates by operation of law, although again there is a dearth of authority on the point. An undischarged bankrupt may not, however, take part in the management of the company without leave of the court which adjudged him or her bankrupt.

Directors can be disqualified on a number of grounds. Principally, these are:

(a) that they have been convicted on indictment of an offence in connection with the formation or management of a company

(b) that in the course of the winding-up of a company it is established in civil or criminal proceedings that they were guilty of fraudulent trading, or guilty of any fraud in relation to the company

(c) that they are or were directors of two companies which have followed each other into liquidation because of insolvency within five years and that their conduct makes them unfit to be involved in the management of a company

(d) that they defaulted persistently in making various statutory returns.

Application for disqualification must come from a limited number of people, depending largely on the ground upon which it is based: the position is set out in the Companies Act 1985 and the Insolvency Act 1985. The procedures are complex and somewhat flexible in that variations can be granted to allow directors to continue with certain activities while precluding them from others. It is, therefore, possible that a disqualification order — which will be made by the court — would preclude directors from involvement with trading companies, or allow them to act only within subsidiaries, or where their powers to act on behalf of the company do not extend to making contracts.

Employing Personnel Overseas

An increasing number of companies have some overseas operations. These range from fairly small pilot projects or agencies to the multi-nationals who have full scale operations in a variety of countries. The first decision which has to be made is whether a native of the particular country is to be employed or whether the post is to be filled by a British employee.

As a general rule the less skilled work will almost certainly best be catered for, in cost terms, by the indigenous population of the country in question. It is usually the more specialised posts which lead to expatriation of expert employees.

Primary Considerations — Work/Residence Permits

Although there is no restriction on the movement of labour throughout most EC countries (see below) many other countries now impose some controls on the employment of non-nationals. If the job under consideration is in such a country, the first question to be weighed in the balance is — can a permit be obtained for a United Kingdom employee to do the work?

The controls in different countries vary greatly, but in most the emphasis, as in the United Kingdom itself, is on keeping such employment as may be available for the indigenous population. The rule regarding the obtaining of work permits in this country may therefore serve as a useful indicator of the difficulties which will be found in other non-EC countries.

For a United Kingdom employer to employ a non-resident it must be shown either:

(a) that there is no suitable person in the United Kingdom to do that job: the Department of Employment will have to be shown that the job has been properly advertised (advertisements for mining engineers in the *New Musical Express*, for example, would not fulfil this condition). The employer will also have to show that no suitable applicants were obtained or

(b) that the work is part of a training course, for example the employed parts of a sandwich course in this country.

It will be apparent from these very limited exceptions to the use of indigenous labour that in most cases it will be both time-consuming and expensive for companies to obtain labour permits for British employees to work in other countries.

Relocation Expenses

If British employees are transferred abroad the company will have to consider the cost not only of their salary, but also of relocating them. In the majority of cases this will mean estimating the length of the job which is proposed. The expenses, dependent on length of tenure, will then relate either to accommodation for employees during their working period or to moving their household completely to the relevant country.

In either case it will be apparent that the costs of sending employees abroad are likely to be considerable. The additional costs will be even more significant if employees fail to come up to expectations or find that they cannot live in that country and so have to be brought home early. Against this, the advantages of employing from the indigenous population of the country are obvious.

Free Movement in EC Countries

The principle of free movement — and the right to work — within the Member States of the European Community (Belgium, Denmark, France, West Germany, Greece, Ireland, Italy, Luxembourg, Netherlands, Portugal, Spain and the United Kingdom) is enshrined in the Treaty of Rome (although this does not apply to Greece, Portugal or Spain until they have been members of the EC for seven years). This means that workers must be allowed access to employment on equal terms with nationals of the country. No work permits are required and workers from other EC countries are entitled to equal treatment in relation to pay, working conditions, training, etc.

EC nationals are subject to the legislation which governs the particular Member State in which they are working, providing they are "based" in that country — see *The Contract Base* below.

Recruitment

Where employers are recruiting in this country for service overseas they will need to be aware of any particular customs, practices and other difficulties in employing persons of one sex or race to a particular post. Both the Sex Discrimination Act 1975 and the Race Relations Act 1976 make special provisions to allow employers to overcome these difficulties when employing people for overseas work. For example, it is not always sensible to employ women for particular jobs in many Moslem countries where there are severe restrictions on their movements, and hence their effectiveness as employees.

Where indigenous employees are being employed in the country in which they are to serve, the company will be well advised to obtain the services of a specialised recruitment agency which has a good knowledge of the restrictions imposed by law. Many countries have anti-discrimination laws which are wider than the British laws. A number of countries have outlawed discrimination on the basis of age and some, notably EC countries, have minimum wages legislation. Above all, the health and safety laws and regulations protecting women, young persons and others in particular industries vary from country to country. Where the employer has a large operation in that country there will usually be suitably qualified staff to deal with recruitment, but recruitment can be a major hazard where the employer is setting up a small pilot project.

The Contract Base

The "contract base" has two, inder-dependent meanings for this purpose. Firstly, the contract base relates to the place where the employee is employed *legally*. Secondly, the contract base can be seen as the legal system under which the contract is made. In both senses the contract base which is chosen will be important.

If a company is contemplating a small overseas operation it will often be advantageous to use existing employees known to be capable of carrying out the required functions and transferring them to the country in question (subject to what has already been said above about work permits, the country's laws and customs etc). Where the contract is of this type, with the employee being "seconded" abroad, the employee's normal base will be Britain. Although British employment law places fairly strict duties on employers, for a small overseas operation it will often be preferable to have these duties imposed on the employment relationship rather than being subject to the individual employment laws of the country concerned. The obvious advantages are operating within a system with which the company's experts are familiar and a saving in overseas legal costs should the relationship turn sour.

In terms of United Kingdom law, employees who "ordinarily work outside the United Kingdom" are excluded from most of the employment protection rights. If employees are made redundant after having been recalled to the United Kingdom, however, they will be entitled to a redundancy payment based on any period of service during which they ordinarily worked in the United Kingdom.

Difficulties of Interpretation

The employee's "ordinary" place of work for purposes of the employment protection legislation has led to considerable difficulties of interpretation. In *Wilson v Maynard Shipbuilding Consultants* AB [1977] IRLR 491 the employee was employed as a staff consultant by a Swedish company. He had worked for 50 weeks in Italy and 40 weeks in the United Kingdom before being dismissed. The Court of Appeal held that the question of whether or not the employee "ordinarily works" outside Great Britain is analysed not merely by looking at where he has *actually* been employed during the contract period, but by looking at the whole of the contemplated period of the contract and ascertaining where the employee was based. The rationale of this decision is that, by the nature of an unfair dismissal claim, the employment has been prematurely terminated; the place where the employee may actually have been working is not, therefore, always indicative of where the employee was ordinarily to work.

In another case *Janata Bank v Ahmed* [1981] IRLR 457, a differently constituted Court of Appeal again held that the contract was the key to where the employee ordinarily works. In this case the employee had worked for the larger part of his period of employment at the bank's London branch. Under the terms of his contract he was liable to be posted to other of the bank's branches and could be recalled to Bangladesh. The Court of Appeal held that the EAT had erred in trying to decide where the employee's "contract base" was, ie whether it was Dacca to where he had been posted originally, or London. The question was whether he ordinarily worked in Great Britain or outside it and, in this case, where he was liable to be posted elsewhere by the bank the contract clearly contemplated that he could work anywhere in the world. The tribunal therefore had no jurisdiction to consider the employee's unfair dismissal complaint.

Termination of Employment

Where employment is being terminated, a clause in employees' contracts of employment entitling the company to recall them to this country at any time, will be helpful to settle employment protection matters on termination. Equally, employers may well be able to avoid overseas law being invoked during employment by using the same method: recalling the employee to this country. There will, however, be certain employment protection rights which are afforded during employment with which the employer will have to comply and which cannot simply be dealt with by recalling the particular employee: for example, minimum wages legislation and health and safety regulations. It is essential for employers who have overseas operations to make themselves aware of such provisions in relation to the particular country in question.

Taxation and Residency

Liability to British income tax is dependent on the employee being resident in this country. We looked above at the question of "where the employee ordinarily works" which is the test for an employer's liability under United Kingdom employment legislation. "Residence" for purposes of tax law is not decided in the same way. It is not fatal to employees' non-resident status that they maintain an abode in the United Kingdom provided that:

(a) all their duties are performed outside this country

(b) any duties performed within the United Kingdom are merely incidental to the performance of other duties outside the country.

In *Robson v Dixon* (1972) IWLR 1493 a KLM pilot was held to be resident in the United Kingdom where he had made only 38 landings in a six year period. The pilot maintained a house in the United Kingdom for his wife and children, as well as a flat in Holland and in this case it was held that the landings in this country were not incidental to his other duties.

The matter of residence is, of course, related to each tax year so that a person who is a non-resident for a whole tax year will not be liable to British Income Tax. It should be noted that a visitor to the United Kingdom who spends more than six months here in any tax year is automatically regarded as a resident (**NB**: the converse does not apply: merely being outside the United Kingdom for six months of the year is not, by itself, enough to provide non-resident status).

Double Taxation Agreements

If employees are not resident in the United Kingdom they will, of course, be subject to local tax liability in the country where they are working. From the complex way in which "residence" is determined it will immediately be apparent that employees may be resident in the United Kingdom *and* in the country where they are employed. In such cases they will *prima facie* be liable to pay tax in both countries on their earnings. The United Kingdom now has "double taxation" agreements with many countries to prevent this from happening. These agreements are complex and are reached individually with separate countries. For further information on double taxation relief you are strongly advised to consult a tax lawyer, accountant or the Inland Revenue.

Disabled Workers: are you Missing Out?

The International Year of Disabled People was in 1981 but disabled people still suffer from many of the myths and superstitions which influence some employers. In 1978, 63.2% of employers were not fulfilling their quota obligations — 3% of the workforce of companies with more than 19 employees should be registered disabled — and the Government is now considering doing away with the Quota Scheme altogether. However, studies show that disabled people can be as or even more productive and reliable than other workers.

Who is a Disabled Person?

The first piece of legislation on disabled people was passed in 1944 in response to a report on the employment plight of disabled persons — a topical subject for a country at war. The Disabled Persons (Employment) Act 1944, together with the 1958 Act of the same name, form a legislative framework upon which little has been built.

The Acts define a disabled person as someone who "on account of injury, disease or congenital deformity, is substantially handicapped in obtaining or keeping employment, or in undertaking work on his own account, of a kind which apart from that injury, disease or deformity would be suited to his age, experience and qualifications". This will include anyone who is physically or mentally disabled.

The most important provision of the Acts — the Quota Scheme — applies only to registered disabled people. Under the Acts, a register of disabled people is maintained by the Secretary of State for Employment. The main conditions for registration are that applicants:

(a) are disabled within the definition set out above and the disablement is likely to last for at least 12 months
(b) are over the age of 16
(c) are ordinarily resident in Great Britain and wish to work in some form of remunerative employment or on their own account in Great Britain
(d) have a reasonable prospect of obtaining employment or work.

Registers are kept at offices of the Employment Service Agency (ESA) and at careers offices. Registration is voluntary but certain benefits, such as the Quota Scheme and designated employments (ie car park and electric lift attendants), only apply to those registered. A green card is evidence of registration.

Finding Employment

The Manpower Services Commission, through its Disablement Resettlement Officers (DROs) and Blind Persons' Resettlement Officers (BPROs), provides a range of services for disabled people and for prospective or existing employers. Many services, such as advice on suitable jobs, etc are offered to any disabled person, regardless of whether or not he or she is registered. Employment Rehabilitation Centres and the Training Opportunities Scheme can help to prepare disabled people for work, but only employers can provide permanent jobs.

The Quota Scheme

The Acts require every employer who employs more than 19 employees to employ a quota of registered disabled people. The quota presently stands at

3% of the workforce. The quota applies to virtually all employers — only sea-going employment has been granted a smaller percentage (0.1%) and the Crown is exempt.

Having said that, there is no effective action likely to be brought against an employer who does not fulfil the quota. The rules are that anyone who does fail must not:

(a) engage staff other than those registered as disabled unless a permit has first been obtained

(b) discharge a registered disabled employee without due cause if to do so would bring him or her under quota.

Breach of these rules is an offence leading, on summary conviction, to a fine not exceeding £1000 or to imprisonment for a term not exceeding three months, or both but, in practice, such convictions are most unlikely.

Permits

Employers are able to get a permit, valid for six months, which will exempt them from the requirement to fill a vacancy with someone from the disabled register. These permits are issued by DROs if they consider that suitable registered disabled people are unlikely to be found to fill a specific vacancy or several vacancies.

The permits do not appear to be difficult to get, certainly for companies employing less than 100 people. Renewal of the permit can almost become automatic.

Employing Disabled People

The ESA's leaflet, *Positive Policies: A guide to employing disabled people* (EPL 56) suggests clear guidelines on employing and ensuring the maximum potential contribution of disabled workers. These include:

- giving full and fair consideration to applications from disabled people for all types of vacancies
- retaining newly disabled employees wherever possible
- providing equal opportunities for training, career development and promotion
- making modifications to equipment, the use of special employment aids or job-restructuring where appropriate
- adapting premises where necessary
- maintaining close co-operation with the local DRO.

Finding Disabled Workers

Advice on people suitable for particular vacancies can be obtained from the local DRO or BPRO who deal with all disabled people through Jobcentres and employment offices. They can interview prospective workers and assess their skills. They can also arrange for expert medical, psychological or technical advice to help in assessing candidates' abilities.

The Job Introduction Scheme operates as a cash incentive to employers to employ disabled workers. Under the scheme, employers will be paid £45 a week for six weeks when they employ a registered disabled person. The idea is that the worker will, in that time, prove to be suitable and be taken on permanently. The six week period may be extended to 13 weeks when disabled people need longer than six weeks to demonstrate their suitability for the job.

During Employment

Certain problems may arise when a disabled worker is taken on unless the employer gives the matter some forethought. For example, an occupational pension scheme may operate in the company and the rules of the scheme must be examined carefully to find out the worker's position.

Employers should also make themselves aware at the start of the nature of the disability so they can gauge possible absences due to sickness and act accordingly; evidence shows in fact that disabled people are less prone to absence than many able-bodied employees. The other main area which could cause difficulty is health and safety. This has two aspects:
- where the safety of the disabled worker is endangered due to premises, nature of job, etc and
- where the safety of other workers is jeopardised by the actions of disabled workers.

The first aspect obviously requires some forethought. No adjustments may be necessary for some workers, or perhaps only minor modifications will need to be made to equipment, the working environment or the organisation of the job. The DRO can give advice on this and arrange grants for adaptations, technical advice and free loan of equipment. Premises modifications could include the provision of ramps, special car parking facilities, etc.

The other side of the coin is the danger that a disabled worker could be to fellow employees. In one case, an epileptic had three fits in the space of two years. During each of those fits, he had attacked and displayed violence to his fellow employees. The EAT held that the tribunal had not been wrong in holding that the subsequent dismissal was fair and related to the man's capability to do the job (*Harper v National Coal Board* [1980] IRLR 260). Lack of capability or any reason which falls within the potentially fair reasons under the unfair dismissal provisions of the Employment Protection (Consolidation) Act 1978 would be "good cause" under the Disabled Persons (Employment) Acts 1944 and 1958 and so would not attract penalties.

Dismissing Disabled People

As regards dismissal generally, disabled workers should be treated in the same way as able-bodied workers. The main area is likely to be capability dismissals, ie general capability or ill-health. Once disabled people are taken on, their capability to do a job is presumably established and it is unlikely that any subsequent dismissal for lack of capability would be fair unless the DRO has been involved.

Ill-health dismissals have always been a thorny subject and are no less so in relation to disabled workers. Generally it comes down to the employer balancing the interests of the company with the interests of the employee, culminating in the question "Is it reasonable in all the circumstances for the employer to go on employing the employee?" The factors to consider are:
- the nature, length and effect of the illness or disability (eg deterioration of a known disability)
- the importance of that particular employee
- the prognosis.
In other words, as with all ill-health dismissals, care should be taken to ensure that the decision to dismiss is fair.

That, however, is not all. The way the dismissal is handled should also be fair. This means that the employee (and in the case of a disabled person, probably the DRO) should be consulted about the problem, alternative opportunities should be looked for and retention on the books should be considered if recovery is likely.

In relation to redundancy, it should be noted that an industrial tribunal has held (*Fashion Industries (Hartlepool) Ltd v Miller and others* EAT 34/80) that an employer who, after a strike, failed to offer re-engagement to two disabled workers because of their disability, had acted unfairly by, in effect, selecting them for redundancy. It was clearly stated in *Forman Construction Ltd v Kelly* [1977] IRLR 468 that in the absence of a clearly defined selection procedure (express or implied by custom and practice), the personal circumstances of an employee whom it is proposed to make redundant must be taken into account. In other words, the fact that a disabled person would have much more difficulty in getting another job should carry some weight.

8 TERMINATION OF EMPLOYMENT

The termination of employment is often viewed with mixed feelings by the employer. On the one hand there may be regret at losing a valued member of staff; on the other, positive relief at the departure of a particularly problematic employee. Concern may also arise over a pressing need to recruit a replacement, or the possibility of unfair dismissal action stemming from the ending of employment. In addition to these points, however, the employer may encounter certain difficulties in actually administering the termination of employment and some of the practical issues which can arise in this situation are examined in this chapter. We also review the law relating to redundancy and procedure at tribunal.

Ending the Contract

A contract of employment can come to an end in various ways. Usually it will be as a result of the employer effecting a dismissal or the employee resigning, although termination can also take effect by mutual agreement or by the operation of law, eg where an unforeseen event makes continued performance of the contract impossible or totally different from what was originally contemplated (frustration of contract). Contracts are normally terminable on notice by either party, although fixed term contracts and certain contracts for performance of specific tasks will expire naturally without the need for notice to be given. However, it is perfectly permissible for notice provisions to be built into these types of contracts to enable earlier termination if required.

Notice to Terminate

Either the employer or the employee can give notice to end the contract and this can be done orally or in writing, unless the contract specifically provides that notice to terminate must be given in one particular form. Even where this is not specified, it is always best to confirm the position by letter where notice has been issued to an employee, or to confirm acceptance of resignations in writing. This has the advantage of formally recording the termination and provides better evidence that notice to terminate was actually given should any subsequent dispute arise as to how or when termination was effected. It also provides a means of outlining the position where notice to end the contract is given in the heat of the moment. Such notice may not be valid in law if it can be shown that the recipient could not seriously have acted upon it. In *Sothern v Franks Charlesly & Co* [1981] IRLR 278, a case concerning the resignation of an employee, the Court of Appeal recognised that situations exist where idle words or words spoken under stress might be used which the employer should know were not meant to be taken seriously. It is therefore important that employers set out in writing their views of particular events and seek further clarification if there is any ambiguity.

Notice to terminate must indicate the date on which the employment will end or contain information which makes that date readily ascertainable. Thus in *Morton Sundour Fabrics v Shaw* (1967) 2 ITR 84, the mere warning to the employee that a redundancy situation would occur at some time in the future was held not to constitute notice of termination. Thus, the employer should make sure that notice of dismissal is clear and that any doubts over a resignation are clarified before acting upon it.

The amount of notice which should be given will be determined from the terms of the contract. If no notice provisions have been detailed the courts will imply "reasonable" notice. This will be dependent on a number of factors such as the position the employee holds, length of service, custom and practice in the industry, etc. S.49 of the EP(C)A lays down statutory minimum periods of notice which must be given, although it is perfectly permissible for longer periods to be agreed and enforced. The parties cannot, however, provide for periods of notice which are shorter than those required by statute. Minimum statutory notice periods are based on the employee's continuous service and are as shown overleaf:

Notice from the employer

After 1 month's service but less than 2 years	1 week's notice.
2 years' service or more	1 week for each year of service up to a maximum of 12 weeks.

Notice from the employee:

1 month's service or more	1 week's notice

Withdrawal of Notice

Occasionally, after notice has been issued and accepted, circumstances may change and the employer or employee may wish to withdraw notice. Perhaps the employee's new job has fallen through, the employer's original notice of redundancy is now unnecessary due to an influx of orders, or the employer may have thought better of the decision to dismiss for conduct, capability, etc and wish to reinstate the employee. The position in law is that notice cannot be withdrawn unilaterally and it is open to either party to refuse to allow a retraction, although an unreasonable refusal could have a bearing on later claims for unfair dismissal or redundancy payments.

Failure to Give Required Notice

Where the employer dismisses an employee for gross misconduct there is no requirement to give notice. Similarly, where the employer commits a fundamental breach of contract — for example refusing to pay the employee — which repudiates the employee's contract, the employee is free to end the contract without notice if he or she so chooses. However, in most cases notice will be required to terminate the contract and failure to give notice will be a breach of contract in itself. However, where an employee leaves without giving full notice it can be more difficult for the employer to recover the loss. The main problem here is for the employer to quantify the value of the lost work for the notice period, which may be determinable in the case of production workers but can be difficult to estimate in other situations. However, even if a loss can readily be ascertained, the cost in time and expense of court procedure and representation usually outweighs any advantage which the employer may obtain from successfully suing the employee and, for practical purposes, employers usually write off this particular loss. The employer is not free to withhold payments as a punitive measure from an employee who has left without serving proper notice unless there is a contractual right to do so. Some contracts do provide that accrued holiday pay or other payments may be withheld if no notice is given or if an employee is dismissed for gross misconduct. This would seem to be the best long term approach for employers who may face a similar situation.

Occasionally, instead of giving too little or no notice, an employer or employee may give too much notice: for example an employee who only needs to give one week's notice may give one month. While this can be convenient, in that it provides more time to seek a replacement, employers sometimes prefer departing employees to go as soon as possible. Where too much notice is given the recipient can accept it, although it can quite rightly be rejected as improper notice and a request made for correct notice to be issued. However, this may merely result in the notice being delayed. Additionally, either party to the contract is quite at liberty to waive the right to receive notice. It is normally the employer who agrees to waive this right but it is quite permissible for an employee to do the same. It is advisable, however, that written confirmation is obtained from an employee who proposes to waive rights, in order to protect the employer from future claims for notice pay.

Determining Final Payments

The calculation of final payments to a departing employee will be important. All payments for work already carried out must be made as well as payment for the notice period itself. S.50 of the EP(C)A specifies that employees who have been given statutory notice by the employer must receive a week's pay for each week of the notice period if they are: ready and willing to work but no work is provided; incapable of work due to sickness or injury; or absent from work on holiday in accordance with their contractual rights. This is so even where an employer may not provide sickness or holiday pay or where this has been exhausted. These rights do not apply where contractual notice is at least one week longer than that required by statute. Any payments for accrued holiday, outstanding bonuses and overtime should also be made. Where employees are in possession of loans or floats of cash it is not open to the employer to deduct these from final pay unless there is a contractual right to do so. Where no contractual right exists, the correct approach is to pay over all payments in full, request repayment of the loan and, if necessary, sue the employee for recovery.

Most final payments will be subject to income tax and national insurance. However, lump sum payments of up to £25,000 made in respect of the termination will not normally be subject to such deductions unless there is a contractual right for employees to receive them. Other final arrangements such as removing the employee from the payroll, issuing a P45 and notifying relevant departments, eg pensions, insurance, etc of the employee's departure should also be made at this stage.

Paying People Off

There are many occasions when employers decide that it is imperative to dismiss employees without warning. In some cases redundancies become necessary and the employer decides to dispense with the consultation process with individuals; in others, it is decided that the organisation can no longer afford to employ inefficient or untrustworthy employees and so a decision is taken to pay off the employees concerned rather than face the inevitable tribunal claims.

Payment in Lieu of Notice

It may be desirable, for whatever reason, not to allow some employees to work out their notice period and in most circumstances this will mean that a payment in lieu should be made. There is some confusion over what pay in lieu of notice means in practice, whether it is taxable and whether it extends the employee's effective date of termination. This has arisen largely because it is common practice to pay "notice pay" rather than give actual notice of impending dismissal, which is what the law really requires employers to do!

Liquefied Damages

Payment in lieu of notice is in fact compensation for breach of contract rather than literal notice pay. The breach of contract arises because the employer fails to allow the employee to serve the notice period. This could give rise to a claim for damages (ie lost notice pay) in the county court but, if a payment equivalent to earnings is made, the employee cannot demonstrate any loss and is therefore unable to sue. The employer, therefore, is paying liquefied damages when a payment in lieu of notice is made.

For this reason, any payment given in lieu of notice should include compensation for any losses the employee incurs by being prevented from working throughout the notice period. Apart from pay, the loss of fringe benefits — use of a company car, mortgage subsidies, etc — should all be taken into account and an approximate value calculated and added to the payment. Any bonuses, regular overtime or shift premia which would have been earned during the notice period should also be included. If the employee would have earned another year of service by working the notice (ie the anniversary of the commencement date would occur during the notice period) an extra week's notice pay and any other benefits, such as extra holiday entitlement, stemming from a further year's service should be given. The general principle is that the employee should not suffer any loss by being prevented from working throughout the notice period.

Payment in lieu of notice should be made in a lump sum. If the employer pays notice pay through the payroll and deducts tax and national insurance, this will not be genuine pay in lieu of notice but contractual notice pay. In these circumstances the notice period will be a normal period of continuous employment, even if the employee is no longer attending work.

Taxation of Pay in Lieu

Pay in lieu of notice which is made in a lump sum as compensation, taking into account the non-cash factors outlined above, will not generally be assessable under Inland Revenue rules or subject to any other deductions, provided the total payment is not in excess of £25,000. There are special rules governing the tax treatment of amounts over £25,000 and these are detailed below (see *Taxation of Payments*). According to Inland Revenue policy there are two circumstances when lump sum pay in lieu of notice should be taxed:

   (a) when the contract of employment expressly provides that a payment in lieu of notice will be made, rather than notice of dismissal given and

   (b) employment where there is a "reasonable belief" that payment in lieu of notice should be made.

"Reasonable belief" is not defined but could mean the kind of occupation or organisation where employees never work out their notice, are always paid in lieu and this is a well known practice throughout the industry.

The situation is further complicated by the fact that some local tax offices will advise employers to tax all payments in lieu of notice, even if they do not obviously fulfil the conditions above. This is because they interpret contractual provision for pay in lieu as any mention of notice periods in the contract or written statement.

Effective Date of Termination

In most circumstances, pay in lieu of notice will not extend an employee's date of termination of employment. If paid in a lump sum as compensation the last working day will be the end of the period of continuous employment. However, if the employee continues to be paid through the payroll, even though he or she does not attend work, this could extend the termination date to the end of the notice period. This can be crucial when determining whether an employee has sufficient service to qualify for unfair dismissal protection. Another point to bear in mind is that dismissal with pay in lieu is regarded as dismissal without notice by a tribunal and statutory notice will be added on to the employee's termination date to determine whether he or she has sufficient service for unfair dismissal purposes.

Conciliated Settlements

It is most desirable to make use of the services of ACAS if an employer wishes to prevent unfair dismissal claims by making a compensation payment to a sacked employee. First of all, it is the statutory duty of a conciliation officer to promote settlement of disputes without a tribunal hearing and it is sensible to take advantage of the machinery set up for this purpose. It should be stressed that an ACAS ratified settlement is the only way to be sure of avoiding tribunal claims. This is because any other agreement (even if drawn up by solicitors) will automatically be void under s.140 of the EP(C)A (contracting out of the provisions of the Act): an individual simply cannot sign away statutory rights, except through the procedure expressly provided for this purpose.

Employers are sometimes reluctant to involve ACAS in settlements as it is felt that this might encourage the employee to make a tribunal claim. It is also sometimes thought that a substantial payment will be sufficiently rewarding to ensure an employee's satisfaction and guarantee no further trouble. This can be an expensive misconception! For example, a senior employee may be given £25,000 as a severance payment: a tribunal may assess the compensation as £50,000, take the £25,000 into account but still award the maximum compensatory award as well. This would have been avoided if an ACAS settlement had been agreed.

A conciliation officer can be called in even if a tribunal claim has not been made by the employee, although the dismissal must have been effected and the officer will need to be satisfied that the employee can claim an infringement of statutory employment rights. The ACAS officer will advise both parties and record the details of the terms agreed on a form COT3 which, when signed by employer and employee, is binding upon both and will prevent the employee from pursuing a claim further.

The wording of the agreement on the COT3 is obviously very important: the usual formula suggested by the conciliation officer is that any payment made by the employer "is in full and final settlement of all claims which could be made to an industrial tribunal arising out of the dismissal". The snag with this is that it prevents only unfair dismissal claims and the employer should endeavour to preclude potential breach of contract claims as well. Something along the lines of ". . .full and final settlement of all claims arising out of the termination of employment" would be preferable. The settlement may also include terms about future references to be provided by the employer, often indicating that certain details should be omitted or even, in some cases, actually dictating the wording of the reference to be used. Employers should beware of any agreement to provide references which misrepresents the employee. Apart from potential negligence suits by future employers, the ACAS settlement itself could be tainted with illegality and thus rendered unenforceable.

Taxation of Payments

Lump sums paid on termination of employment will only be subject to PAYE if, as with pay in lieu of notice, they can be looked upon as income from employment or a contractual payment. If the payment is in any way for work performed or a reward for services rendered it will be fully assessable. Any sum provided for in the contract as compensation will be fully taxable, for example where a service contract provides for a set payment in the event of termination as "compensation for loss of office".

However, where the payment is not expressly provided for within the contract and is made ex-gratia it will be taxed according to a special formula if it exceeds £25,000.

Employers should also note that non-monetary gifts will be subject to Inland Revenue scrutiny and could potentially be taxable. Once again, anything which could be looked upon as a reward for services rendered will be regarded as an emolument and hence be fully taxable. A gift which is truly compensation for loss of office, such as a company car being retained as part of the termination package, will be subject to the special rules mentioned above. The amount to be taxed is defined as the object's value at the date when it is given (ie second-hand value) and this amount must be added together with other termination payments.

The Early Retirement Option

Many companies would like to see some of their employees retire earlier than normal State pensionable age, in order to unblock promotion channels, to allow new blood into the company or, perhaps, to reduce the size of the workforce.

This option is not always well received. However, some employees may have done their sums and decided that early retirement is right for them. Usually, the financial demands on their income have been reduced because their children have grown up, the mortgage is paid, etc and although their income will be reduced by retiring early, it is an option they wish to take for all kinds of personal reasons. Other employees, however, are reluctant to retire early and in such cases it is usually left to the personnel manager to break the news to the employee and, hopefully, to obtain his or her agreement. Apart from handling the emotionally fraught situation, the personnel manager must be able to spell out the financial realities of the early retirement decision.

Information First

Personnel managers cannot talk to an employee sensibly about early retirement without thoroughly researching what the employee's pension options are, the possibility of State benefits supplementing the employee's income, etc. These are overriding considerations for an employee who is considering the early retirement option. Where will his or her income come from? How much will it be?

Early Retirement Incentives

The Job Release Scheme allows people in the year before retirement age to give up their jobs in return for a weekly allowance until normal retirement age. The employer must appoint a replacement from the registered unemployed.

While the allowances are being paid the State benefits cannot be claimed, eg unemployment benefit, sickness benefit, supplementary benefit. Such retired people may not take up paid employment or go into business on their own account unless their earnings will not exceed £4 (net) per week. The allowances vary with age and marital status.

There is also a special scheme for disabled men aged 60-63 which provides for a taxable allowance. Further information is contained in *Croner's Reference Book for Employers* and application forms can be obtained from Jobcentres or Employment Offices.

Company Pension Schemes

There is a multiplicity of occupational schemes but all schemes take into account the fact that, if an employee retires before the normal age, life expectancy and pension span will be longer than if retirement took place at the normal age. Consequently, the annual pension has to be smaller and it is not uncommon for pensions to be reduced by ½% for each month the employee has retired before the normal retirement age.

Additionally, the pension fund has to forgo interest over the years before normal retirement age is reached thereby cutting back the amount accumulated to pay pensions. Early retirement greatly devalues pension rights. Further enquiries of pension fund managers may reveal additional options, eg to defer the pension until normal retirement age, to commute part of the pension for a tax-free cash sum (this, of course, will cut back the employee's pension even more), etc.

Employees generally expect to do rather better financially out of early retirement than the actuaries will allow. Consequently, employers may have to consider improving the terms for early retirement, either by increasing their annual contributions or making a lump sum payment to the pension scheme at the time the employee retires to make good the investment losses to the pension scheme. There are other methods of boosting the retirement income of an employee who retires early, for instance buying annuities for a lump sum or giving a golden handshake for investment.

When early retirement is part of a redundancy programme, it is possible to offset such improved pension arrangements against State redundancy payments. Obviously, negotiating problems will arise if this tactic is used when the employer wants to encourage voluntary early retirement/redundancy. If this option is not taken up, statutory redundancy payments based on age and length of service are payable in addition. Any pension income is taxable.

When early retirement is at the employee's request the employer has discretion as to whether to agree unless there is a contractual right to retire after the completion of appropriate lengths of service.

State Pension Arrangements

State pensions are not payable until statutory retirement age (60 and 65 for women and men respectively) is reached. The amount of pension payable is subject to the employee having made the appropriate amount of contributions. It is important to check that early retirement does not substantially decrease the basic pension that will be paid.

Other State Benefits

Unemployment benefit can be claimed provided the early retired person:
- has sufficient contributions
- is unemployed or does not earn more than £2 per day
- is available for and willing to work.

The benefit is paid after the first three waiting days for one year but, if payment in lieu of notice has been given, the claimant will be prevented from claiming until the notice period has expired.

Additionally, people choosing to retire early will lose the first 13 weeks' unemployment benefit because they have left their job "without just cause". However, if they have retired early because they volunteered to be made redundant, this exclusion does not apply. Similarly, if the claimant refuses to accept or apply for suitable employment after being directed to do so by the Department of Employment, the unemployment benefit can be disallowed.

Unemployment benefit will not be paid if the person is in receipt of sickness, invalidity or widow's benefit. However, it is unaffected if the person receives basic industrial disablement pension or gratuity, basic war pension or gratuity, mobility allowance or attendance allowance for severe disablement.

Anyone over 60 years of age receiving an occupational pension in excess of £35 per week will have unemployment benefit reduced by 10p a week for every 10p by which the pension exceeds £35. This provision does not apply in cases where pension payments are made solely by way of compensation for redundancy. Further considerations are that unemployment benefit is taxable and tax refunds will be withheld while unemployment benefit is being paid. At the end of the unemployment period or the end of the tax year (whichever comes sooner), tax liability will be assessed after taking account of any benefit received during the year, and only then will a refund be made.

"In Sickness or in Health"

The retiring employee may be able to claim sickness or invalidity benefit or allowances, provided the appropriate contributions have been paid. Once again these benefits depend on the employee having:
- actually paid Class I or Class II contributions of at least 25 times the lower weekly earnings limit for that year in any one tax year since 6.4.75
- paid or been credited with at least 50 Class I or Class II contributions in the tax year which ended in the previous calendar year.

This contribution requirement can often be difficult for employees retiring for ill-health reasons, although there are non-contributory severe disablement and other allowances such as attendance allowance, invalid care allowance and mobility allowance that can be claimed by those not eligible for sickness benefit. Some employees who retire early may be in receipt of disablement benefit which gives a further boost to their income.

The Balancing Act

The decision to retire early will be based on all the factors of individual personal circumstances, ie severance payments, spouse's income, buying a smaller house, investment income, income from State benefits, etc. If the income is sufficient early retirement can be attractive. Very often it provides the opportunity to start a new career, a new business, to have more time to pursue hobbies and to spend time with family and friends.

Assistance in working out the financial implications of early retirement is very often necessary and the personnel manager has a very valuable counselling role to play so that the employee can assess properly the value of agreeing to early retirement. The employer can also work out what additional compensation will be necessary, either in the form of a golden handshake or an enhanced pension to persuade the employee to accept early retirement.

Mutual Agreement to Retire

No matter how sensible the suggestion that the employee retires early may be, an employer cannot force an employee to resign. Discussion may be lengthy and wide-ranging so it is necessary for employers to have all relevant facts to hand. The course of these negotiations should be recorded by letter, or the meetings minuted, so that there can be no doubt that the employee has agreed the terms.

An EAT case that looked at the features of "mutual agreement" to terminate employment is *Sheffield v Oxford Controls Co Ltd* [1979] IRLR 133. Here an employee's willingness to resign was influenced not so much by the threat of dismissal but by the terms he was able to negotiate for himself. The terms were to his satisfaction and he initialled an agreement to resign. The EAT decided that there was no dismissal because the contract was terminated by mutual agreement.

As neither party to the mutual agreement is taking unilateral action, the question of giving or paying notice technically does not arise. The financial value of notice is usually part of the agreement and forms part of the inducement. Clearly, if the employer forces early retirement on a reluctant employee this will constitute a dismissal and so might give rise to an unfair dismissal claim.

Recent Developments

A recent case (*Birch and Humber v University of Liverpool* Court of Appeal 23.1.85) has indicated that agreed early retirement may not constitute a redundancy dismissal even if it can be shown that the arrangement was made in a situation that amounted to redundancy. Employers should take care about the way they enter into discussion with employees about redundancy and early retirement. In this case the employer introduced a "Premature Retirement Compensation Scheme" which was expressly stated not to be a redundancy scheme. Staff who applied were taken to have mutually agreed to the early retirement package, even though a redundancy situation existed. They were not entitled to a redundancy payment because they had not been dismissed.

Finally, it should be remembered that, with effect from November 1987, it will constitute unlawful sex discrimination to have different mandatory retirement ages for men and women.

Identifying Redundancy

Redundancy is one of the potentially fair reasons for dismissal provided for in s.57 of the EP(C)A. Unlike dismissal on grounds of capability or conduct, employers who want to justify dismissal on the grounds that the employee in question is redundant must be able to demonstrate more than just a "reasonable belief" that a redundancy situation exists. The definition of redundancy is clearly set out in the legislation and a strict standard of proof is required for an employer to show that the circumstances of a dismissal fit that statutory definition.

Place of Employment

A redundancy situation arises when an employer ceases carrying on the business in which the employees were employed or ceases to do so at the place where the employees were employed. Similarly, a dismissal is on grounds of redundancy if it is because the employer's requirements for employees to do work of a particular kind cease or diminish or if the requirements for them to do such work at the place where they were employed cease or diminish.

Since a redundancy can be defined in relation to the place of employment, the question of what is meant by "the place where the employee was so employed" has been examined in a number of cases. In *Mumford v Boulton & Paul Ltd* (1971) ITR 76 the Court of Appeal's finding indicated that what was important were the terms of the contract, rather than where the employee actually worked, and this was followed in a subsequent NIRC decision. In *Sutcliffe v Hawker Siddeley Aviation Ltd* [1973] IRLR 304, it was held that "the words where he was so employed' . . . do not mean where he in fact worked. They mean where under his contract of employment he could be required to work'." The employee, who could be required to work anywhere in the United Kingdom, was therefore not redundant when he was dismissed for refusing to accept a posting to another part of the country, even though there was no further work available at his current place of employment.

Fewer Employees Needed

An employer might decide he needs fewer employees for a variety of reasons. The EAT has held that, even if the amount of work remains the same, employees who are dismissed when that work is reallocated among the rest of the workforce are redundant (*Delanair Ltd v Mead* [1976] IRLR 340). In *Carry All Motors Ltd v Pennington* [1980] IRLR 455, this principle was applied when a manager took on his clerk's duties as well; the dismissed clerk was redundant. However, an employer who took on extra employees in anticipation of additional work which did not materialise could not claim they were redundant when he had to dismiss them: the requirement for the employees never actually materialised, therefore it could not have ceased or diminished (*O'Hare v Rotaprint Ltd* [1980] IRLR 47).

It should be noted, however, that the dismissal of employees for replacement by self-employed independent contractors *can* amount to redundancy. The NIRC in *Bromby & Hoare Ltd v Evans* (1972) ICR 113 held that "requirements" means "needs" and if an employer no longer needs employees because the work can be done more economically by contractors that falls within the statutory definition of redundancy.

Contractual Work

The question of what is work of a particular kind has also raised problems and in two important cases the Court of Appeal addressed itself to this matter. In *Nelson v BBC* [1977] IRLR 148 the employee was dismissed when his work in the Caribbean Service disappeared, but was not held to be redundant since, under his contract, he could be required to work elsewhere but had refused to do so. In *Haden Ltd v Cowen* [1982] IRLR 314, the employee tried unsuccessfully to apply this argument to his own case. He failed because, although his contract stated that he could be required to undertake any duties falling within the scope of his capabilities, the Court of Appeal held that this clause referred to his job at the time of dismissal — Divisional Contracts Surveyor, and not to quantity surveying in general.

Reorganisation

It is often the case that a reorganisation of some kind within a company can result in a change in the requirements for certain employees. Whether any subsequent dismissals are for redundancy will depend largely on the nature of the reorganisation. The abolition of two old jobs and the introduction of a new one, which incorporates parts of the previous duties but is significantly different in terms of the work to be done, can justify dismissal on grounds of redundancy of the two original jobholders (*Robinson v British Island Airways Ltd* [1977] IRLR 477). In *Murphy v Epsom College* [1983] IRLR 395 the Robinson case was used as authority for holding that a plumber was dismissed as redundant when his employers wanted a more specialised heating technician instead.

Where the reorganisation takes the form of a change in the hours of work, rather than of the work being done, several cases have indicated that this is unlikely to constitute a redundancy within the meaning of the statute. In *Johnson v Notts Combined Police Authority* [1974] IRLR 20 two clerks who were dismissed for refusing to accept changed hours were held by the Court of Appeal not to be redundant. A change in hours of work alone is not a change in "work of a particular kind". This finding has been followed in several other cases, such as *Lesney Productions & Co Ltd v Nolan* [1977] IRLR 77, in which the employees on night-shift were dismissed as redundant because their work had dropped off, whilst those on day-shift who refused to accept a new shift pattern and were subsequently dismissed were held not be redundant. The reorganised day-shift was intended as an economy measure to cut down overtime; there was no reduction in the work done by the employees. The EAT confirmed this in *Maher v Photo Trade Processing Ltd* EAT 451/83.

Lay Off and the Contract

Where employees are employed with normal hours of work, for instance 09.00 hours to 17.00 hours, employers can only reduce their hours or stop work on a particular lay off day if they have the contractual right to do so. Alternatively, they may obtain employees' agreement to such a temporary or permanent change. Where employers unilaterally take these steps to change hours, employees can sue for loss of wages through the courts.

In *Needs v CAV Ltd* [1983] IRLR 360 the Queen's Bench considered claims for wages by an employee who had been laid off for two days because of an industrial dispute. They decided that there was no general right at common law to lay off without pay.

Employees might also seek other remedies through a tribunal by claiming constructive dismissal and/or redundancy payments.

Claiming Redundancy Pay

S.88 of the EP(C)A states that if employees, in response to a diminution of work, are laid off or their hours of work are reduced to the extent that they earn less than half pay, they can serve their employer with notice to terminate their employment and their intention to claim a redundancy payment. However, this can only be done where there is a contractual right (express or implied) to lay off. The conditions for claiming redundancy payments are as follows:
- the employee must have been laid off or kept on short time for four or more consecutive weeks
- if the lay off or short time was not continuous, the employee must have been laid off or kept on short time for a series of six weeks out of 13 (of which no more than three were consecutive)
- the employee must give the employer notice of his or her intention to claim a redundancy payment within four weeks of the end of the lay off or short time period.

The only defence to such a claim is for the employer to write, within seven days of the notice being received, stating that he reasonably expects within four weeks to provide work again without further lay off or short time for a period of not less than 13 weeks. Additionally, he should state that he will contest the claim for redundancy payments. If the employer is going to contest the claim he must produce some evidence of future work (*Taylor v Dunbar Buildings* (1966) ITR 249). This work must be the same as that which the employee was employed to do — not alternative work. In *Reid v Young and Son* EAT 714/82 it was held that, provided employees have complied fully with the legislation, the question of whether they acted unreasonably in turning down alternative work should not arise.

If the employer does not contest the claim the employee must, in order to get the redundancy payment, give at least one week's notice (more if the contract requires) to terminate the contract. This notice to quit can be given orally but it must be served within four weeks of the giving of the notice to claim redundancy pay (*Fabar Construction v Race* [1979] IRLR 232). If the employer contests the claim and the employee goes to a tribunal for his or her redundancy pay, notice to quit must be given within three weeks of receiving the tribunal's decision.

The Technicalities

Where the employer lays off in breach of contract (ie without the contractual right to do so), the employees are still entitled to full payment. Therefore, they cannot claim under s.88 but, of course, they can resign and claim constructive dismissal and/or redundancy pay in the usual way (*Power Duffryn Wagon Co Ltd v House* (1974) ICR 123).

Fair Redundancy Selection

The law governing fair selection for redundancy is found in s.59 of the EP(C)A which states that:

"Where the reason or the principal reason for the dismissal is that the employee was redundant, but it is shown that the circumstances constituting the redundancy applied equally to one or more other employees who held similar positions and who have not been dismissed and either:

(a) the reason (or if more than one, the principal reason) for which he was selected related to his trade union membership or activities or

(b) he was selected for dismissal in contravention of a customary arrangement or agreed procedure relating to redundancy and there were no special reasons justifying a departure from that arrangement,

then the dismissal shall be regarded as unfair".

The General Guidelines

The case of *Williams and others v Compair Maxam Ltd* [1982] IRLR 83 led the Employment Appeal Tribunal to set down five useful principles to be followed by employers who recognise trade unions when redundancies are necessary.

1. The employer should seek to give as much warning as possible of impending redundancies to enable the union and individual employees to take early steps to acquaint themselves with the relevant facts, consider possible alternatives and, if necessary, obtain alternative employment, either in the company or outside.

2. The employer should try to reach agreement with the union on the criteria to be applied in selecting employees for redundancy and, when the selection has been made, the employer should consider, with the union, whether the selection actually was made in accordance with those criteria.

3. Whether or not agreement can be reached with the union, the employer should seek to establish criteria for selection which, so far as possible, do not depend solely upon the opinion of the person making the selection, but can be checked objectively against such things as absence records, efficiency at the job, experience or length of service.

4. The employer should try to ensure that the selection is made fairly in accordance with such criteria, and any representations made by the union should be taken into consideration.

5. Finally, the employer should always consider whether alternative employment can be offered instead of redundancy.

It must be stressed, however, that these principles are for general guidance only: departure from them does not mean dismissal will be automatically unfair, nor that they should be followed by every company regardless of size and circumstances.

For instance, in *A Simpson & Son (Motors) v Reid and Findlater* [1983] IRLR 401, an industrial tribunal held that the company had unfairly dismissed two employees because they had not followed the guidelines set out above. The EAT rejected the decision and substituted a finding of fair dismissal. The observations contained in the Compair Maxam case, they said, have no application to a case such as this which concerned a small, non-unionised company. Although the selection of two employees out of three was made by one person it was not disputed that great care had been taken in deciding which two had to go.

LIFO — Maybe!

One common agreement on selection is "Last in — first out, other things being equal". In *Beardmore v Westinghouse Brake & Signal Co Ltd* [1976] IRLR 310 this was the procedure and Mr Beardmore was selected because, although not the most junior member of staff, his employer considered he lacked personality, ability and leadership. This dismissal was held to be fair by the tribunal, but the employee's appeal was allowed: the tribunal should have specified in more detail the reasons for the employer deciding that other things were not equal. The moral of this case is clear: if you apply such criteria, make sure your selection can be justified by reference to such documents as timekeeping/absence records, disciplinary warnings, annual appraisal records, etc.

Redundancy and Reasonableness

The question of reasonableness in a redundancy dismissal is important: many employers have fallen foul of tribunals because they failed to consult redundant employees, or give adequate warnings, or consider alternative work, before dismissing them. The fact that there is no recognised trade union in respect of employees, and that they are genuinely redundant, will not necessarily prevent tribunals deciding that employers have acted unreasonably, so making the dismissals unfair.

Consultation in the context of redundancies is normally associated with recognised trade unions, prescribed time limits, specific information, etc. Even where there is no recognised trade union, or the number of redundant employees is very small, the requirement for consultation of some kind with the employees concerned has been clearly established.

In *Paine & Moore v Grundy (Teddington) Ltd* [1981] IRLR 267 the EAT held that it was a general principle of good industrial relations that employers should take reasonable steps to get together as much information as possible before coming to any decision to dismiss on grounds of redundancy. This case was sent back to the tribunal for it to find out whether the reasons behind the two employees' poor attendance records (which formed part of the basis of their selection for redundancy) had been looked into. Consultation could have shown that prolonged periods of absence had been due to an accident, from which the employee had fully recovered. Future absences would, therefore, be unlikely and failure to consult could well render the employee's selection and subsequent dismissal for redundancy unfair on that basis (*Wimpey Asphalt v McGuire* EAT 370/81).

The other main reason for the importance tribunals place on individual consultation is evident in the case of *Vokes Ltd v Bear* [1973] IRLR 363. The employee was a works manager and was dismissed for redundancy with no prior warning and without any attempt by the employer to find him alternative work in one of the other 300 companies in the group. The dismissal was held to be unfair for this reason, particularly since one company in the group was advertising for a senior manager at the time of dismissal. In the NIRC's opinion, the employer had not done all that was reasonable and failure to consider alternative work rendered the dismissal unfair.

It should be noted that failure to offer alternative employment because the employer does not think it suitable, is not necessarily an acceptable defence. Consultation might well reveal that the employee would be prepared to accept an alternative job (contrary to expectations), rather than face redundancy (*Ladbroke Courage Holidays v Asten* [1981] IRLR 59). If the employer has failed to check this before dismissal a tribunal will probably consider he has acted unreasonably. What is "suitable" alternative work should be left up to employees to decide; whether a transfer to another post within the company involves demotion is for them to worry about — that post should still be offered if available (*Avonmouth Construction Co Ltd v Shipway* [1979] IRLR 14). Consultation with a recognised trade union is not necessarily an acceptable reason for the employer not consulting an individual employee (*Huddersfield Parcels Ltd v Sykes* [1981] IRLR 115). The fairness of a redundancy dismissal will only be unaffected by a failure to offer alternative work if the reasons behind the employer's actions are: that there is no other work available — there is no obligation to create new jobs (*Pond v Louis Edwards & Sons* EAT 122/80); or that the employee is not believed to be capable of doing the jobs which are vacant at the time (*England v Bromley* EAT 210/79).

Would the Outcome Differ?

As is often the case when an employer has failed to follow the proper procedure, tribunals sometimes take into account whether failure to consult the employee prior to a redundancy dismissal has had any effect on the eventual outcome. In *British United Shoe Machinery Co v Clarke* [1977] IRLR 297 the EAT held that it is open to tribunals to consider whether, had there been consultation, it would have made any difference. If they decide that it would not, they can either make a finding of fair dismissal or hold that the dismissal was unfair but award nil compensation. The difficulty that arises, of course, is in assessing what the outcome would have been had the employer "acted reasonably". The EAT warned tribunals not to make unrealistic assumptions about the outcome of searches for alternative employment. However, in *Abbotts v Wesson-Glynwed Steels Ltd* [1982] IRLR 51 the tribunal took account of the fact that — although consultation would have made no difference to the outcome — the employee's dismissal would probably have been delayed for 14 days. Compensation of two weeks' pay was therefore awarded.

Taking a Case to Tribunal

Over the last few years or so it has become increasingly obvious that the EAT and higher courts are severely restricting the possibility of making a successful appeal against decisions of industrial tribunals by reducing the number of areas that can be considered as points of law, saying that these are matters of fact for the tribunal to decide and deprecating the use of leading cases where guidelines have been suggested on the correct approach for the tribunal to take. The moral of this is that the employer must put everything either into settling the matter or into the defence at the tribunal hearing.

Any defence will improve immeasurably if the story is told to the tribunal coherently. This means proper preparation which will be time-consuming even if it is done by a legally qualified representative.

Preparation

Good preparation of tribunal cases begins even before the reply form (IT3) has been returned to the tribunal. It is important that the applicant's complaint form (IT1) gets to the right person; ideally this is the manager who will be responsible for collecting information and possibly seeing the action all the way to a tribunal hearing itself. All correspondence either from or about the applicant should be channelled through this manager.

The reply form (IT3) should be returned within 14 days to the regional tribunal office. An extension of time will readily be granted if it is requested in writing. Failure to return the IT3 may prevent the employer from taking any further part and this, in almost all cases, means the action will be lost.

Investigation

The manager in charge of the case should investigate the matter thoroughly before completing the IT3. The story may have been told for the umpteenth time but those people who played a part in the dismissal must be questioned again rigorously — they should be put under a bit of pressure just as they will at the tribunal hearing. It is rarely possible to defend a case effectively by a written defence, so witnesses will have to attend the hearing: forget about affidavits since these are of little value — tribunals like to be able to question witnesses.

The employer must give sufficient information on the form to show the reason for dismissal and must highlight the procedures followed, showing that the company acted reasonably towards the employee.

Further and Better Particulars

The information given by the applicant, eg wages, hours, job title, etc, should be checked. If it is not clear what the applicant is claiming, or if the detail is obscure, further and better particulars can be sought directly from the applicant. The procedure is to write requesting details of the grounds relied on, relevant facts and the argument that will be put forward.

For instance, the simple statement "I was frequently victimised by them" needs more definition: who victimised? when did it happen? what did they do? what did they say? how many incidents? was anyone else present? is discrimination being alleged? Without more details it would be impossible to prepare the case properly. Once the further information is received it should be thoroughly checked out. The tribunal has the power to dismiss an application or strike out the notice of appearance if requests for further information, backed up by a tribunal order, are not complied with.

The Employer's Information

Accurate and detailed information in chronological order relating to the events leading to the dismissal should be given on the IT3 — "who, where, what, when". If there is a failure to follow a reasonable procedure and it can be explained away adequately the reasons should be stated, eg "Dismissal rather than a written warning was given because the applicant had shown such an intransigent attitude at the disciplinary hearing that a warning would not have persuaded him to do as requested".

The manager should make sure that all the relevant documents are collected together but these do not have to be sent to the tribunal.

The detailed summary of events on the IT3 will help the ACAS conciliation officer in his or her job of securing a settlement or withdrawal of the application. Furthermore, to hold things back so that the applicant can be taken by surprise at the tribunal hearing might result in an adjournment or postponement and costs may well be awarded against the party causing delay.

Finally, the manager should check that there is no statutory bar to the applicant presenting his or her case. Some common examples are:
– the applicant has insufficient qualifying service
– the applicant is beyond the normal retirement age
– the applicant is ordinarily employed outside Great Britain
– the applicant has not applied within the three month time limit.

If such a bar appears to be present, a preliminary hearing should be requested to see if the tribunal has jurisdiction to hear the complaint. At such a hearing the employer only needs to bring evidence and witnesses which have a bearing on these technical matters. The tribunal will not hear evidence about the dismissal itself until such matters have been decided.

Letters which will accompany the IT3 should be photocopied and sent by recorded delivery to the regional office of the tribunals.

Pre-Hearing Tactics

Tactics before the hearing revolve around strategies to get the applicant to withdraw the claim or to settle the matter on terms acceptable to the company.

The applicant may be looking for remedies which cannot be obtained from the tribunal, eg pay in lieu of holiday, a reference, "clearing his or her name", etc. The conciliation officer can usually do a good job in explaining to an applicant that the tribunal can only award compensation or, rarely, reinstatement or re-engagement. However, it may be possible to settle the claim on the basis of a reference and payment of contractual debts.

Pre-hearing assessments may be used successfully to get rid of hopeless cases, especially where the applicant is less than enthusiastic about going to tribunal. Requests for further and better particulars can also be used to reveal glaring weaknesses in the applicant's case (or the employer's for that matter). This will probably be the first time that the applicant realises how closely his or her allegations will be scrutinised and that any assertions will not be accepted without challenge.

Managers may also find the applicant making a tactical ploy by applying for witness orders for all and sundry — to the extent that a small firm would have to close for the day. An interlocutory hearing could be requested by individual employees to have the orders withdrawn if there is little relevant evidence that they can give, while those with important evidence will probably be at the hearing anyway.

With the help of the conciliation officer the parties may be able to come to a financial settlement. Any manager who is in charge of a case must become familiar with the way in which compensation is assessed. This does not mean knowing what the maximum award is, since a sensible assessment can form the top line for any negotiations.

Unwinnable Cases

Sometimes the case is so clear that, with the best will in the world, there can only be one outcome — an unfair dismissal finding. The manager in charge of the case may wish to avoid publicity and the ignominy of having the company's manager told off by the tribunal, by paying compensation. However, some applicants refuse to settle: they want their day in court! In such circumstances a sensible move might be to make a direct offer based on the likely calculation of the unfair dismissal award. Set out the calculation clearly, do not label the letter "without prejudice" and make it clear that, although the company does not accept that the dismissal is unfair, it is prepared to offer the sum in settlement. The applicant should be encouraged to discuss the letter with a solicitor or a citizens' advice bureau. The letter can be introduced in evidence at the subsequent hearing if the applicant refuses to settle and the chairman is likely to bear in mind the fact that the applicant has wasted the tribunal's time. In the majority of cases, however, the applicant is likely to accept the offer.

Finally, reinstatement or re-engagement might seriously be considered, especially if the applicant has requested this remedy. Reinstatements and re-engagements can be made on terms agreeable to the parties (ACAS is obliged to ensure that the terms are equitable). This usually means on the basis of back pay whilst unemployed and, frequently, the employee being given a final written warning.

The employee will have continuity of employment preserved by statutory regulation. If applicants refuse (unreasonably) an offer of reinstatement or re-engagement, employers are entitled to argue that they have failed to mitigate their loss and that they should not be compensated. This particular tactic is becoming popular in cases arising from dismissals for trade union activities or non-membership of a trade union in a closed shop situation. The reason is simple: the special award is very large and the joinder provisions threaten future industrial relations within the company.

Conciliated Agreements

The fact that discussions have taken place through the conciliation officer cannot be placed before the tribunal because such evidence is inadmissible. However, tribunals do expect employers to try and buy off trouble since this will save public money being spent on a hearing. It should be noted that an offer of a settlement does not imply that the company accepts that the dismissal was unfair.

In some cases settlements are more cost-effective than fighting and winning cases at tribunal. It is important to remember that ACAS can also be called in to help before a tribunal claim is made. Once an agreement has been reached for the employee to leave the company on the payment of an agreed sum, the conciliation officer can record it all on a COT3 and effectively prevent the employee from going to tribunal. Of course, the conciliation officer will tell the employee what rights are being signed away.

Postponements

Postponements are often used tactically to delay hearings to the extent that the applicant allows the case to die or withdraws it. This cannot be recommended because memories will dull over time and compensation may become payable when an early hearing would have resulted in none or a smaller amount. Clearly, the loss caused to the applicant can be estimated more accurately over a long period of time, eg the applicant's new job may fold once his references are received and a longer period of compensation may be appropriate. However, when there are genuine reasons postponements are usually granted.

Preparing for the Hearing

It is extremely useful to interview all potential witnesses and take a statement of their evidence beforehand. The statements are to enable the representative to check out discrepancies between the evidence given by different witnesses; to remind witnesses of situations several months after the events (although these statements should not be read by the witnesses to the tribunal) and to act as a check list of evidence for each witness so that the representative can tick off each section as the witness goes through the evidence.

All the appropriate documents should be gathered together to create a "bundle" of evidence (original copies) which should be numbered consecutively.

Not all the documents appertaining to the ex-employee will be relevant and placed in the bundle but all the contents of the employee file should be taken to the hearing just in case. Don't forget, the statement of terms and conditions of employment, written company disciplinary/grievance procedures and pay records for at least six months will nearly always be required as evidence.

Collecting the Evidence

Consideration should be given to preparing material for the tribunal's better understanding of the situation. For example, quite complex reorganisations or alleged constructive dismissals can be understood more easily if an organisation chart before the changes, together with one illustrating the new structure is drawn up. Office and building plans can also explain easily the escape route of an alleged thief almost caught red-handed. Photographs can also be used to good effect. Consider the use of exhibits, eg of bad workmanship, etc. For instance, a damaged side panel from a coach was brought to the second day's hearing of a case to refute the applicant's allegation that damage was only slight.

Another important aspect of preparation concerns whether or not applicants have mitigated their loss. They will usually attempt to show that they have actively sought employment. The employer may cross-examine and present evidence which has a bearing on both of these points. A collection of local newspapers or trade magazines will provide evidence about the availability of suitable jobs. Enquiries at the local jobcentre may also indicate how many jobs are available in the particular trade or profession. Questions can be put in cross-examination with regard to these advertisements — whether the applicant has seen them, applied for them, etc.

Witnesses

Witnesses should be selected to give direct evidence about the event. Try and avoid hearsay evidence, ie "she said she was not going to take any notice of the reprimand, but I wasn't there when she said that to her manager". However, a tribunal can and does allow hearsay if it is germane to the case and if the employer took it into account when deciding to dismiss.

In deciding which witnesses to take to the hearing, the person who conducted the investigation beforehand must be included. More witnesses do not equate with "weight" of evidence — an applicant alone can be believed in spite of larger numbers of witnesses appearing for the company. It is the quality of the witnesses that counts; they must be convincing.

Finally, a pre-hearing conference of the company's witnesses is very useful. This is not the time to rehearse the evidence; rather, it should be used to explain the ground rules of the tribunal hearing:
- explain what will happen, where to meet, what to wear (business-like attire but comfortable), how to address the tribunal members ("Sir" or "Madam"), what oath or affirmation is to be taken before the hearing
- check through the statements with each witness and see if there is more to add or be changed
- explain how you will ask the questions (not leading questions) and remind witnesses that they should not look at you but at the tribunal when they answer (turn the chair round to face the tribunal) and that it is important to talk slowly and loudly so that all can hear
- explain some of the lawyers' tricks, eg oversimplifying situations by requiring short speedy answers of "yes" or "no", etc. Explain that they should qualify first and then answer and, if pressure is brought to bear, appeal to the chairman to be allowed to answer in their own way to avoid misleading the tribunal
- find out background information about the witnesses which will enhance their credibility, eg many years of management experience in several

industries is a point that can be brought to the tribunal's attention with a question about previous work experience.

It goes without saying that a visit as an observer to a tribunal hearing will be very beneficial to all the participants.

Organising the Paperwork

Most representatives will have to deal with the problem of paperwork at the tribunal. A loose-leaf file divided into sections is an ideal way of keeping the papers in order and giving ease of access. The sections can be prepared in advance as follows:

(a) opening statement — this gives details about the company (size, departments, products, etc), chronological order of events, persons giving evidence and the documents that will be submitted. This statement, however, is often dispensed with at the chairman's discretion

(b) main case — usually this includes the "proofs of evidence" and perhaps an outline of questions to be asked to elicit the information; use open-ended questions, eg "what did you do?","what happened next?", etc

(c) cross-examination — outline of questions for the applicant, etc — particularly those areas that are in dispute; leading questions can be used

(d) closing statement ("submissions") — difficult to prepare in advance of hearing the evidence but it should:
    (i) highlight the evidence that supports the employer's reason for dismissal and the reasonableness of the decision to dismiss
    (ii) explain why some evidence should be preferred and
    (iii) consider if the ex-employee has contributed to the dismissal if the tribunal does not find the dismissal fair and suggest a percentage reduction. If evidence has already been presented about the employee's loss of earnings and this has been cross-examined, it will also be sensible to present arguments about the failure to mitigate

(e) potential compensation until the date of hearing
(f) important dates in chronological order
(g) correspondence with the ex-employee and the tribunal
(h) industrial tribunal forms IT1 and IT3
(i) copies of case law (if you intend to use any).

The Day of the Hearing

Barring last minute settlements at the door of the tribunal, the case and all the witnesses will have to be assembled ready for the hearing. The manager presenting the company's case should ensure that all the necessary photo-copying of documents has been done beforehand (five copies in all). Company witnesses should be shepherded to the Respondent's Room. Hearings usually start at 10.00 hours but it is worth checking to see if the case is a "floater", ie waiting until a tribunal completes another hearing. The wait could be a long one and, in London, the parties might find themselves hurtling in a taxi to another tribunal centre if there is a spare tribunal available.

There should be ample opportunity to meet the applicant or his or her representative before the hearing starts. Perhaps a settlement can be obtained, new evidence checked out and the witnesses for the applicant established.

The next step is to make the acquaintance of the tribunal clerk who will explain the procedures, note down the names of the witnesses and case law that is to be used and the preferred methods of taking the oath. When the tribunal is ready the clerk will escort all the parties into the room where the hearing will take place.

The employer sits on the left hand side facing the tribunal. The representatives should arrange their witnesses behind them.

Make sure that messages are passed on pieces of paper to the company representative — don't break concentration. Giving evidence and addressing the tribunal can be done from a seated position but witnesses usually seat themselves at a separate table on the right hand side between the tribunal and the applicant when they give evidence.

Tribunal Procedures

The way the tribunal tackles the case is entirely at its own discretion but the usual pattern is as follows.

1. If the employer acknowledges that the employee was dismissed, the employer will give evidence first (but the chairman has discretion).
2. The employer's representative will give an opening statement (usually dispensed with) and then call witnesses.
3. Each witness should be taken through their evidence, then cross-examined by the other side; further questions may be asked by the tribunal and then the witness can be re-examined by the employer's representative about facts previously presented (not new facts).
4. When the employer's witnesses have all given evidence the other side will present their witnesses and the procedure will be repeated.
5. Both sides will then summarise their case in turn. This is often dispensed with if all parties agree.
6. The tribunal retire to consider their decision.

Sometimes, however, tribunal chairmen are not content to let the parties present their own cases. They may adopt an inquisitorial approach asking most of the questions themselves and controlling the proceedings totally. Whatever style is adopted, the representative has little choice but to go along with it. Most cases have a few critical points that the tribunal has to be sure about and an experienced chairman will know precisely what questions are necessary to establish the fairness or otherwise of the dismissal.

If any members of the party wish to leave the room during the hearing it is good manners to seek the chairman's permission. If any witness wishes to leave the hearing after giving evidence, once again the chairman's permission should be sought. It must also be remembered that it is a cardinal sin to discuss the case with any witness still giving evidence during the lunch break.

Cross-Examination

Every company witness will be cross-examined by the other side and no doubt some searching questions will be asked by the tribunal members. After that the company representative will be asked if he or she has any re-examination. This may be a useful opportunity to get the witness to restate central parts of the evidence. When the company's witnesses have been heard, the applicant can present his or her evidence and call witnesses. The company's representative must take verbatim notes of the applicant's evidence and highlight conflicting evidence. These are areas where the applicant *must* be cross-examined unless the matter is of little significance to the case.

Leading questions can be asked, eg "I put it to you that you did re-enter the premises after clocking out" etc. It is useful to prepare a few obvious questions to prevent "drying up" before the hearing. It is not essential to be good at cross-examination: pick out the areas you wish to cross-examine — ask a few halting questions and the chairman will usually help you out by formulating the questions for you.

Finally, do not forget to cross-examine about mitigation of loss. It is sometimes unclear from the proceedings when this should be done and if there are signs that the chairman is impatient it will probably mean that you need not concern yourself with compensation because the applicant's case will be dismissed. There is no harm in asking the chairman from the outset how the case is to be conducted, eg will the tribunal hear the evidence, retire for a decision and then hear evidence about compensation/mitigation afterwards or hear all the evidence including that on compensation before making the decision.

Closing statements can then be given by both parties. Keep this brief: include any references to case law if appropriate but most cases do not need such embellishments. Then, await the decision.

Appeals and EAT Procedure

The Employment Appeal Tribunal is composed of lay members headed by a judge acting as a chairman. It avoids formality as far as possible and any party may appear in person or be represented by anyone he or she chooses. The Employment Appeal Tribunal Rules 1980 (SI 1980 No. 1608) give the EAT power to regulate its own procedure.

The notice of appeal and a copy of the industrial tribunal decision must be lodged with the Registrar within 42 days of the date the decision was sent to the parties. Extensions of time are allowed only in wholly exceptional circumstances and the EAT can consider whether or not the application would fail when deciding whether to extend the time limits (*De Mars v Gurr Hohms & Angier Bird Ltd* (1973) ICR 35). The Registrar has a vetting function and an appeal will not be registered if it does not allege an error of law. If the notice is rejected, a new notice may be served within the remaining time limit or 28 days whichever is the longer. The papers will be placed before a judge for a decision and the complainant (appellant) can be asked to attend to show why the appeal should not be dismissed.

Grounds for Appeal

If the appellant claims that there is an error of law he or she must establish that the tribunal has:

- misdirected itself in law, misunderstood the law or misapplied the law, eg applied the wrong statutory provision, overlooked a section of the Act or overlooked a case decided by a higher court which is binding upon it or
- misunderstood the facts or misapplied the facts, eg made a finding of fact and then ignored it or
- reached a conclusion unsupported by evidence or reached a decision which no reasonable tribunal could have reached, although they have not misdirected themselves in law, or misapplied the facts (*Watling v William Bird and Son Contractors Ltd* (1976) ITR 70).

It is not always easy to establish a point of law on which to appeal; some issues can be a mixture of fact and law. For this reason taking legal advice is advisable; it is important to take care because costs can be awarded for unnecessary, improper or vexatious actions. Findings of fact made by a tribunal can be challenged as being wrong in law only if there is no evidence to support them or there was misdirection. (*Chiu v British Aerospace plc et al* [1982] IRLR 56).

In cases of constructive dismissal where the ex-employee is alleging a fundamental breach of contract, the EAT has said that this involves a mixture of fact and law. However, the EAT cannot substitute its own decision for that of the tribunal if there was evidence that would justify the tribunal's decision. (*Woods v W M Car Services Ltd* [1981] IRLR 347).

It is settled and accepted practice that the EAT will not allow new issues to be raised on appeal which were not considered by the industrial tribunal but where the matter concerns tribunal jurisdiction, eg whether a claim was made within the time limit, an appeal can be allowed.

There is a similar practice concerning evidence. In rare circumstances the EAT can hear fresh evidence but only if some reasonable explanation can be given for it not being put before the tribunal in the first instance, if the new evidence is credible and if it would have or might have had a decisive effect upon the decision (*International Aviation Services (UK) Ltd v Jones* [1979] IRLR 155).

Chairman's Notes

When appeals are made the industrial tribunal chairman's notes are often requested by the parties. These can only be regarded as an aide memoire and where they appear to conflict with the findings of fact made by the tribunal it is the findings that must take priority. As a general rule these notes will not be provided unless cause is shown. Usually if the grounds for appeal are the allegation that there was no evidence to support a finding of fact or the tribunal had misunderstood the evidence or the finding of fact was perverse (*Webb v Anglian Water Authority* [1981] IRLR 494) the application will be granted. Even then the appellant must specify exactly the finding that is being attacked and state what the finding should have been. Where an unrepresented party brings in a representative for the appeal the application for the chairman's notes will be treated in a more generous fashion. The EAT Practice Directions 1981 make it clear that the chairman's notes are supplied for the use of the Appeal Tribunal and not for parties to embark on a "fishing" expedition to establish further grounds of appeal.

Complaints of Bias

If the ground for appeal is an allegation of the chairman's bias, the EAT Practice Directions require that:

(a) the notice of appeal must give full and sufficient particulars
(b) the allegations must be specific and not general in character
(c) the Registrar may require affidavits dealing with the matters upon which the complaint is based or can require further particulars of the complaint
(d) the complaint will be drawn to the notice of the chairman of the industrial tribunal so that he or she can have the opportunity of commenting upon it.

Jurisdiction of the EAT

Recent cases have further clarified the scope of the EAT's jurisdiction. In *IMI Yorkshire Imperial Ltd v Olender* (1982) ICR 69 the EAT refused to hear an appeal concerning an order for reinstatement of three workers who had been dismissed for sleeping on the job. The employer had complied with the order but wished to establish that dismissal was a legitimate action to take in such a matter. The EAT said they thought the matter was essentially for negotiation and declined to establish the principle for the future as it would discourage employers from displaying generous behaviour.

INDEX OF CASES

Abbotts v Wesson-Glynwed Steels Ltd
  [1982] IRLR 51 246
Airfix Footwear Ltd v Cope [1978]
  IRLR 396 197
Alderton v Richard Burgon Association
  Ltd QBD 1974 CLR 318 195
Anderson and Chambers v Oak Motor
  Works Ltd (unreported) 179
Armour v Skeen [1977] IRLR 310 36
Associated Dairies Ltd v Hartley
  [1979] IRLR 171 92
Association of Patternmakers and Allied
  Craftsmen v Kirwin [1978] IRLR 318 . .127
Avonmouth Construction Co Ltd v
  Shipway [1979] IRLR 14 245
Barber v Tricentrol Cars (Leeds) Ltd
  (unreported) 177
BBC v Beckett [1983] IRLR 43 117
Beardmore v Westinghouse Brake &
  Signal Co Ltd [1976] IRLR 310 244
Beloff v Pressdram Ltd (1973)
  1 AER 241 188
Bevan Harris Ltd t/a Clyde Leather
  Co v Gair [1981] IRLR 520 158
Birch and Humber v University of
  Liverpool Court of Appeal 23185 239
Boychuck v H J Symons Holdings
  [1977] IRLR 395 91
British Aircraft Corporation Ltd v Austin
  [1978] IRLR 332 91
British Leyland (UK) Ltd v Ashraf
  [1978] IRLR 330 . . . . .26, 27
British Railways Board v Herrington
  (1972) AC 877 30
British United Shoe Machinery Co v
  Clarke [1977] IRLR 297 . . . . .130, 246
Bromby & Hoare Ltd v Evans (1972)
  ICR 113 240
Brooks (W) & Son v Skinner [1984]
  IRLR 379 178
Burdett-Coutts and others v
  Hertfordshire County Council [1984] IRLR
  91 116
Carry All Motors Ltd v Pennington
  [1980] IRLR 455 240
Chapman v Beacon Auto Electrics Ltd

(unreported) 18
Chiu v British Aerospace plc et al [1982]
  IRLR 56 255
Cleminson v Post Office Engineering
  Union [1980] IRLR 1 133
Conway v George Wimpey (1951) 1 AER
  363 37
Costain Engineering Ltd v Draycott
  [1977] IRLR 17 .21
Courage Home Trade Ltd v Keys [1986]
  IRLR 426 27
Cox v ELG Metals Ltd (1985) ICR 310 17
Cresswell and others v Board of Inland
  Revenue [1984] IRLR 190 152
Dairy Produce Packers Ltd v
  Beverstock [1981] IRLR 265 178
Dalgleish v Kew House Farm Ltd [1982]
  IRLR 251 202
D'ambrogio v Human Jacobs Ltd [1978]
  IRLR 236 197
De Mars v Gurr Hohms & Angier
  Bird Ltd (1973) ICR 35 255
Delanair Ltd v Mead [1976] IRLR 340 240
Donoghue v Stevenson (1932)
  AC 562 . . . . .28, 29
Drym Fabricators Ltd v Johnson (1981) ICR
  274 19
Eales v Halfords COIT 1179/51 90
East Lindsey District Council v
  Daubney [1977] IRLR 181 . . . . . .130, 174
England v Bromley EAT 210/79 245
Fabar Construction v Race [1979]
  IRLR 232 242
Fashion Industries (Hartlepool) Ltd v
  Miller and others EAT 34/80 227
Fogarty v Austin Morris (unreported) . . .178
Ford v Warwickshire County Council
  [1983] IRLR 126 193
Forman Construction Ltd v Kelly [1977]
  IRLR 468 227
Freud v Bentalls Ltd [1982] IRLR 443 130
Frizzell v Fladers & others t/a P J
  Contracting COIT 847/232 91
Gilbert v Kembridge Fibres Ltd [1984]
  IRLR 52 27

258

Gismatic Ltd v Neal EAT 129/83 197
Goodeve v Gilsons CA 31185 22
Gorris v Scott (1874) LR 9 32
Green (E) & Son (Castings) Ltd and
    others v ASTMS and another [1984]
    IRLR 135 128
Greensides v J T Ellis and Co Ltd
    (unreported) 212
Gunn v British Waterways Board
    . . . .(unreported) 179
Haden Ltd v Cowen [1982] IRLR 314 241
Hanson v Fashion Industries (Hartlepool)
    Ltd [1980] IRLR 393 24
Harper v National Coal Board [1980]
    IRLR 260 226
Henderson v Granville Tours Ltd [1982]
    IRLR 494 14
Hennessy v Craigmyle & Co Ltd and
    ACAS [1985] IRLR 446 28
Huddersfield Parcels Ltd v Sykes [1981]
    IRLR 115 245
Hughes v Lord Advocate (1963) AC 837 . . .33
Igbo v Johnson Matthey Chemicals
    Ltd [1986] IRLR 215 . . . . .26, 27
IMI Yorkshire Imperial Ltd v Olender
    (1982) ICR 69 .256
In re Polemis (1921) 3 KB 560 . . . . .32, 33
Inner London Education Authority v
    Lloyd [1981] IRLR 394 202
Inner London Education Authority v
    Nash [1979] IRLR 29 26
International Aviation Services (UK)
    Ltd v Jones [1979] IRLR 155 256
International Sports Co Ltd v Thomson
    [1980] IRLR 340 175
Iran National Airways Corporation v
    Bond (unreported) 20
Janata Bank v Ahmed [1981] IRLR 457 . . .222
Johnson v Highland Regional Council
    SCOIT 1480/84 170
Johnson v Notts Combined Police
    Authority [1974] IRLR 20 241
Jones v Associated Tunnelling Co Ltd
    [1981] IRLR 477 118
Joseph v Joseph (1967) 1 CH 78 24
Ladbroke Courage Holidays v Asten
    [1981] IRLR 59 245
Lesney Productions & Co Ltd v Nolan
    [1977] IRLR 77 241
Limpus v London General Omnibus
    Company (1862) I H & C 526 37
Macarthys Ltd v Smith   [1980] IRLR 209   11

Mackay v River Borra Board COIT
    F116/220 175
McKew v Holland & Hannon & Cubbitts
    (Scotland) (1969) 3 AER 1621 34
McWilliams v Sir William Arrol & Co
    (1962) 1 AER 623 31
Maher v Photo Trades Processing Ltd
    EAT 451/83 241
Malik v BHS COIT 987/12 90
Massey v Crown Life Insurance [1978]
    IRLR 31 189
Mayhew v Anderson (Stoke Newington)
    Ltd [1978] IRLR 101 91
Moody v Telefusion Ltd [1978]
    IRLR 311 113
Morton Sundour Fabrics v Shaw (1967)
    2 ITR 84 229
Mumford v Boulton & Paul Ltd
    (1971) ITR 76 .240
Murphy v Epsom College [1983]
    IRLR 395 241
National Car Parks Ltd v Diamond
    EAT 397/83 159
Needs v CAV Ltd [1983] IRLR 360 241
Nelson v BBC [1977] IRLR 148 240
Nethermere (St Neots) Ltd v Gardiner &
    Taverna [1983] IRLR 103 198
Nettleship v Weston (1972) 2 QB 691 30
Norfolk County Council v Bernard
    [1979] IRLR 229 179
North East Coast Shiprepairers Ltd v
    Secretary of State for Employment [1978]
    IRLR 149 204
O'Brien v Prudential Assurance Co
    [1979] IRLR 140 174
O'Hare v Rotaprint Ltd [1980] IRLR 47 . .240
O'Kelly and others v Trusthouse Forte
    [1983] IRLR 369 190
Osborne v Bill Taylor of Huyton Ltd
    [1982] IRLR 17 .16
O'Sullivan v Thompson-Coon QBD
    1973 14 KIR 108 196
Paine & Moore v Grundy (Teddington)
    Ltd [1981] IRLR 267 245
Parkes Classic Confectionery Ltd v
    Ashcroft (1973) 7 ITR 43 118
Parsons (Albert J) & Sons Ltd v
    Parsons [1979] IRLR 117 . . . . .18, 216
Paviour (J A) & P Thomas v Whitton's
    Transport (Cullompton) Ltd [1975]
    IRLR 258 204
Pedersen v London Borough of Camden

[1981] IRLR 173 118

Pentney v Anglian Water Authority
(1983) ICR 464 .93

Philco Radio & Television Corporation v
J Spurling Ltd (1949) 2 AER 882 34

Pond v Louis Edwards & Sons EAT
122/80 245

Power Duffryn Wagon Co Ltd v House
(1974) ICR 123 243

R S Components Ltd v Irwin [1973]
IRLR 239 210

Read v Tiverton and Bull [1977] IRLR
202 36

Ready Mix Concrete v Minister of
Pensions (1968) 1 AER 433 . . . . . .186, 188

Reid v Young and Son EAT 714/82 242

Reiss Engineering Co Ltd v Harris
[1985] IRLR 232 162

Riddell v Reid (1943) AC 1 28

Roberts v Sutcliffe Catering COIT
24663/77/D 90

Robinson v British Island Airways Ltd
[1977] IRLR 477 241

Robson v Dixon (1972) IWLR 1493 223

Rose v Plenty and Co-op Retail Services
Ltd [1976] IRLR 60 37

Ross Foods Ltd v Lamb EAT 833/77 175

Royle v Globtik Management Ltd (1977)
ICR 552 21

Saddington v Valetta Modes Ltd EAT
280/83 153

Sakals v United Counties Omnibus
Company Ltd [1984] IRLR 475 135

Schmidt v Austick Bookshops [1977]
IRLR 360 90

Scott v Shepherd (1773) 2Wm B1 892 33

Secretary of State for Employment v (1)
Deary and others (2) Cambridgeshire
County Council [1984] IRLR 180 25

Sheffield v Oxford Controls Co Ltd
[1979] IRLR 133 238

Simpson (A) & Son (Motors) v Reid
and Findlater [1983] IRLR 401 244

Smith v Leechbrain & Co (1961) 3 AER
1159 34

Sothern v Franks Charlesly & Co [1981]
IRLR 278 229

Spencer and Griffin v Gloucestershire
County Council [1985] IRLR 393 155

Sterling Engineering Co Ltd v Patchett

(1955) 1 AER 369 161

Stevenson, Jordan and Harrison Ltd v
MacDonald and Evans (1952) 1
Times Law Reports 101 186

Strathclyde Regional Council v Syme
(unreported) 176

Superlux v Plaisted (1958) CA 43

Sutcliffe v Hawker Siddeley Aviation
Ltd [1973] IRLR 304 240

Tabor v Mid-Glamorgan County
Council (unreported) 179

Talbot v Hugh M Fulton [1975] IRLR 52 . .89

Tate v Leeds Polytechnic Students'
Union COIT 1473/151 190

Taylor v Dunbar Buildings (1966)
ITR 249 242

Taylorplan Catering (Scotland) Ltd v
McInnally [1980] IRLR 53 176

Tesco v Nattrass (1972) AC 153 36

The Wagon Mound (No. 1) (1961)
1 AER 404 .32, 33

Tocher v General Motors Scotland Ltd
[1981] IRLR 55 .25

Todd v British Midland Airways Ltd
[1978] IRLR 370 20

Tolley & others v Booths Distilleries Ltd
EAT 316/81 131

Trusthouse Forte v Adonis EAT 788/83 . . .119

Turner v Vestric [1981] IRLR 24 130

Turriff Construction Ltd v Bryant and
others (1967) 2 KIR 659 119

USDAW v Leancut Bacon Ltd [1981]
IRLR 295 129

Vokes Ltd v Bear [1973] IRLR 363 245

Waring and Gillow Ltd v Hodgson EAT
30/84 21

Watling v William Bird and Son
Contractors Ltd (1976) ITR 70 255

Webb v Anglian Water Authority [1981]
IRLR 494 256

Williams and others v Compair Maxam
Ltd [1982] IRLR 83 . . . . .243 Wilson v
Maynard Shipbuilding Consultants AB
[1977] IRLR 491 . . . . .20, 221

Wimpey Asphalt v McGuire EAT
370/81 245

Woods v W M Car Services Ltd [1981]
IRLR 347 255

Young (W) & Sons v Smeaton EAT
113/82 174

SUBJECT INDEX

A

Absence recording .54
ACAS . .14, 27, 125, 144, 214, 233, 247, 249
Acceptance, promotion 157
Accident records .62
Acts of Parliament .3
Administrative arrangements, employee
    death 181
Administrative departments, planning for
    strikes 138
Advertisements
    clarification of contractual terms 118
    discriminatory .54
Advertising, job vacancies 101
Advisory service, personnel
    management 48
Agency workers .194
Alcohol, at work .176
Allowances, early retirement 236
APEX 170
Appeals
    grievance procedures 88
    tribunal cases .255
Appearance, employees 89
Application forms 57, 102
Apprentices, employment rights 23
Apprenticeship .203
Assessment, job candidates 105
Associated employers 17
ASTMS 170
Auditing, personnel procedures and
    policies 56
Autonomy, personnel managers 46

B

BACS 68
Bailees, employees as 41
Bailment, liability in 38, 93
Balloting, strike action 136
Bankers' Automated Clearing Services
    Ltd 68
Bankruptcy 218
Basic skills, personnel secretaries 52
Behaviour, standards 155
Bills 4
Blind Persons' Resettlement

Officers 224, 225
Board membership, termination 217
Bodily fatigue, VDU operators 167
Breach of provisions, redundancy
    consultation .128
Bridlington Principles 122
Bumping agreements, redundancy 25
Business
    operation during strikes 143
    transfers 129

C

Capability dismissals, disabled
    workers 227
Car parks 40
Career guidance, counselling 98
Case law 7
Cash handling, employees 164
Cashless pay .67, 68
Casual staff, employees 190
Causal connection, between breach of
    duty and damage 31
Chain of causation, damage 33
Change, management 151
Check-off agreements 131
    unfair dismissal and 134
    withdrawal 132
Civil Service Medical Advisory
    Service 168, 169
Cloakrooms 40
Clothing
    accommodation 93
    employer provision 92
Co-operatives, members as employees . .19
Code of practice
    race discrimination 15, 63, 103
    sex discrimination 14
Code of Practice on Disciplinary Practice
    and Procedures in Employment,
    ACAS 14, 214
Code of Practice on Picketing 142
Codification, laws .7
Collective agreements
    check-off arrangements 132
    incorporation into contracts 118

Collective bargaining 122
  disclosure of information for 125
Collective consultation 126
  redundancy 127
College courses, apprentices 203
Commencement, Acts.................6
Commission, European
  Community 9
Commission payments
  changes 207
  sales representatives 206
Commission for Racial Equality ....
  ....15, 100, 103
Committee stage, bills 5
Common law rules, interpretation 8
Communication
  organisational change and 153
  personnel managers 49
Communications
  vehicles 73
  workforce 72
Companies, directors' reports 77
Companies Act 1948 78
Companies Act 1967 78
Companies Act 1985 .....78, 216, 217, 218
Company cars, sales representatives ...208
Company directors, employment
  status 215
Company image, employee appearance
  rules and 90
Company negotiators, strike action 136
Company pension schemes 236
Company performance, employee
  involvement 80
Company policies, documentation 60
Company policies and procedures,
  creation 49
Company property, recovery, deceased
  employees 182
Company rules 214
  drinking at work 178
Compensation, dismissal 233, 249
Comptroller of Patents 164
Compulsory redundancies,
  minimisation 97
Computer payroll systems 66, 70
Computers, personnel departments 52
Conciliated agreements 249
Conciliated settlements 27, 233
Conciliation, pre-complaint 28
Conciliation officers . .27, 233, 247, 248, 249
Conditional offers, employment 110

Conduct of Employment Agencies and
  Businesses Regulations Act 1976 195
Conflict management, personnel
  management 50
Consolidating legislation 6
Constitution, works councils 75
Constructive dismissal 255
Consultation
  dismissal 130
  employee involvement 80
  employee mental health 175
  health and safety 129
  incapacity dismissals 175
  recognised trade unions 126
  redundancy 96, 244
  terms of apprenticeship 204
  transfer of business 129
Contagious Diseases (Animals) Act
  1869 32
Continuing relationship,
  homeworkers 197
Continuous service
  accrued 24
  temporary workers 193
Contract, liability in 39
Contract base, employment 221, 222
Contracting-out, State pension
  scheme 124
Contractors
  non-employees....................18
  self-employed 240
Contracts 53, 109, 113, 115
  agency workers 195
  apprenticeship 203
  changing 116
  check-off arrangements and 132
  conflicting terms 117
  ending 228
  illegal 22
  job changes and 152
  sales representatives 205
  understanding 53
Contracts of service 18
Contractual position, homeworkers ...196
Contractual rights, temporary
  workers 192
Control, homeworkers 197
Control test, employee or independent
  contractor 186
Council of Civil Service Unions 169
Council of Ministers, European
  Community 9

Counselling
    career guidance 98
    early retirement 238
    employees 81
    skills 82
    techniques 83
    work-related 82
Credit transfer, payments 68
Criminal courts, tachograph
    tampering 212
Cross-examination, tribunal hearings . .254
Custody rule, employers' property . .42, 43
Customer objections, employee
    appearance 91
CVs 102

D
Damage
    causal connection with breach of
    duty 31
    chain of causation 33
    employers' property 44
    recoverable 33
    remoteness of causal connection 32
Dangerous things, duty of care 31
Data protection
    payroll systems 70
    personnel records 64
Data Protection Act 1984 . . . . . . .52, 64, 71
Death, at work .180
Decision making, counselling
    interviews 85
Decisions, European Community 10
Delegated legislation 7
Demotion 159
Department of Employment, Code of
    Practice on Picketing 142
Design, application forms 104
Direct discrimination 54
Directives, European Community 8, 11
Directors
    disqualification 218
    as employees .18
    employment status 215
    service contracts 216
    termination of board membership . . .217
Directors' reports
    companies 77
    small companies 16
Disabled Persons (Employment) Acts
    1944 and 1958 . . . . .224, 226
Disabled workers 223

statement relating to 78
Disablement Resettlement
    Officers 224, 225, 226, 227
Disciplinary procedures 214
    auditing 59
    demotion 159
Discipline, tachographs and 211, 213
Discrimination, application forms 103
Discriminatory requirements, employee
    appearance rules 89
Dismissal
    consultation .130
    directors 216
    disabled workers 226, 227
    on dress or appearance grounds 92
    events leading to 247
    incapacity 174
    individual consultation 127
    loss of driving licence 209
    reasonableness, small companies 14
    strikers 142
Disputes procedure, precluding
    industrial action 146
Disputes procedures, no-strike
    agreements 148
Disqualification, directors 217, 218
Diving Operations at Work Regulations
    1981 112
Dockworkers, employment protection
    exclusion 22
Documentation, company policies 60
Documents, formal 73
Double taxation 223
Downgrading, employees 160
Drafting, bills 4
Dress, employees 89
Drink, at work .176
Drivers 211
    disciplinary action 214
Driving licence, loss of, reason for
    dismissal 209
Drug offences, outside work 179
Drugs, employees 179
Duty of care, employers 28, 166

E
Early retirement 235
EC Regulation 3820/85 211
EETPU 23, 147
Effective date, termination 233
Electrical Contractors' Association 23
Electronic funds transfer 68

Employee handbooks 73
Employee involvement reports 77
Employees
  appearance 89
  cash handling .164
  counselling 81
  death 180
  distinguished from independent
     contractors 185
  drugs 179
  duty of care owed to 30
  inventions 160
  liability for employers'
     property 41
  mental illness 174, 175
  need for fewer, redundancy 240
  new 54
  objections to employee appearance . . .91
  paying off 231
  personal history records 55
  property, employers' responsibility . . .38
  recruitment 99
  resistant to change 154
  rights to trade union membership and
    activities 123
  stress 171
Employers
  associated 17
  checklist of employment status 190
  duty of care 28, 30, 166
  employee liability for property 41
  liability in bailment 93
  management of change 151
  provision of protective clothing and
    equipment 92
  responsibilities for employees'
    property 38
  trade union recognition 120
Employers' Liability (Compulsory
  Insurance) Act 1969 s.5 38
Employment
  acts outside the scope of 37
  conditional offers 110
  contracts 113, 115
  disabled people 224
  offers of 57, 108
  offers of alternative 245
  outside Great Britain, employment
    protection exclusion 19
  personnel overseas 219
  place of, redundancy 239
  termination 228

termination of overseas 222
Employment Act 1980 . . . . .6, 121, 136, 204
Employment Act 1982 . . .6, 77, 78, 136, 143
Employment agencies, briefing 54
Employment Agencies Act 1973 194
Employment Appeal Tribunal 255
  interpretation of EP(C)A s.140 24
  jurisdiction 256
  redundancy selection guidelines 243
Employment of Children Act 1973 6
Employment contracts see Contracts
Employment interviewing, effective . . .106
Employment law .47
  personnel managers as specialists 49
  small companies 13
Employment protection, exclusions 18
Employment Protection Act 1975
  s.99 . . . . .96, 126
  s.126 . . . . .121, 122
Employment Protection (Consolidation)
  Act 1978 . . . . .6, 8, 17, 18, 87, 114,
    142, 185, 204, 217, 218, 226
  s.1 114
  s.8 62
  s.49 . . . . .24, 229
  s.50 213
  s.57 239
  s.57(3) 14
  s.58(13)(b) 134
  s.59 243
  s.62 143
  s.88 . . . . .141, 242
  s.89(3) 141
  s.133(3) 28
  s.140 . . . . .23, 195, 234
  s.140(1)(b) 27
  s.140(2) 27
  s.141 19
  s.141(5) 21
  s.142 204
  Schedule 11 184
  Schedule 12 183
Employment Rehabilitation Centres . . .224
Employment rights, signing away 23
Employment Service Agency 224, 225
Employment status, directors 215
Equal Opportunities Commission . . .14, 63
Equal opportunities policy, ...63, 103
Equal Pay Act 1970 . . . . .15, 114
Equal pay regulations 11
Equipment
  employer provision 92

ownership, inference of self-
employment 188
Ethnic monitoring 63, 103
European Communities Act 1972 11
European Community
directives 8, 11
free movement of workers 220
structure 9
temporary workers draft directive . . .194
European Court of Justice 8, 9, 11, 12
European Parliament 9
Evidence, tribunal hearings 250
Exclusion clauses
fixed term contracts 204
liability 39
Exclusive service, inference of contract of
employment 189
Executive search consultants 100
Exemption, political levy 133, 134
Expenses
incidental, inference of self-
employment 188
sales representatives 209
Expertise, personnel managers 49
Express prohibition 37
Express terms, contracts of
employment 113, 117
External agencies, recruitment 100

F
Facial dermatitis, VDU
operators 167
Facilities, trade union activities 125
Factories Act 1961 . . . . .28, 73, 92, 199
s.133 199
Factories (Home Work) Orders 199
Family credits 69
Family income supplement 69
Fidelity bonding 112
Fifth Directive on Company Law 13, 73
Final payments, employees 213
Financial settlement, pre-hearing 248
First reading, bills .5
Fishermen, share, employment protection
exclusion 22
Five Fold Grading Scheme 105
Fixed term contracts 27
exclusion clauses 204
Fixed term probation 201
Flying pickets 142
Formal documents 73
Forms 73

design and use .65
Freelance agents, non-employees 18

G
Genuine occupational qualifications 54
Going concern, business transferred
as 129
Golden rule, interpretation 8
Great Britain, employment outside,
employment protection exclusion 19
Grievance procedures 86
auditing 60
Grievances, handling 88

H
"Headhunters" 100
Health hazards, VDUs 167
Health and safety 35, 48
clothing 91
consultation 129
small company provisions 15
Health and Safety at Work, etc Act 1974
. . . . .15, 28, 91, 112, 123, 199
s.2 . . . . .92, 127
s.6 130
s.37(1) 35
Health and Safety Executive 168, 180
record keeping requirements 62
Heavy goods vehicles, tachographs . . .210
Home Work (Lampshades) Order
1929 199
Homeworkers 196
new technology 199
statutory rights 198
trade unions and 199
Hours of work
changing 241
fixed, contract of employment 189
salesforce 205
House of Commons 5
House of Lords 5, 11
House-magazines 73

I
Ill-health dismissals
consultation 130
disabled workers 227
Illness, drinking as 176
Implied terms, contracts of
employment 109, 113, 117
Incapacity dismissals 174
Incentives, early retirement 236

Incidental expenses, inference of self-
   employment 188
Income tax, resident status and 222
Independent contractors 185
Indirect discrimination 54
Individual consultation 126
   dismissal 130
   redundancy 245
Induction, new employees 54
Industrial action, unofficial 149
Industrial relations 47
Industrial Relations Code of
   Practice 87, 93, 97, 126, 146
Industrial tribunals 246
   procedure 253
   tachograph records 212
Information
   disclosure to workforce 58, 80
   recognised trade union right to 124
   redundancy consultation 127
   tribunal cases .247
Information trace, tachographs 210
Inland Revenue, record keeping
   requirements 62
Insolvency Act 1985 . . . . .217, 218
Institute of Personnel Management,
   recruitment code 101
Integration test, employee or independent
   contractor 186
Internal promotion 156
Internal sources, recruitment 99
Interpretation, statutes 7
Interpretation Act 1889 8
Interviews
   counselling 84
   recruitment 104, 106
Invalidity benefit, early retirees 238
Inventions
   employees 160
   patentable 161
Investigation
   employee mental health 175
   tribunal cases .246

J

Job applicants 57
Job changes
   and contracts of employment 152
   legal position .152
Job descriptions 57
Job flexibility 147

Job Release Scheme 236
Job security
   agreements 94
   policies 60
Job vacancies, advertising 54, 101, 118
Jurisdiction, Employment Appeal
   Tribunal 256

L

Last in first out 244
Law, points of, grounds for appeal 255
Law making, process, UK 3
Law making process, European
   Community 9
Lay-offs 241
   in breach of contract 243
   during strikes .141
Layout, application forms 104
Leading questions 254
Learning, counselling skills 86
Leave, overstaying 26
Legal aspects, employee death 182
Legal enforceability, no-strike agreements
  148
Legal obligations, personnel records 61
Legal position
   job changes 152
   promotion 158
Legal rights, recognised trade unions . .123
Legislation 3
   European Community impact 11
Legislative aspects, application forms . .103
Letters, official 73
Liability
   in bailment 38, 93
   in contract 39
   employees, for employers property . . .41
   employers 38
   exclusion clauses 39
   in negligence 40
   occupier's 41
Liability insurance, compulsory 38
LIFO 244
Limited companies, contracts of service
   with 188
Liquefied damages, pay in lieu of
   notice 232
Listening skills, counselling 85
Literal rule, interpretation 8
Lockers 40
Loss, mitigation 249, 251, 254

M

Maintenance departments, planning for
  strikes 139
Management
  advising 48
  change 151
  conduct during strikes 141
Management commitment, job security
  agreements 98
Management teams, strikes 137, 138
Manpower planning 96
Manpower Services Commission 224
Marketing departments, planning for
  strikes 139
Mass picketing 142
Maternity allowance 69
Maternity rights 55
  small companies 15
Medical certificates 63
Medical examinations, prospective
  employees 112
Mental illness, employees 174, 175
Mergers 12
Minimum notice periods 229
Miscarriages, VDU operators 167, 168
Mischief rule, interpretation 8
Misconduct, drinking as 178
Mitigation, loss 249, 251, 254
Multiple test, employee or independent
  contractor 187

N

National Health Service employees,
  employment rights 23
National Maritime Board Agreement ...22
National Radiological Protection
  Board 168
Negligence 28
  liability in 40
Negotiations, strike settlements 140
"Neighbour" principle, duty of care 29
New technology
  homeworkers 199
  office use 167
Night Work of Male Young Persons
  (Medical Examinations) Regulations
  1983 112
No-strike agreements 145
  legal enforceability 148
Non-executive directors 215
Notice
  failure to give 230

statutory minimum 24
termination of contracts 229
withdrawal of 230
Notice-boards 59, 73
Notifiable accidents 62

O

Obligation, mutuality, contracts of
  employment 198
Occupational pension schemes 124
Occupier's Liability Act 1957 41
Offers
  clarification of contractual terms 118
  employment 57, 108
  revocation 110
Office-holders, non-employees 19
Offices, Shops and Railway Premises Act
  1963 73
Operation, during strikes 140, 143
Oral communications, workforce 72
Organisational change,
  implementation 153
Output, standards 155
Overseas employment, UK personnel 219
Ownership, inventions 163

P

Paperwork, tribunal hearings 252
Parliament, procedure 5
Parliamentary draftsmen 4
Participation, workforce 147
Partners, non-employees 19
Partnerships, contracts with 188
Patent rights, assignment to employer 163
Patentability, inventions 161
Patents, case law 162
Patents Act 1949 160
Patents Act 1977 ....160, 161, 162, 163
Pay statements, itemised 62, 67
Pay-slips, design 67
Paying off, employees 231
Payment
  deceased employees 181
  in lieu of notice 232
  method of, inference of employment
    status 189
  methods of 68
  on termination, taxation 234
Payroll systems 66
  state payments through 69
  statistics 70
Pension schemes, administration 47

Period of incapacity for work 55
Personal history records, employees 55
Personal liability 35
Personal obligation, inference of self-
  employment 188
Personal problems, counselling 83
Personal qualities, personnel
  secretaries 51
Personnel, employed overseas 219
Personnel manager's
  expertise 49
  role 45
Personnel policies 50
Personnel procedures, auditing 56
Personnel records 61
  auditing 58
  data protection .64
Personnel secretaries 51
Personnel skills, secretaries 53
Photosensitive epilepsy, VDU
  operators 167
Physical setting, recruitment
  interviews 105
Picketing 142
Place of employment, definition of 239
Political levy 132
Pregnancy, VDU use during . .167, 168, 170
Premises, trade union activities 125
Preparation
  recruitment interviews 104
  tribunal cases .246
Probation
  employees 200
  fixed term 201
Probationers, rights 202
Production departments, planning for
  strikes 139
Professional and Executive Recruitment
  Service 100
Promotion 155
  acceptance 157
  unsuccessful 158
Promotion schemes, fair 157
Protective awards, breach of redundancy
  consultation provisions 128
Protective clothing, employer
  provision 92
Public communications, during
  strikes 138
Purchasing departments, planning for
  strikes 139

Q
Qualifying days, SSP 55
Qualifying service, unfair dismissal
  rights 13
Quota Scheme, disabled workers . .223, 224

R
Race discrimination 14, 37, 53, 103
Race relations, code of practice. .15, 63, 103
Race Relations Act 1976 . . . .15, 37, 53, 220
Radiation emission, VDUs 167, 168
Re-engagement 116, 249
  strikers 143
Reasonable care, duty of 29
Reasonableness
  employee appearance rules 89
  redundancy dismissals 244
Recognised trade unions 59
  consultation 126
  legal rights 123
  redundancy consultation 96
  redundancy selection 243
Recognition
  trade unions 120, 147
  withdrawal 121
Recommendations, European
  Community 11
Record keeping, personnel
  secretaries 54
Records
  design and use .65
  storage 65
Recruitment 99
  auditing 57
  secretarial knowledge of 53
Recruitment code, IPM 101
Recruitment consultants 100
Recruitment interviewing, effective 106
Recruitment interviews 104
"Red circling", employees 160
Redundancy 12
  bumping agreements 25
  compulsory 97
  consultation 96, 127, 128, 130
  counselling 83
  disabled workers 227
  early retirement and 236, 239
  reasonable dismissal 244
  selection .98, 243
  statutory definition 239
Redundancy payments
  claiming 242

employee death 183
employment outside Great Britain 21
lay off as result of strike 141
Redundancy programmes 95
Redundancy rebates 16
References 57, 165
taking up 111
Registered disabled people 224
Registered dockworkers, employment
protection exclusion 22
Regulations, European Community 10
Rehabilitation of Offenders Act 1974 ... 165
Reinstatement 249
Relocation expenses, personnel
employed overseas 220
Reorganisation, redundancy 241
Report stage, bills 5
Representational rights, trade unions .. 122
Representations, redundancy
consultation 127
Residence, for tax law purposes 222
Residence permits 219
Restraint clauses, sales
representatives 209
Restrictive covenants, sales
representatives 210
Retirement
counselling 83
mutual agreement 238
Royal Assent, bills 6
Royal Assent Act 1967 6

S

Safety, cash handling employees 164
Safety representatives 123, 127, 130
Safety Representatives and Safety
Committees Regulations 1977 129
Safety wear 91
Salary administration, personnel
function 47
Sales departments, planning for
strikes 139
Sales representatives, employment 205
Sales targets 206
Sales territories 208
Second reading, bills 5
Secondary action, trade disputes 136
Secretaries, personnel 51
Security, cash handling 165
Security departments, planning for
strikes 139
Selection

auditing 57
redundancy 98, 243
Self-certificates 63
Self-employment 185
inferences of 188
Servants, as bailees 41
Service contracts
directors 216
failure to renew 218
Settlements, strikes 144
Seven Point Plan 105
Severance packages, job security
agreements 98
Sex discrimination 11, 12, 14, 36,
53, 63, 103
code of practice 14
Sex Discrimination Act 1975 .... 12, 36, 37,
53, 220
Sex Discrimination Act 1986 13
Sex monitoring 63
Share fishermen, employment
protection exclusion 22
Ships, employment protection
exclusion 21
Sickness benefit, early retirees 238
Skills, personnel secretaries 52
Small companies, employment law 13
Social skills, counselling 83
Staff
reliability 165
single status 147
State benefits, early retirees 237
State pension scheme, contracting-out . 124
State pensions, early retirement and ... 237
Statistics, payroll systems 70
Statute law 7
Statutes, interpretation 7
Statutory instruments 7
Statutory maternity pay 55, 61, 69, 194
Statutory minimum notice 229
Statutory notices 73
Statutory obligations, personnel
records 61
Statutory requirements, itemised pay
statements 67
Statutory rights
exclusion 23
homeworkers 198
temporary workers 192
Statutory rules, interpretation 8
Statutory sick pay 54, 61, 69, 194
records 63

Statutory terms, contracts of
    employment 113
Stop and search, employees 166
Storage, records 65
Stress, employees 171
Strikers, dismissal 142
Strikes 135
    conduct during 141
    employer considerations 136
    planning for 138
    settlements 144
Subscriptions, trade unions 131
Supervisors, probationers 201

                        T
Tachograph evidence, internal
    disciplinary action 213
Tachographs 210
    false records 211
    tampering 211
Tactics, pre-tribunal hearing 248
Taxation
    lump sum payments 234
    pay in lieu of notice 233
Technical skills, personnel secretaries . .52
Techniques, counselling 83
Temporary workers 191
    continuous service 193
    EC draft directive 194
Termination
    contracts 116
    effective date .233
    employment 228
    mutual agreement 238
Terms, strike settlements 144
Terms of employment
    harmonisation 147
    sales representatives 205
    written statements 58, 65, 109,
    ·114, 115, 117, 192, 205
Theft, employers' property 44
"Thin skull" cases, damage 34
Time limits
    claims 256
    records storage 65
    redundancy consultation 127
Time off work, trade union membership
    and activities .125
Trade disputes 136
Trade Union & Labour Relations Act
    1974 136

Trade Union Act 1913 . . . . . . .133, 134, 135
Trade Union Act 1984 . . . . .7, 133, 136, 150
Trade Union and Labour Relations Act
    1974 . . . . .135, 148
Trade union membership and activities
    dismissal for 123
    time off work .125
Trade unions
    homeworkers and 199
    membership 73
    non-recognition 123
    recognised see Recognised trade unions
    recognition 120
    representational rights 122
    subscriptions .131
    view of VDU health hazards 169
Trade Union and Labour Relations Act
    1974, s.18 132
Training
    new methods .154
    personnel function 47
    policies 61
Training Opportunities Scheme 224
Transfer of Undertakings (Protection of
    Employment) Regulations 1981 . . .7, 11,
    12, 126, 129
Transfers, business 129
Treaty of Rome 8, 11, 12, 220
Trespassers, duty of care owed to 30
Tribunal hearings, preparation 250
Truck Acts 68, 164
TUC 122

                        U
Unemployment benefit, early
    retirees 237
Unfair Contract Terms Act 1977 . . . . .23, 39
Unfair dismissal 116, 249
    check-off agreements and 134
    consultation and 130
    directors 216
    mental health .175
    pregnant VDU operators 170
    small company provisions 13
    trade union membership and
    activities 123
United Kingdom, ordinarily working
    outside 221
Unofficial action .149
grading, employees 156

V

VDUs, risks 167
Vicarious liability 35
"Vredeling" Directive 13

W

Wages Act 1986 ....6, 7, 16, 114, 198
Wages Council Orders 73
Wages Councils 192
Welfare 48
Witness, tribunal hearings 251
Word of mouth recruitment 100
Word processors 52
Work
  changing standards 155
  death at 180
  fixed hours, contract of
    employment 189
  ordinary place of 221
  of a particular kind 240
Work permits 219

Work-related counselling 82
Worker directors 74
Workers, free movement within EC ...220
Workers' co-operatives, members as
  employees 19
Workforce
  communication with 49, 72
  information 58
  participation 147
Works councils 74
  checklist 76
  constitution 75
  forming 75
Works rules, incorporation into
  contracts 119
Written communications, workforce 73
Written statements
  health and safety policy 15
  terms of employment 56, 58, 109,
    114, 115, 117, 192, 205
Written terms, apprenticeship
  contracts 203